In appreciation of
volunteer service performed by

Beth Hallum

April "kick-off" '97

Cedar Mill Community Library

THROUGH THE GARDEN GATE

THROUGH THE GARDEN GATE

· · · · · · · · · · · · · · · · · · · ·

by Elizabeth Lawrence

Edited by Bill Neal

THE UNIVERSITY OF NORTH CAROLINA PRESS

Chapel Hill ❧ *London*

Library of Congress Cataloging-in-Publication Data
Lawrence, Elizabeth, 1904–1985.
    Through the garden gate / by Elizabeth Lawrence ; edited by
Bill Neal.
        p.   cm.
    ISBN 0-8078-1907-7 (alk. paper)
    1. Gardening.   2. Gardening—North Carolina—
Charlotte.   I. Neal, Bill.
SB455.3.L39   1990   89-27890
635—dc20   CIP

Elizabeth Lawrence's columns presented here originally appeared in the Charlotte *Observer* between 1957 and 1971. The
editor and the University of North Carolina Press gratefully ac-
knowledge the permission of the Charlotte *Observer* to reprint
this material.

Design by April Leidig-Higgins

Manufactured in the United States of America
94 93 92 91 90   5 4 3 2 1

The paper in this book meets the guidelines for permanence
and durability of the Committee on Production Guidelines for
Book Longevity of the Council on Library Resources.

 CONTENTS

✒ INTRODUCTION

I met Elizabeth Lawrence for the first time on a cold winter day in December 1974. It was not the sort of day to pick for a garden tour in North Carolina, even when the garden belongs to the author of a classic book entitled *Gardens in Winter*. Sky, air, and ground were wet and cold in a particularly penetrating, southern way. But my stay in Charlotte was to be a brief one, and the invitation had been accepted. I drove the leafless streets until I came to Ridgewood Avenue. One block away I could already see the first evidence of a garden "where at all times of the year . . . there is some plant in perfection of flower or fruit." Miss Lawrence's own words reproached me in my doubt.

Even from the street, I could see a garden that was a galaxy of blossoms. Camellias by the walk bloomed brilliantly against the gray sky, and beyond, a witch hazel wreathed the door in gold. I'm not sure that we had even finished introducing ourselves before Miss Lawrence ushered me into the living room, saying, "I want you to see what I found today."

Along a wooden table, a dozen little flowers, all different, spilled over caper jars under a wide, uncurtained window. Outside, a thicket of emerald bamboo screened the glass; through it flowed the light of the tropics on this, one of the darkest days of the year. Miss Lawrence could have been quoting *A Southern Garden*: "I like to leave flowers in the garden when the weather is pleasant, but in winter I bring them in out of the cold. On many chilly days I cut little bouquets of wintersweet and spring heath, a blue viola, perhaps a paper-white narcissus, a camellia, an iris, and a few spikes of the pale blue flowers of rosemary."

Later I would visit Elizabeth Lawrence often. She would meet me at the door with secateurs in hand and say, "Go to the garden, clip what you like. Then we'll talk." I never had nerve enough to take more than one small piece of ivy for rooting, now moved four times. In those days, I was a graduate student at Chapel Hill, and my "garden" was sandwiched between the back door of an apartment and a laundry line. My plants came from ditches, construction sites, and waste areas. But Elizabeth interrogated me about it as if my plot were Kew; every plant, even my weeds, interested her. I learned very quickly to have at least one date for her: "Elizabeth, *Thalictrum aquilegifolium* bloomed May 7," I practically shouted almost as soon as I saw her on one visit. But she was patient and gracious in talking to me and many, many others, even strangers who just appeared at her door with a flower or leaf to identify.

In 1988, when I came across one of her Sunday columns in a back issue of the Charlotte *Observer* in the library of the University of North Carolina in Chapel Hill, those talks came back vividly, and I began to search out more columns.

There were all the gardens and gardeners she loved—Bill Hunt of Chapel Hill; the Dormons of Louisiana; Mittie Wellford, Hannah Withers, and Elizabeth Clarkson of Charlotte; Carl Krippendorf of Ohio—the folks who populated the books she wrote, as well as filled each other's borders with slips and cuttings passed by hand or through the mail. There, too, were the other fast friends, all members of "that great fraternity, the Brothers of the Spade" (*Gardening for Love*), known only through letters or from the market bulletins.

Many people whom we now know through her books made their first appearances in the *Observer*. Mrs. Radau, whom we would later meet in *Gardening for Love*, had sent Elizabeth a shoebox full of dried flowers, seed pods, and cones.

Many of Mrs. Radau's plants are familiar—some grow in my own garden—but I would not have known what they were if she had not put their names on them, and I had never realized how beautiful they are when they are really looked at. . . . I might have guessed the slender, papery, cinnamon-colored cones of the tulip tree, and could surely have named the tiny, delicate cones of the alder, but I wouldn't have been able to distinguish the cone of the spruce pine from that of our old field pine, though they are very different when laid side by side. There were cones of three species of magnolia: the large ones of *Magnolia grandiflora*, the smaller ones of *M. virginiana*, and the very slender ones of *M. pyramidata* with their tapered and curiously twisted seed vessels. Some of these things fall to the ground, and are there for the gathering, but others must be picked from the limbs of tall trees. As I unpacked the shoebox I wondered how Mrs. Radau had collected them. She must have an army of small boys at her command. I wish I had one small climber to swarm up the empress tree, and cut for me some bare branches tipped with tawny velvet, winter buds.

Such detail and close observation are the province of the expert gardener. I once carelessly expressed a lack of appreciation for Japanese maples. Elizabeth said, "Then you have never crawled beneath one in October." She was on her knees in the garden twelve months a year. Once she and Bill Hunt searched out autumn cyclamens by matchlight on the steep slopes of the Hunt Arboretum in Chapel Hill, and in her own garden one January she discovered the delicious fragrance of *Crocus laevigatus* 'Fontenayi', remarking later, "I did not know this for a long time, as you must get on your knees on the cold ground in order to find it out."

"Just as vividly before me are the gardens of books," she wrote. When Elizabeth Lawrence wasn't in the garden, she was most likely in the library. She learned Latin early on in grade school, but her love for the language blossomed upon reading Virgil. "I wish that Saint Mary's, instead of sitting their pupils down to *Omnia Gallia divisa est*, had allowed us to translate *Quid faciat laetas segetes*, 'What makes the crops joyous?' As it is, I came to the *Georgics* late in life, when I might have been enjoying it all along." She quoted Shakespeare and all the classic English herbalists, Thoreau, almost every writer who ever created a garden in reality or fiction. Her memory was prodigious, not only for the botanical names of plants but for the picturesque common plant names of the English cottager or the southern farmwife and for the verses of the poets who wrote of the flowers she loved, even the ditties of her childhood.

In the *Observer* columns she went to great lengths to acquaint readers with the best European and American garden writers: her beloved "German Elizabeth," Mrs. Loudon, Dean Hole, Gertrude Jekyll, Alice Morse Earle, and Vita Sackville-West, with whom she corresponded. "Gardening, reading about gardening, and writing about gardening are all one; no one can garden alone," she wrote. And in 1983, in one of her last essays, she wrote, "Gardens are so perishable; they live on only in books and letters; but what has gone before is not lost; the future is the past entered by another door." There are many doors to past and future beauty; Elizabeth Lawrence's writing is one of the most easily opened.

The Charlotte *Observer* published the first of Elizabeth Lawrence's Sunday columns on August 11, 1957. Miss Lawrence then was fifty-three years old, the author of the now classic *A Southern Garden* (1942). *The Little Bulbs* appeared in print the year the columns began; *Gardens in Winter*, in 1961. She had left her legendary Raleigh garden in 1950 and moved to Charlotte with her mother to live next to her sister, and just a few houses down from her good friend Elizabeth Clarkson and the beautiful bird sanctuary Winghaven. By 1957 her garden on Ridgewood Avenue had achieved some maturity, though the columns are quick to tell that nothing was static in Elizabeth's world. Plants failed, were discarded, were tried again. Those that succeeded usually did so too well for the small scale of her urban garden. She likened her manner to that of E. A. Bowles, who "seemed to garden just about the way I do. He would never have enough room, no matter how big his garden, and was always stuffing some shrub into a place too small for it."

The great lesson of the *Observer* columns is fearlessness. Elizabeth's garden was an experiment, evaluated daily, even hourly, a place where aesthetics and sentiment did battle: "A pomegranate tree was one of the first plants to come into my garden when I started to make a new one, and it was one of the first to go, for I could never find a place where the burning scarlet of the flowers was not at war with its surroundings. Now I often wish I had kept the pomegranate and let everything else go." And she wrote, I "cannot bear for people to say (as they often do) that I am better at plant material than design; I cannot help it if I have to use my own well-designed garden as a laboratory, thereby ruining it as a garden" (*Gardening for Love*).

Elizabeth wrote seven hundred and twenty columns for the *Observer*, in longhand, as she never learned to type. The one hundred and forty-four columns in this collection span the range of her interests: gardening literature and lore, plant culture, the demands of an ever-changing modern landscape (even interstate highways), friends and visits, the church calendar.

The articles are arranged by the month in which they were originally published, and within that month, from the earliest published to the latest. In a few instances, I moved a later column to the beginning of the month to establish an easily recognizable time frame. Columns that obviously were meant to correspond with a historical date are also sometimes repositioned. Thus an article printed in May in honor of Shakespeare's birthday has been moved to April. But otherwise, I wanted to preserve the sense of anticipation that devoted readers must have felt each Sunday morning when picking up the *Observer*. Where would she range next? In August she wrote of daffodils, and in February she wrote of roses. In other words, she wrote as gardeners think. The columns are printed here entire; only topical and dated information on local meetings and so forth has been deleted.

From the beginning of this project, I felt I was looking through these columns into the garden as Elizabeth Lawrence knew it. Any attempt to update cultural or theoretical practice seemed unwise and to run the risk of attributing words to Miss Lawrence. This is a record of growth and understanding, a walk through the garden with a friend. Elizabeth knew well that plants in the South and elsewhere never behave as many authorities would have us believe. She is interested in successful gardeners; if they plant by the signs, it is only part of the wonder we know in the garden from childhood. And science is equally wondrous in this world, though one of its practices haunts her. Over the years of these articles, she sensitively and intuitively rejects chemicals in the garden. The horror of one dead bird on the garden path in the 1950s leads her to embrace the conclusions of Rachel Carson's *Silent Spring*. From literature Elizabeth knew well that universal struggles are often fought in the backyard. Upon her death, her obituary in the Charlotte *Observer* remarked to the same effect that she was "the Jane Austen of the gardening literary world."

L. H. Bailey, who gave us *Hortus*, wrote, "It is necessary to state again that fixity or rigidity in botanical nomenclature is unattainable." For this book, I chose to stick with what Elizabeth Lawrence wrote. When Elizabeth Lawrence pronounced the botanical name of a plant, it echoed with an authority that we are unlikely to hear ever again. Latin was her second language, and I cannot bear to change the words she spoke. Her voice is too clear. *Hortus Second* was Miss Lawrence's reference when the *Observer* articles were written. Subsequent changes in nomenclature are given in the index.

The Charlotte *Observer* gave Elizabeth Lawrence her first wide readership with these articles, and I am grateful to it for that gift and for granting the rights of republication for this book. I owe thanks to the University of North Carolina Press for first publishing Elizabeth Lawrence's *A Southern Garden*, and for adding this volume to her writings in print. Particularly, I wish to thank David Perry, Johanna Grimes, and Suzanne Bell. To Nigel Smith, I owe thanks for constant and diligent research. Edith Eddleman kindly took time away from her magnificent borders at the North Carolina Arboretum and her international lectures to read the manuscript closely and to weed out the errors of time and typing. To Bill Hunt, I and all Southerners owe thanks for an unrelenting devotion to friendship and plants.

And for inspiration, friendship, and dedication, I am inexpressibly grateful to an innovative gardener, a fellow Brother of the Spade, Gene Hamer.

Bill Neal
Carrboro, North Carolina
August 1989

THROUGH THE
GARDEN GATE

THROUGH THE GARDEN GATE

· · · · · · · · · · · · · · · · · ·

This is the gate of my garden. I invite you to enter in: not only into my garden, but into the world of gardens—a world as old as the history of man, and as new as the latest contribution of science; a world of mystery, adventure and romance; a world of poetry and philosophy; a world of beauty; and a world of work.

Never let yourself be deceived about the work. There is no royal road to learning (as my grandmother used to say). And there is no royal road to gardening—although men seem to think that there is.

"Gardening is becoming very popular now that labor-saving devices have taken the hard work out of it," your editor said to me. I gave him a withering look (but he did not wither, and when I questioned this I could see him thinking that I did not know what I was talking about).

"Is there a machine," I asked, "to dig a hole and plant a shrub for you? Is there a machine to get up early in the morning and pick all of the dead daylilies off the stalks. Is there a machine that gets on its knees and plants petunias . . . or sweeps the walks . . . or digs and divides and replants daffodils?" (You can see that your editor is not a gardener.)

I, too, once had illusions about carefree gardening—all play and no work. When my mother and I left our old and dear and sprawling garden in Raleigh and came to Charlotte to make a new garden and a new life, I believed what I had been told, and what I had read in books and newspapers. I thought I could plan a garden that would require very little upkeep.

There would be no grass to cut, for ground covers would provide the green carpet. There would be no hedges to clip—ivy-covered fences would take the place of them. There would be no spraying to do, for I would use only disease-resistant and pest-free plants.

Now, after seven years, I find that the new garden—although about a quarter of the old one's size—demands exactly as much time of me as the old. It demands every single moment that I have to spare, and every ounce of strength that I have left in me.

Any garden demands as much of its maker as he has to give. But I do not need to tell you, if you are a gardener, that no other undertaking will give as great a return for the amount of effort put into it.

August 11, 1957

𝒥 JANUARY

. . . .

Frost

As I look out at silvered evergreens on a morning when thin ice coats the garden pool, the delicate work that has been done in the night reminds me of what V. Sackville-West said in *The Garden*, that frost must be forestalled as an enemy, and used as a friend. "Wise old winter," she says, "scorns the sensuous lies of summer," and

> Etches the finer skeleton
> For more perceptive eyes.

Lovely as it all is from the window, it is even lovelier close at hand. Well wrapped, for it is impossible to linger over detail while longing for warmth, I go out of doors to examine this fine needlework before it vanishes.

Leaves outlined with silver stitching stand out as individuals: the scalloped circle of the ground-ivy, the trefoil of *Oxalis braziliensis*, the heart, the fan and the fleur-de-lis. Blades of iris and yucca are sprinkled with glistening crystals, and the columbines are dusted with a powder as fine as confectioner's sugar.

Frost does its most elaborate work on the evergreen herbs. Fennel turns to a gossamer web; the silvery lavender and lavender-cotton are newly painted; wooly plants like lambs-ears and mullein are patches of snow; the coarsely picoted leaflets of burnet are frost encrusted, and then when the sun comes up they are hung with diamonds.

Beautiful as it all is, the gardener cannot forget frost, the foe, and as soon as the crystals have turned to diamonds I look about to see what has escaped.

Everyone is hanging on the words of the weatherman—even on the Gulf Coast. "This is a lovely spring morning after a night of drizzle," Mr. Morrison wrote from Pass Christian early in December, "but in the garden it is the time of year that is least certain, for it can turn cold any minute, and nothing is entirely asleep. Until the cold strikes one can expect almost any kind of bloom. The azaleas are outdoing themselves, and the camellias are in fine flower. The Paper-White narcissus that you sent me from Dr. Mayer proved to be the elegant, starry, large-flowered form that we used to see in the catalogues as French."

About the same time, Mrs. Sheets wrote that in Reidsville, North Carolina, sleet was falling on the buds of the Algerian iris. "'Fairy' roses still bloom," she said, "and yesterday I saw several open blossoms on the California poppies. Daylily buds were caught by a hard freeze, but a few camellias escaped. Perhaps there will be at least one flower in bloom for Christmas!"

Here, we escaped with only a cold rain. The lowest temperature before Christmas was 22 degrees and things went on blooming in spite of the frost. Someone left an orange daylily in our mail box, irises at Queens College, camellias bloomed in the Clarkson's garden ('Lady Clare', 'Cup of Beauty', 'Triphosa', 'Berenice Boddy', and 'Debutante'), and in mine I picked sasanquas until Christmas Day. The last one was 'Pink Snow', only slightly yellowed like old silk. After Christmas Dawn it was still blooming. A low of nineteen did little more than turn the petals to ivory.

There were blooms on the autumn cherry all through December, and frost did not harm the snowdrops, the arbutus, the wintersweet or the winter clematis. There were Chinese violets and white rain lilies, Elizabeth Clarkson's aster (from Texas) and her little pink wallflowers and a single spike of *Alstroemeria pulchella*, which has never before bloomed for me so late in the year. The Algerian iris bloomed between freezes, and so did the little bulb that came to me as an iris but proved to be *Moraea polystachya*.

Last summer two California gardeners sent me bulbs of the moraea. They bloomed from the second day of November until the week before Christmas, much earlier and much more freely than those that winter in North Carolina. Some crocuses that had escaped the squirrels and the chipmunks bloomed early in the month, and on the eighteenth I found a single flower of *Crocus laevigatus* 'Fontenayi' visited by a bee almost as large as itself.

On Christmas Eve I found a sweet olive blooming freely and fragrantly in against a warm chimney. As I picked a sprig, I thought of Mrs. Sheets, and hope that she found at least one flower in bloom on Christmas Day.

January 7, 1962

The Loudons

One morning last summer I found in the mail a delightful little volume of essays on nineteenth-century gardeners, by Geoffrey Taylor. One of them tells the story of the Loudons. John Loudon was forty-seven and already a celebrated landscape gardener, editor, and author of the *Encyclopedia of*

Gardening, when he met Jane Webb in February 1830. He had asked to be introduced to the author of a novel called *The Mummy*, and was disconcerted when, instead of the middle-aged gentleman that he had expected, he was presented to a young woman of twenty-three; but he quickly recovered. "I believe that from that evening he formed an attachment to me," Mrs. Loudon wrote demurely, "and, in fact, we were married on the fourteenth of the following September."

Although she had been a gardener from childhood, Mrs. Loudon was not able to hold her own in conversation with her husband, his family and his friends. Heartily ashamed of her ignorance, she turned to the library, but the books were so technical that she was forced to ask for help. She found Mr. Loudon as eager to teach as she was to learn.

It was fortunate that she was so eager to share his work, for she would have had a poor time if she had expected a normal family or social life. Even while his man-servant was dressing him for his wedding (he had lost his right arm) he was dictating his *Encyclopaedia of Cottage, Farm, and Villa Architecture* to a secretary whose duties were soon to be taken over by his bride. Their only child, Agnes, was fitted into their life of travelling in search of plants, growing them in their garden in Bayswater, and writing about them.

The garden in Bayswater was small, only a quarter of an acre, but two thousand species, and no telling how many varieties, of trees, shrubs, vines, roses and herbaceous plants grew within its walls. The lawn was so thickly planted with several hundred sorts of bulbs that the grass could never be cut. There was also a hot house for tropical plants, and an alpine house with six hundred pots. There was even a collection of mosses.

Mrs. Loudon had material at hand for any number of garden books, and having found that there were none for the amateur, she set out to write them for the Victorian ladies who were beginning to take an active interest in gardening. A quarter of a century earlier, Jane Austen's heroines would never have gone beyond directing the gardener, but a lady of Mrs. Loudon's day might put on her gloves and weed her own flower bed.

So Mrs. Loudon wrote *Botany for Ladies*, *Gardening for Ladies*, and *The Ladies' Companion to the Flower Garden*. She wrote and illustrated the five quartos of her *Ladies' Flower Garden of Ornamental Plants*, dealing with annuals, perennials and bulbs. These are now in great demand for their quaint hand-colored engravings. I bought the text of the volume on bulbs for a dollar. It had been priced at a hundred dollars before some book-ghoul tore out the fifty-eight plates to use as decorations for lamp shades and scrap baskets.

Since Bayswater, a suburb of London, has winters very like ours, Mrs. Loudon's books have a particular interest for gardeners in these parts. The bulbs that she writes about are those found in Southern gardens: mont-bretias, red spider lilies, the spring starflower . . . and many more that we could grow, but don't.

In *The Ladies' Companion to the Flower Garden* she gives a "monthly calendar of work to be done," that we might do well to follow. One of the January chores is to kill slugs and snails "as they will begin to be active this month." The easiest way, she says, is to throw them into a large vessel of water.

Although I do not know even the names of some of Mrs. Loudon's eighteen books, I hope in time to track them all down, and if I can't hope to possess them all, to at least have the pleasure of reading them.

January 25, 1959

Amorphophallus Rivieri

Elizabeth Clarkson called one spring day to ask what *Amorphophallus rivieri* is. I told her that I didn't know, but would look it up in *Hortus Second*. It proved to be a member of the arum family, commonly known as devil's tongue, and also as the sacred lily of India and is properly called hydrosme.

Elizabeth said she had found tubers at Mr. Furr's, and thought she would try one in her garden. She came home with one for herself, one for me, and one for Dr. Mayer. Although they are tropical bulbs, native to Cochin-China and the East Indies, all three have survived out of doors for six winters. Elizabeth says that hers, planted in a border with light shade, blooms every spring. Mine rarely blooms. Its blooming this year, early in May, stirred me up to make some notes and have its picture taken.

The flower comes ahead of the leaves, suddenly pushing up out of the ground, and opening before you know it is there, looking something like an enormous and sinister calla lily. The spathe, by my measurement, is sixteen inches long. From it rises the very dark, red and green spadix which measures nearly two feet in length. The color of the spathe is a mingling of livid brown, wine red, and olive green. It is paler at the base, with a mottling of green that merges into the very dark green stem. The flower has a most unpleasant odor that is said to attract the carrion-loving insects that pollinate it, but the scent is not noticeable unless you stick your nose in it.

Although the flowers are impressive, I really grow the devil's tongue for its decorative foliage. The great leaves measure a yard or more across. They are finely divided, and their mottled stalks are handsome too. Some think they are like palm leaves, and call the plant snake palm.

While browsing about in search of information about *A. rivieri*, I came upon an interesting description of *A. titanum*, which was sent from the Botanic Gardens at Florence to the Royal Gardens, Kew, and flowered ten years later, in June 1889. The spadix was six inches in diameter, and over three feet tall. It stood in the center of a bell-shaped spathe over two feet across. The spathe began to unfold at five in the afternoon, began to close soon after it was fully open, and was shut before midnight. "The stench was overpowering," Mr. Weathers says, in *The Bulb Book*, "and was said to resemble that of rotten fish and burnt sugar."

Mr. Houdyshel lists another aroid, *Sauromatum venosum*, the lizard lily, which I think would be fun to add to the garden curiosities. "The long serpent-like spathe wriggles along the soil surface," he says; "I have seen persons jump, at their first look."

This reminds me of Vita Sackville-West's "Joke plants," one of which is the 'Monarch of the East', *Sauromatum guttatum*. "The monarch rejoices in the decadent livery of green and purple, with bruises on the pale green," she says in *A Joy of Gardening*. The joke is that you can set the tuber down in a saucer with no soil and no water, and within a few weeks it will show signs of flowering.

Other jokers, if you are interested (though they do not appeal to me half so much as the lizard lily), are the gas plant—if you can set alight that eerie blue flame; the obedient plant, *Physostegia virginiana*—if you can push the flowers into a new position, tell them to stay there, and make them obey you; and the humble plant, *Mimosa pudica*. "So humble is the Humble Plant that a mere touch of the finger or a puff of breath blown across it will cause it to collapse instantly into a woebegone heap, like the once popular Ally Sloper." It soon rises again, and then you have the fun of doing it all over. I don't remember Ally Sloper, but I like the idea of having an humble plant. I think I shall order some seeds from Mr. Saier.

January 24, 1960

Animals in the Garden

"My garden is, I think and hope, a happy one," Phyllis Reiss, an English gardener, said on one of her broadcasts. "The birds have become so tame that in winter time they share their scraps on the lawn with my cocker spaniels, and the cat has kittens in an old yew cheek by jowl with a starling feeding its young and a tit nesting in a box a couple of feet away—all quite undisturbed by each other and by an old owl who has lived in the top of the tree for years—so I really do think it is a friendly garden!"

I wish I could say the same, but my garden is not a happy one. How can it be when I find the body of a little rabbit drowned in the pool on a bright morning in spring, or a baby bird dashed from its nest by a summer storm, to say nothing of the torture that goes on before my eyes.

I know, of course, that dogs and wild things may become friendly. We once had a cocker who liked to romp with a wild rabbit, and I know of two cats who are said to have no taste for birds. One of the cats lives at Briarwood with Caroline Dormon, who has taught the shiest birds to eat out of her hand. The other is an enormous golden creature, called Butterball, who spends his days on a sunny ledge in Mrs. Henderson's rock garden. He was lying there, looking dreamily into the woods, while his mistress spoke of his virtues. I thought he winked at me.

In my garden I have never seen a cat eat a bird, or even approach one, although I do find little piles of soft feathers here and there. It is the chipmunks I fear for. When my cat had the run of the place, it seemed to me that I never went out without meeting her on her way down the long path with a wretched little beast in her mouth. When she had kittens (which was often) I was confined to the house during all daylight hours.

But now that she has gone to the country to live, the chipmunk population has increased alarmingly, and the garden is so riddled with tunnels that the stone walls are sagging, and the shrub borders and flower beds seem about to cave in. Even while I am wondering how I can reduce the numbers of little animals going so confidently about their business, I suffer every time a stray cat wanders in from the street, and crouches before one of the holes, waiting for its hapless victim.

It is comforting to find that I am not the only person torn by the imbalance of nature. In his collection of essays, *The Points of My Compass* (Harper and Rowe), E. B. White writes of his enemy the fox.

"I shot a fox last fall," he says, "a long, lucky shot with a .22 as he drank at the pond. It was cold murder. All he wanted at the moment was a drink of water, but the list of his crimes against me was a long one, and so I shot him dead, and he fell backward and sank slowly into the mud.

"The war between me and the fox is as senseless as all wars. There is no way to rationalize it. The fox is not even the biggest and meanest killer here—I hold that distinction myself. I think nothing of sending half a dozen broilers to the guillotine. . . . I have plenty of convictions but no real courage, and I find it hard to live in the country without slipping into the role of murderer."

I find it hard to live anywhere without slipping into the role of murderer. Last spring I sent Ulysses up on a ladder to clear out the nests that the sparrows had built under the eaves. He cleared them out, baby birds and all. And yet the young of the sparrows must be as dear to them as young wrens are to wrens.

I had supposed that as I grew older I would become hardened to the suffering of small animals, but I find that as my gardening fingers thicken, my skin grows thinner than ever. And even at moments when the garden seems to be happy, a shadow falls, and there comes to mind an echo from childhood:

He hears the cry of the little kit fox,
And the lemming in the snow.

January 6, 1963

Mrs. Radau's Shoebox

Some years ago I saw an advertisement in the *Mississippi Market Bulletin* for a shoebox full of dried plant material for winter bouquets. I sent for one, and when I opened it I couldn't name a single thing in it. This fall I ordered another, from a different person, Mrs. Radau of Saucier, Mississippi, but this time I asked her to label everything. Many of Mrs. Radau's plants are familiar—some grow in my own garden—but I would not have known what they were if she had not put their names on them, and I had never realized how beautiful they are when they are really looked at.

The first thing I took out of the box was a spray of crape myrtle berries. They are small, round, oxford gray, and satiny, and set in little pale brown, star-pointed saucers. I know, of course, the prickly balls of the sweet gum, but I am not at all sure that without the label I could have named the granular sand-colored balls of the sycamore, and I know I wouldn't have recognized the sticky brown burrs of the Chinquapin, with spines as sharp as needles.

I might have guessed the slender, papery, cinnamon-colored cones of the tulip tree, and could surely have named the tiny, delicate cones of alder, but I wouldn't have been able to distinguish the cone of the spruce pine from that of our old field pine, though they are very different when laid side by side. There were cones of three species of magnolia: the large ones of *Magnolia grandiflora*, the smaller ones of *M. virginiana*, and the very slender ones of *M. pyramidata* with their tapered and curiously twisted seed vessels.

Some of these things fall to the ground, and are there for the gathering, but others must be picked from the limbs of tall trees. As I unpacked the shoebox I wondered how Mrs. Radau had collected them. She must have an army of small boys at her command. I wish I had one small climber to swarm up the empress tree, and cut for me some bare branches tipped with tawny velvet, winter buds.

Along with the cones there were pods of two kinds of garden okra, one long and thin and curved like a scimitar, the other large and straight, and striped in pearl grey and silver. There were enormous toast-colored pods of some kind of Louisiana iris, and some olive-sheen hibiscus bolls, covered with silky hairs as fine as gossamer. I wanted to make a wreath of these things, but I knew I never would, so I arranged them in a circle in a round wicker tray, and added some mimosa pods (also from the box) the color of amber, and almost as translucent.

Some little white balls on very long thin stems were marked buttonwort. I couldn't find this name in any botany or horticultural dictionary, but after a while I thought of hat pins, and looking in *The Natural Gardens of North Carolina* I found a picture of them, growing in a grassy marsh with tall pines in the background. Dr. Wells also calls them pipeworts, and gives a choice of three Latin names, none of which, I am sure, are ever heard outside of a classroom.

Some other buttons, larger and on shorter, stouter stems, were honey colored, and looked like small empty honey combs. I put these in a brown bottle. They were labeled "wild sun flower of some kind." There were several tall spikes of small thickly clustered, seed vessels of a rich chocolate color. These were marked dockweed. Dock is a name attached to many different plants, but I take this to be garden patience, *Rumex patientia*, an old-world weed that is naturalized in this country, and grows in waste places. There were also some great cottony plumes in tones of rosy fawn, on tall reedy stems. These were marked papyrus grass.

I shall write more about Mrs. Radau later on, as she has listed seeds of rare native trees and shrubs and wild flowers, that she collects on her plantation near the Gulf Coast.

January 27, 1963

Moss

I always wanted a moss garden, but I never knew how to go about making one. Now, I find that it is only a question of time. As a garden ages, moss comes.

It has begun to grow in great patches in a damp place at the foot of a down spout, and it grows in narrow velvet strips between the bricks around the pool, and it is beginning to carpet the bare ground under the pines, and to embroider the rocks of the retaining walls.

All that is needed is bare ground, or rocks, or fallen trees, or walls, or roofs—there is even a kind, *Muscus calvarius*, that grows on human skulls if they are left exposed. This is the moss that is frequently used as a ground cover in Japanese gardens. In the pictures it looks like a very coarse sedum. The Japanese devote whole gardens to moss collections. At the Moss Temple, near Kyoto, there are said to be twenty kinds.

Mosses are the first plants to appear on naked rocks and bare ground and burnt-over places, and when these are available they will come of their own accord. The book says (though I have not found it so) that bits brought from the woods are easily established if the natural surroundings are noted, and duplicated as nearly as possible, and if some of the rock, soil, or rotten wood on which the mosses are growing is brought along. "Press them down gently," the book says. "The rhizoids will soon grow and make firm contact with the soil beneath." In transplanting mosses I think the main thing is not to let them dry out, but city water is a doubtful benefit, and water from a zinc can is said to be poisonous.

As mosses form seed beds for the higher plants, continuous and patient weeding is needed to keep them in good condition. Like a carpet they need sweeping, and I find it is best done with a small, stiff whisk broom that brushes away the leaves and other debris that gathers on them, without taking up tufts of the moss itself, as a rake is sure to do.

Mosses like shade and humidity. Most of them prefer moisture in the air, but not too much of it in the soil. Like other plants they are divided into lime-lovers, lime-haters, and those-that-are-not-particular.

As mosses are not in the trade they will have to be gathered from the woods. I would like a collection, if only for their charmingly descriptive names, such as willow moss, apple moss, palm tree moss, foxtail feather moss, and silvery thread moss.

There is something soothing in mossy recesses—perhaps because the plants are on such a small scale, perhaps because they bring with them the silence and serenity of the deep woods. "The beauty there is in mosses," Thoreau says, "will have to be considered from the holiest quietest nook." The mosses, Ruskin said, are "the first mercy of the earth," because they tenderly cover the ruins of war and time. "No words that I know of," he said, "will tell what these mosses are. None are delicate enough, none perfect enough, none rich enough. How is one to tell of rounded mosses of furred and beaming green—the starred divisions of rubied bloom, fine filmed as if Rock Spirits could spin porphyry as we do glass—the tracery of intricate silver, and fringes of amber, lustrous, arborescent, burnished through every fiber into fitful brightness and glossy traverses of silken change, yet all subdued and pensive and framed for simplest, sweetest offices of grace."

I have been trying to identify, with the aid of a book lent to me by Mittie Wellford, the various mosses that have appeared in my garden, the feathery, the spiky, the cut-velvet; "mosses like little fir-trees, like plush, like malachite stars"; but I despair of ever distinguishing the genera, much less the species and varieties. Still, I hope in time to learn the names of the common kinds.

Most mosses are small, some so small that they can scarcely be seen by the naked eye, but the common hair moss (*Polytrichum commune*)—though sometimes only two or three inches tall in dry places—may grow to a height of a foot or more. This is the kind that is frequently used as a ground cover.

January 3, 1965

A Witch's Garden

Behind her house, Carolina Tillett says, there is a dark wood where toadstools grow. She thinks she would like to make it into a witches' garden. She thinks she would like to grow her own poisons for "the charmed pot":

Double, double, toil and trouble
Fire burn, and cauldron bubble.

I told her I would make a list of herbs suitable for witches' broth, as it is a subject I have given some thought to. Hemlock would be at the top of the list, a handsome plant that likes to grow in shady places; and yew, also a lover of shade, would be next. The witches in *Macbeth* put both of these in their pot: "root of hemlock digged in the dark," and

Gall of goat and slips of yew
Slivered in the moon's eclipse.

Shakespeare called the yew "double-fatal" because the wood was used for bows, and the berries were thought to be poisonous. Some think the "cursed hebenon" that Hamlet's uncle poured in the king's ear was distilled from yew, but others think henbane (*Hyoscyamus niger*), a magic herb and a favorite of witches, was the plant Shakespeare had in mind. Henbane is a strong narcotic. An old writer says that if it is eaten in a sallet or pottage it brings frenzie, "and whoso useth more than four leaves shall be in danger to sleepe without waking."

The plants Ben Jonson names for a witch's broth are

Hemlock, Henbane, Adder's Tongue bane
Nightshade, moonwort, Leopard's-bane.

Adder's Tongue is an unfernlike little fern, *Ophioglossum vulgatum*, that looks like an arum. I have not found anything about its use by witches, but it was supposed to have great power for evil, to keep grass from growing near it, and to poison cattle. It was also an ancient wound herb, and was used in the "Green Oil of Charity."

Nightshade is the deadliest herb of all. It belongs to the devil. "This kind of nightshade," Gerard says, "causeth sleep, troubleth the mind, bringeth madness if a few berries be inwardly taken, but if more be given they also kill and bring present death. . . . If you will follow my counsell, deale not with the same in any case, and banish it from your gardens . . . three boyes of Wisbich in the Isle of Ely did eat of the pleasant and beautiful fruit hereof . . . two whereof died in less than eight hours. . . ." The third boy, he goes on to say, drank a quantity of honey and water and recovered. Deadly nightshade is *Atropa belladonna*, named for Atropos, the Fate whose duty it was to cut the thread of life. A witches' garden should have enchanter's nightshade, *Circaea*, for the sake of its name, though it has no evil properties, and is not known to have been used in enchantments.

Moonwort, *Botrychium lunaria*, has magical powers if gathered by moonlight. If its leaves are stuffed in keyholes, it will open locks, no matter how fast, and horses who step on it will lose their shoes. Alchemists prized it, too, for changing quicksilver to pure silver.

Leopard's bane, *Doronicum pardalianches*, so called because it was supposed to destroy wild animals, was also said by some old writers to be poisonous to human beings, but Gerard said John de Vroede "ate very manie of the rootes at sundrie times, and found them very pleasant in taste, and very comfortable." The roots were once in good supply in apothecaries' shops.

As witches like plants that are poisonous, or that stir up passions of love and hatred, mandrake, an ancient aphrodisiac, belongs to their gardens. Gerard says, "Mandrake is called Circaea, of Circe the witch, who by art could procure love; for it hath been thought that the root thereof served to win love."

Rue was used in pagan rites before witches took it for their own incantations, and then the Christians called it the Herb of Grace, and used the sprigs to sprinkle holy water. It is said to quicken the sight, and also to bestow second sight. It is one of the plants that must not be given away, but will prosper only when stolen.

Witches are enabled to fly by anointing themselves with an ointment containing the juice of smallage, wolf bane, and cinquefoil.

January 9, 1966

Cordial Flowers

The cordial flowers are those that cheer the heart. They are the rose, the violet, alkanet and borage, borage being the foremost. The old saying "I, borage, always bring courage" is a translation of an older adage, *Ego borago gaudia semper ago*. "The leaves and floures of Borage put into Wine," Gerard said, "make men and women glad and merry, and drive away all sadness, dullness and melancholy. Syrrup made of the floures of Borage comforteth the heart, purgeth melancholy, and quieteth the phrenticke or lunaticke person. Syrrup made of the juice of Borage with sugar . . . is good against swooning, the cardiac passion of the heart . . . and falling sickness."

Pliny said borage steeped in wine would raise men's spirits, and the soldier who drank from the cool tankard, "wine and water with lemon juice, spices and borage," was assured of success in battle. But the herbalists found in borage qualities to soothe as well as to exhilarate. Pliny believed it was Homer's nepenthe, which caused complete forgetfulness.

Borage is used in the claret cup; an old recipe calls for a bottle of claret, a pint of water, a tablespoon full of sugar, a teaspoon full of mixed spices (cloves, cinnamon, and allspice), thinly cut lemon rind, and a sprig of borage. Only the best wine should be used. Some say the cup should be iced. Others shudder at the thought, but all agree that it must be chilled. All parts of borage are used—a number of old recipes call for the roots, and others use the leaves or flowers. The blue flowers are pretty floating on summer drinks or fruit punches.

Gertrude Foster recommends red rhubarb, boiled for twenty minutes, as a drink for children. Strain, add four ounces of sugar, two tablespoons of raspberry juice, and serve with nutmeg and crushed borage leaves. She says rhubarb puts a protective coating on the teeth.

Fr. Butler's Cordial Water, described in *The Queen's Closet Opened* by the cook to Queen Henrietta-Marie (1655), calls for both borage and bugloss. Parkinson says, "Borage and Buglosse are held to be both temperate herbs, being used both in the pot and in drinkes that are cordiall, especially the flowers, which of Gentlewomen are candied for comfits."

The distilled water of roses, Gerard says, "is good for the strengthening of the heart, and refreshing of the spirits. . . . Of like vertue also are the leaves of these preserved in Sugar, especially if they be only bruised with the hands . . . , and so heat at the fire rather than boyled." He also tells how to make a conserve of roses which "taken in the morning fasting, and last at night, strengtheneth the heart, and taketh away the shaking and trembling thereof." Both fruits and petals strengthen the heart, and the Romans liked to find the petals floating in the wine cup.

Gerard said candied violets are "most pleasant and wholesome, and especially comfort the heart and other inward parts." He considered violets the chief ornament of the garden, as well as being delightful to look on, and pleasant "to smell to" in garlands, nosegays and posies, "speaking nothing of their appropriate vertues . . . for they admonish and stir up a man to that which is comely and honest." Along with their cordial virtues of comforting and strengthening the heart, violets are said to moderate anger and to induce sleep.

All four of the cardinal flowers go into metheglin, the traditional drink of Wales: The rose, "take of sweet-bryar a great handful," violet-flowers, violet leaves, bugloss and borage. Added to these are rosemary and strawberry leaves, and a great many other herbs and spices, including a trace of ginger. The herbs are boiled in water which is then strained; a quantity of honey is added, and the mixture is fermented with ale-barm (a sort of yeast). They say it is heady stuff, and I feel sure it will warm the heart.

As I was reading Gerard, and the astronauts were being shot into space, I was startled to come upon a question he asked in 1597: "Who would looke dangerously up at Planets, that might safely look downe at Plants?"

January 23, 1966

Mrs. Sheets's Wildflowers

I have been exchanging notes with Mrs. Olen Sheets of Reidsville about the wildflowers in her rock garden. "I think the things that give me most pleasure," she wrote early in December, "are shortia, wild ginger (*Asarum shuttleworthii*), trailing arbutus and the Christmas fern and ebony spleenwort. Also twayblade and goodyera. Even now I enjoy walking in the garden and finding them green and fresh on a blustery day. Trailing arbutus and shortia are happy in my new moist bed which I made for wildflowers when I found that water is the secret of keeping them alive. I am surprised to see some arbutus still growing down on the trail where it had no water at all this very dry summer. It was brought from Olen's home, in Ashe County, and we got it up with the roots intact, which makes a difference in how things survive. Shortia is easier: all it asks for is leafmould, shade, and water."

Trailing arbutus characteristically grows in both wet and very dry places; for it occurs on the mountain tops in the great forest and in the hot sun of the Sandhills. "No other species associated with it in the forest," Dr. Wells says in *The Natural Gardens of North Carolina*, "has been able to accompany it in its excursion to the desert."

Asarum shuttleworthii, which we must now call *Hexastylis* as we are at the mercy of the taxonomists, not only looks pretty in winter but smells good when the heart-shaped leaves are crushed. Though it is a mountain species it is easily cultivated in the Piedmont. It is one of the seventy-eight herbaceous endemics of the southern highland flora.

Another is the lily-leaf sedge, *Carex fraseri*, now called *Cymophyllus*. It came to me from the Gardens of the Blue Ridge nearly ten years ago and has been growing at the foot of the bird bath ever since. The rosette of dark, finely ribbed leaves (an inch wide and a foot or more long) seems content to be in complete shade, but perhaps it would bloom more with a little sun. When it does bloom the flowers usually appear in March, but sometimes in April, and once in January. They are odd hat pins, small white heads of tiny flowers on very slender stems. The lily-leaf sedge is rare indeed, occurring only in a few places in our mountains in North Carolina and adjoining states.

I always think of galax as a mountain plant, and of course it is, but it also occurs plentifully in the Piedmont, and even in the coastal plain as far east as Onslow and Beaufort counties. In my garden, where it grows in deep shade, the leaves turn a deep Indian red in winter, and the pointed leaves of a nearby clump of epimedium take on the same tones.

I had thought of the little evergreen creeper, *Saxifraga virginiensis*, as a rare wildflower of the southern mountains, but I find it grows mostly in the Piedmont counties, including Mecklenburg, that it is not at all uncommon. There seems to be a difference of opinion as to its habitat. Some botanists say it grows in acid soil, some say the pH varies; some say it grows among shady rocks, and others that it is usually found in full sun. In my garden it seems happy in crevices of shady stone steps, and on some that get a lot of sun. The tiny white flowers are among the earliest of the wild things. I find that I failed to make a note of its blooming last spring, but I remember it as coming with the early daffodils.

When the delicate foliage of the false rue-anemone (*Isopyrum biternatum*) disappeared at the end of its first spring in my garden, I thought they had gone for good, but to my delight they came up again early in November. At first I couldn't be sure of them, because the three-parted leaves look just like the new fall foliage of columbine, which seeds itself all about, but the columbine soon grows taller, and the isopyrum makes a thick, close mat only a few inches tall. It seems to be beginning to spread, and I hope it will soon make a bright green winter carpet, as it does in the Ohio garden from which it came.

January 21, 1968

Homer's Asphodel

For years and years I have been pursuing the asphodel. I want it because it is beautiful and because I like to grow the plants of the poets, but it has continued to be rare in gardens and the trade, though it has been in cultivation since the days of the early herbalists. Once, long ago, I had it from Wayside Gardens, and it died during its first summer. Then, last year Marion Becker gave me a plant from her garden in Cincinnati, and that died during its first summer.

I think I know now why I lost it. I was misled by Pope's translation of the *Odyssey*:

They rest at last where souls unbodied dwell
In ever-flowing meads of Asphodel.

What Homer really said was, "Past streams of Oceanus and the White Rock, past the gates of the Sun they sped, and the land of dreams, and soon they came to the mead of asphodel, where dwell the souls, the phantoms of men outworn." Like Pope, I thought of it as growing in water meadows, and so I planted it in low damp places, though dampness seems to be just what it dislikes.

In Mrs. Becker's garden it grows on a hillside, and in a council ring. The council ring, a feature designed by Jens Jensen, and inspired by the Indians, is a circular stone wall, just high enough to sit on, with a fire pit in the center. Mrs. Becker's has no place for a fire; it is covered with large white pebbles, and in it there are clumps of yucca and asphodel. I think the asphodel likes the drainage of the hillside, and the mulch of pebbles, for it grows and blooms and reseeds.

This year Mrs. Becker gave me a seedling which I have planted to itself on a paved terrace, where the soil is never soggy, and where I can enjoy its small fountain of silvery leaves all winter. The leaves are never marred by cold, even in the most severe winters. This time I hope it will thrive, bloom and renew itself, for I know of no commercial source for plants, though one source supplies seeds. This source recommends part shade, and calls it a tender perennial, but it can't be very tender if it survives outdoors in Ohio. It is listed as *Asphodeline lutea*. The books say it blooms in summer, but the one time it bloomed in my Raleigh garden the first flower opened on March 28. The flowers are bright yellow stars arranged in a long spike on a tall leafless stalk.

Theophrastus called it a ferule plant. King's spear is one of its ancient names, and the French call it Jacob's staff. "It provides many things useful for food," Theophrastus said. "The stalk is edible when fried, the seed when roasted, and above all the root when cut up with figs; in fact, the plant is extremely profitable." Even in the Middle Ages the roots were considered a delicacy and called *Cibo Regio*, food for a king. It was because they were so generally eaten that the Greeks planted asphodels on graves as food for the dead, and they therefore became associated with death and the underworld. Persephone appears crowned with asphodel. It was also used as a repellent for rats and mice, as an antidote for snake bite, as a medicine, and as a specific against sorcery.

Pope also wrote of "Happy souls who dwell in yellow fields of asphodel, or amaranthine flowers." For amaranth is also associated with death. It means never fading. The *Oxford English Dictionary* calls it an imaginary flower, but I have read elsewhere that it is considered to be *Gomphrena*, the little globe amaranth that is grown as an annual, and dried for winter bouquets. This, they say, is the flower Milton had in mind, the "Immortal amarant, a flower which once in paradise, fast by the tree of life began to bloom." It was removed to heaven when Adam and Eve were driven from the garden, and there it "grows, and flowers aloft, shading the fount of life."

January 19, 1969

Bud-Hunting

On one of those cold misty days of mid-winter, when the lichens are like jewels, and the mosses greener than ever, I made a tour of the garden to be sure I was not missing anything. I found I was missing a good deal. For one thing, a flower of butcher's broom, *Ruscus aculeatus*.

I was not expecting it, as I had read somewhere that ruscus blooms in spring, but it must have been blooming for some time as I found, when I looked more closely, that little applegreen berries had already begun to form. Most of the old berries were still plump and red and shining, but some were beginning to shrivel. This season's crop will be gone before the end of the year.

The flower is a tiny, colorless, six-pointed star, as delicate as a snowflake. I took the dark wine-colored dot in the center to be the three stamens, as it was a male flower. I haven't yet come upon a female flower. *Ruscus* is the name Virgil gave to the genus (the Romans also called it myrtle). In the *Georgics* he says one of the chores of the husbandman is to cut the shoots in the woods. The new shoots were eaten like asparagus when they first appeared, and the old ones used for brooms. The buds were pickled like capers. I would hate to have to gather a spoonful.

Another thing I had missed, though I had been looking for them, was the berries of the compact form of *Ophiopogon japonicus*. Two bright beads were lying on the ground beside the plant Mr. W. O. Freeland gave me a year or so ago. Evidently some little animal had been a better searcher than I, for one of them had been nibbled. I hope he will remember, next year, that he didn't like the taste. The berries were greenish but they were turning blue, and looked as if they would be the brilliant, almost true blue of the type. The tiny leaves, an eighth of an inch long, are slightly curved. They come up very thick and make an almost flat ground cover. Mr. Freeland says the miniature form spreads as fast as the type, but doesn't get out of hand because the runners are short. Mine is planted between flagstones, and has made a nice little patch of green already.

On a dreary day, the first week in December, I spent a morning weeding and bud-hunting. I looked first for *Sternbergia fischerana*. I have two bulbs. One that I planted ten years ago hasn't bloomed for several years, and doesn't show any sign of doing it now. The other was planted a year ago this fall, and it bloomed at the end of January 1969. The tip of a bud was showing, so there will be one again this January. I have never but once had a bloom before Christmas, though Billy Hunt often has flowers for Thanksgiving. This species comes from the Caucasus, and is impervious to cold.

Then I looked at a patch of hoopskirt daffodils that I have had for twenty years. I had been looking at it for some time, and had found only the threadlike leaves, but now the pointed buds were up. They usually flower after the New Year. I found a few buds of 'Nylon', too, but none of 'Taffeta'. I hadn't much hope for 'Taffeta'. It makes a nice bit of foliage, but I haven't had a flower for years. I looked for crocuses, and in front of the house (which faces south) I found *Crocus imperati*. The bud opened soon afterward, which is unusual, for I seldom have flowers before January.

This is Beverley Nichols's favorite. "You may say 'what does it matter whether they come up in January or in March, provided they do come up?'" he admonishes his readers. "However if you were capable of asking that question you would not be reading me at all, for unless you long to defeat winter, to make your gardening year an endless chain of blossom, this would all be a sorry bore for you."

I missed the buds of *Crocus laevigatus* 'Fontenayi', but on the eleventh of December I found two pretty lilac flowers. I can usually count on finding this species before Christmas, and sometimes even in November, but last winter the buds did not open until after the New Year, and so in 1969 this species bloomed twice—at the beginning of the year and at the end. Both of these crocuses are deliciously fragrant, but I did not know this for a long time, as you must get on your knees on the cold ground in order to find it out.

January 4, 1970

✒ FEBRUARY

· · · · · · · · · · · · · · · · · ·

Catalogues

Along with the first days of spring come the spring bulb catalogues, the only thing that can keep a gardener indoors when buds begin to swell. The minute the postman brings one, I drop whatever I am doing, until I have found out whether it has anything new to offer. This spring I found several new offerings—all of them very expensive. It was painful to have to decide which to order at once, and which to leave for another season—especially as they might not be available another season.

I finally decided upon a new amarcrinum, because the two known to gardeners so far, *x Amarcrinum* 'Howardii' and *x A.* 'Delkin's Find', have proved to be such very satisfactory bulbs for late summer and fall; but $7.50 is a lot to pay for a bulb that may not bloom this season (or at all), and even if it does, may not be any better than the ones I already have. The new hybrid is called 'Dorothy Hannibal'. The only comment that its introducer, Houdyshel, makes, is that the flowers are a very pretty pink, and that it flowers at all seasons in southern California. It does not follow that it will flower at all seasons in North Carolina. The flowers of the other two are also a very pretty pink, and established bulbs usually put up the first scape in July and bloom on until frost.

The amarcrinums are a rare kind of hybrid, a cross between two genera. One parent is a crinum, the other an amaryllis. Like the crinums they respond to generous quantities of fertilizer and water, but they thrive without either.

If I could have only one crinum, 'Cecil Houdyshel' would be it, for it out-flowers them all, putting up one scape after another, from late May through August. I keep it in the back of the border, as the scapes are nearly four feet tall—twice as tall as those of the amarcrinums, which must go near the front—and the large mass of foliage is rather untidy. While this eight-year-old crinum is not so handsome as a clump of lilies in full bloom, no lily has ever bloomed in my garden for three months, or bloomed for so many years with increasing vigor.

Crinum 'Cecil Houdyshel' and the amarcrinums can be planted in the fall, but I think planting them in March gives them a better start. Ismenes should not go into the ground until April; then they can be planted at intervals to make the blooming season longer. Once, some left-over bulbs that I planted in mid-July bloomed as soon as they were planted and bloomed very well. The flaring cups of the frosty white flowers have blunt, finely fringed lobes, and green stripes inside; the narrow petals are slightly recurved. There are six or seven flowers on a stout, 30-inch scape that rises from a clump of broad, dark, shining leaves.

Just before frost, or when the foliage has been killed back, the bulbs can be dug and stored in peat moss for the winter. The roots must be intact, but the foliage should be cut away and the bulbs stored in a fairly warm place. For the past few years I have left mine in the ground. They are perfectly hardy, but bloom better if they are taken up.

Ismenes are called Peruvian daffodils. If they are not listed as ismenes in the catalogue look for *Hymenocallis calathina*. In my garden, ismenes and tuberoses are planted for a succession of sweet-smelling white flowers from June until frost. The pale wands of the tuberoses begin to shoot up soon after the middle of July, and there are always more coming when frost cuts them down at the end of October, or sometimes not until the end of November. In this climate there is no advantage in taking the tubers up; on the contrary, they bloom better for every year that they are left in the ground, and the clumps need never be touched except to keep them from encroaching on their neighbors, or to slice off a chunk to give away. Mine are the tall single variety called 'Mexican Everblooming'. I think 'The Pearl', a dwarf double form, is more tender.

Montbretias can be planted at any time in the spring, and left in the ground over winter; but they will have to be divided from time to time and spring is the time to divide them. Two forms are common in gardens: one with half-open flowers of an ugly red, and the other with wide flowers of a brilliant orange-yellow. The latter blooms brightly and steadily through the heat of July and August. It is not to be found in the catalogues, but sometimes turns up at the curb market. I got mine through an advertisement in the *Mississippi Market Bulletin*. The spring catalogues offer a number of the Earlham hybrids, an improvement on the old montbretias, with large flowers in patterns of yellow, orange and red. These bloom for weeks, the later ones carrying bright colors into the fall.

February 16, 1958

Young Gardeners

Alvin Cain, who wants to enliven the interest of his three-year-old daughter in gardening, has asked me how to go about it. This is a subject on which I am an authority, for I spent many years enlivening the interest of two children in particular, and those of the neighborhood in general. Their response was gratifying.

As long as nothing is accomplished, children love to join in whatever is being done—especially out of doors. They love to clip anything that doesn't need clipping, to rake up leaves and then scatter them, and above all they love water. But they are wary of having their efforts directed to any good purpose; the way to hold their interest is to give them gardens of their own, and to allow them to care for or neglect the plants in their own way. The flowers must be theirs to pick, to arrange, to play with, or to throw in the path to wither.

A child's garden requires an open sunny place where the soil is good, for she cannot be expected to persevere in planting a neglected corner where nothing will grow. It should be small. A plot a yard square is about right for a three-year-old. The ground must be prepared beforehand, but she should be allowed to do the planting herself. If she puts the bulbs and plants in upside downwards, they can be righted later. A child wants her own tools and they should be good strong ones of regular size. A trowel, a fork and a watering pot will be enough, but the watering pot should be small.

When I was eight, my mother told me the Parable of the Sower, and gave me a package of radish seeds. Things like radishes and lettuce are appealing because they grow from seed so quickly, and can be eaten on the spot—dirt and all. But I think for very little children it is better to start with plants.

At this time of the year it is not too late to put out spring flowers like English daisies, forget-me-nots and pansies. Children love pansies, especially when you buy them already in bloom. Mr. Cain should take his small daughter to the greenhouse and let her pick her own plants—even if her choice is not practical. She will probably want cactus or a sedum in a pot. Children love little plants in pots.

When spring flowers bloom out, they can be replaced with long-blooming summer annuals: petunias, verbenas, zinnias and marigolds. And in the fall, when these are gone, a child loves to plant bulbs. If fall crocuses are planted they will come up and bloom right away. For spring there are daffodils, tulips and hyacinths.

There are some plants that I always keep in my garden for the sake of young visitors. At dusk they like to watch the slow-motion opening of moonflowers; they love flowers with names like foxglove, sweet William and Johnny-jump-up; and flowers, like four-o'clocks, that tell the time. *Sedum spectabile* is popular because, once you perfect the technique of separating the thin upper surface from the lower part of the fleshy leaves, you can blow them up to make dolls' hot water bottles. Best of all is the balloon vine with its silken balloons that float on the pool, or explode if you squeeze them, and its round black seed with a little white heart printed on it; or the Passion vine, with hollow pods that can be cut in half to make little boats. For even more than reaping and sowing, children delight in playing in water, and a shallow pool, not more than a foot deep, is the greatest attraction of a garden.

I hope Mr. Cain will not be disappointed if his words fall on barren ground, and his little girl does not grow up to be a gardener. Recently one of the children whose interest I enlivened (now thirteen) asked me the name of a flower in a pot. It was a hyacinth. The other (now fifteen) said, "I never did see what you find to interest you in growing flowers."

February 22, 1959

Gardens of Childhood

There is a garden in every childhood, an enchanted place where colors are brighter, the air softer, and the morning more fragrant than ever again. And in later years a familiar scent brings it to mind. When "Elizabeth" first wandered into the bare and desolate German garden that was to become her own, she wrote in her diary:

I don't know what smell of wet earth or rotting leaves brought back my childhood with a rush, and all the happy days I had spent in a garden. Shall I ever forget that day? It was the beginning of my real life, my coming of age as it were, and entering into my kingdom. Early March, gray, quiet skies, and brown, quiet earth; leafless and sad and lonely enough out there in the damp and silence, yet there I stood feeling the same rapture of pure delight in the first breath of spring that I used to as a child.

It was the scent of lavender on the streets of Athens that suddenly brought Grandmama's garden before my cousin Harriet. "When I got back to my room," Harriet wrote, "I just sat and wrote. I think I remember every flower, bush and shrub in that garden. I remember the big rose bush, the small red ones, the sweet one with the tight petals, and the old-fashioned white rose climbing on the window. I know where the tuberoses were, the sage (which I disliked), the roses that did not do so well, the lemon verbena, a grape vine by the back porch, rosemary, and a plant from which dolls' hot water bottles could be manufactured! There were two lilac bushes by the side porch next to Grandmama's room. The lavender was under the bay window—and how I loved it."

Harriet's letter brought the garden back to me, just as it was when we picked althea (called rose of Sharon in those days) and petunias and four-o'clocks to make the flower people who inhabited the wonderful play-house made by the roots of the Big Tree. It was the garden of my child-hood, too. I think of it as drenched with sunlight and fragrance, but with pools of shade. It was a Low Country garden (though in middle Georgia) with gravel paths and grass-bordered flower beds, the grass kept neatly clipped by Uncle Colding.

I remember the central bed as being in the shape of a heart, but when I asked Harriet about this, she said she would draw a plan. In the plan she made the bed a triangle. "In my mind's eye I see it all very clearly," she said, "but on paper it looks like a vagueness." To me the plan was very clear: the lemon verbena in the long border just where I remembered it, the roses in the central bed and along the white-washed rail fences, the fig tree at the end of the path, and the rose of Sharon by Grandmama's porch—there were porches for every exposure, and the windows that opened on to them came down to the floor. I remember the sage that Harriet didn't like (it was red salvia), but not the tuberoses under the parlor window, nor the lilacs in the shrubbery.

I wish I knew the names of the roses. They probably came from the gardens from which Mr. Sam Hjort made his collection of old roses, and he must still grow at least a few of them. Looking over his catalogue I wonder if the big red rose (Harriet says there were very few pink ones) was the 'Princesse de Sagan', a very dark red tea with semi-double flowers. The small red roses were almost certainly 'Louis Phillippe', the dear and fragrant and almost everblooming China rose that used to grow in nearly every dooryard.

I think the reason that Grandmama's garden is so well remembered is that children were allowed to pick as many flowers as they needed, for there was nothing rare or choice in the flower beds: petunias, four-o'clocks, roses—the more they were picked, the better they bloomed.

February 7, 1960

Winter Blooms

Each year, as the days come and go, I like to think of the flowers that belong to them. The year begins with *Viburnum tinus*, the flower of Saint Faine, which is said to bloom on New Year's Day, when

Raine comes but seldom, and often snow,
And yet this viburnum is sure to blow.

In these parts I have, once or twice, known a few rosy buds to be open at the turn of the year, but flowers are scarce before February or March.

Helleborus niger is called Christ's herb, but it blooms all through January, and so it stands for Saint Agnes (the twenty-first) and for the Conversion of Saint Paul (on January the twenty-third). It belongs to Saint Agnes, who was martyred when she was fourteen, because it is the emblem of purity, but Henry Bright always thought of the snowdrop in connection with her, as Tennyson described her with the first snowdrop of the year on her breast.

An old English *Kalendar of Flowers* begins with the second of February:

The snowdrop in purest white arraie
First rears her head on Candlemas daie;
While crocus hastens to the shrine
Of primrose lone on St. Valentine.

Candlemas, the feast of the Purification, used to be considered the end of the Christmas season. It was celebrated at church by lighting a great many candles, and at home by taking down the Christmas greens.

Herrick, who wrote four poems on the ceremonies of Candlemas, describes another custom:

Kindle the Christmas Brand and then
        Till Sunne-set, let it burne;
Which quencht, then lay it up agen,
        Till Christmas next returne.

Part must be kept wherewith to teend
        The Christmas Log next yeare;
And where 'tis safely kept, the Fiend,
        Can do no mischiefe (there).

English snowdrops (*Galanthus nivalis*), called Candlemas bells, or Mary's tapers, are the emblem of hope. They are not often seen hereabouts, as their place is taken by the snowflake, which grows so much better with us, but I have had them in my garden by the second of February or before. The one that does best for me is the variety 'Scharlokii', a garden form that comes from Germany. In mild seasons it blooms on Candlemas Day. One of the stories of the garden of Eden is that it was snowing when Adam and Eve were driven out, and the Angel, touching the flakes, turned them to flowers as a sign that spring would come.

English poets, at least from the time of Chaucer, have considered Saint Valentine's Day, "whan every byrd cometh ther to chese his make," as the first day of spring; but Hesiod reckoned it from the evening when "the star Arcturus leaves the holy stream of Ocean and first rises brilliant at dusk. After him . . . the swallow appears to men when spring is just beginning." I never think of the crocus as hastening to the shrine of the lone snowdrop on the fourteenth of February, for in my garden the flowers are usually past their prime by then, and the species have been blooming one after another all through the fall and winter.

Last year there was not much in bloom in mid-February, but usually the gardens in the neighborhood are full of flowers. Looking over my notes for past years I find *Scilla siberica* and *S. tubergeniana*; *Iris reticulata*; campernells; early trumpet daffodils, and many others such as 'February Gold' and 'March Sunshine'; early azaleas ('Coral Bells') and such shrubs as forsythia, spiraea and flowering quince; wild plums and some of the Oriental magnolias; spring starflowers and a number of other small early-flowering bulbs.

Just to read about them (as I write this on a cold day in January) makes me feel that spring is already here. But the astronomers say that it is not spring until the sun crosses the equator (about the twenty-first of March) and the meteorologists say it is not spring until the average daily temperature is 48 degrees. I called the weatherman to ask him when this would be in Charlotte, and he says that that temperature is normal for the second of March.

February 12, 1961

Graveyard Roses

As long as humans have died, roses have been planted on their graves. There was an ancient belief that one of the properties of the flower is to prevent decay:

The rose distils a healing balm,
The beating pulse of pain to calm;
Preserves the cold inured clay,
And mocks the vestige of decay;
And after death its odours shed
A pleasing fragrance o'er the dead.

Parsons, in his invaluable book *On the Rose*, says the Romans considered roses so important to the dead that they left money in their wills to provide gardens to furnish flowers and plants for their tombs; and those too poor for such bequests, asked to have these words inscribed on their head stones:

Have pity on me, all who pass
And scatter roses on the grass.

The Romans must have carried this custom to England. Parsons quotes Evelyn as saying, "The white rose was planted at the grave of a virgin. . . .

The red rose was occasionally used in remembrance of such as had been remarkable for their benevolence; but roses in general were appropriated to the graves of lovers." Popular ballads prove the truth of the last: for example, the one about Fair Margaret who died for pure true love, and Sweet William who died for sorrow:

Out of her breast there sprung a rose
And out of his a brier.
They grew till they grew to the top of the church,
And when they could grow no higher,
There they entwined in a true lovers knot
For all lovers true to admire.

Lovers of old roses know that the church yard is the place to look for them. Perhaps they are planted there because the brief bloom of the flower is a reminder of the short term of human existence, or because people plant near the dead the flowers they love best. Whatever the reason, they flourish among the graves long after they have disappeared from the trade.

I wish I knew the name of the rose that grows in the Edgewater cemetery on the Hudson River. Joseph Mitchell writes about it in *The Bottom of the Harbor*. It is a peaceful place, where the caretaker does a good deal of gardening, he says, and

old men and old women come in the spring, with hoes and rakes, and clean off their family plots and plant old-fashioned flowers on them. . . . Coarse, knotty, densely tangled rose-bushes grow on several plots, hiding graves and gravestones. The roses that they produce are small and fragile and extraordinarily fragrant, and have waxy red hips almost as big as crabapples. Once, walking through the cemetery, I stopped and talked with an old woman who was down on her knees in her family plot, setting out some bulbs at the foot of a grave, and remarked on the age of the rosebushes. "I believe some of the ones in here now were in here when I was a young woman, and I am past eighty," she said. "My mother—this is her grave—used to say there were rosebushes just like these all over this section when she was a girl. Along the riverbank, beside the roads, in people's yards, on fences, in waste places."

And she said *her* mother . . . told her she had heard from *her* mother that all of them were descended from one bush that some poor uprooted woman who came to this country back in the Dutch times potted up and brought along with her. . . . "I know why they do so well in here," the old lady's mother would say. "They've got good strong roots that go right down into the graves."

And this brings up another ancient belief, that flowers with petals as red as blood spring from the ground where the dead have lain: there are poppies in Flanders field, and

I sometimes think that never blows so red
The rose as where some buried Caesar bled.

February 4, 1962

Chaenomeles

I have been making a list of flowering shrubs (those that drop their leaves), one for each month of the year. The list begins with the Chinese witch hazel, and ends with wintersweet. For February I have in mind the flowering quince; though the height of its bloom is often a month later, there are other shrubs for March, and I can think of none so colorful in February.

The cultivated quinces are forms of two species, *Chaenomeles japonica*, and *C. lagenaria*; and of *C. x superba*, a hybrid between these two. As *C. japonica* is dwarf, and *C. lagenaria* is tall there is a great variety in habit. The flowers are white, spectrum red, and tones between red and orange. They bloom between Thanksgiving and Easter. *C. japonica* is a prostrate shrub that spreads very slowly to three or four feet. I used to have it in Raleigh in the shady rock garden, where the small coral flowers appeared freely in March, with a few at almost any time of the year. I do not know the dwarf hybrids but several are available. 'Roxana Foster' was described in Mr. Foster's 1953 catalogue as very low and spreading and growing slowly to a height of two or three feet. He says the large flowers are borne in profusion all over the plant. "In color it is deep shell pink in the center blending to carmine rose at the tips of the petals. It begins to bloom at midseason, and blooms over a long period."

Mr. Foster no longer ships flowers, but this is one of the two dozen or so varieties listed by Walter B. Clarke and Co. Mr. Clarke, who died several years ago, developed all of the West Coast forms. He described his 'Pink Lady' as low and spreading, but in my garden it grew very quickly to a height of seven feet. 'Pink Lady' has small flowers of a clear begonia rose. It blooms a little in fall and winter as well as in spring, and the plants have few or no thorns.

'Apple Blossom' is the loveliest of all if it is an enormous bush. It is much too large for my garden, but I must have it for it is the most beautiful shrub of early spring. In spite of continued hacking it is at least 10 feet tall, and has a spread of more than 15 feet. Some years the pink tinted flowers begin to open in January, once as early as the 10th. If they are frozen there are more to come. 'Early Apple Blossom' is even more precocious, and is a smaller and more compact shrub, but it is extremely rare, and I doubt whether it is in the trade at present, unless Mr. Foster could be persuaded to yield one up.

In old gardens through the South there is a beautiful white quince. I have never known what it is, perhaps just an unnamed hybrid. It has bloomed out-of-doors as early as New Year's Day, and can be forced very easily. The nice thing about these strong-growing varieties is that they can be cut ruthlessly. The white-flowered quinces in the trade are 'Candida', 'Nivalis' and 'Snow', all forms of *Chaenomeles lagenaria*, and all vigorous. 'Snow' grows taller than wide, is almost thornless and has pure white flowers to two and a half inches across—or so Mr. Foster says. The Clarkes think it the best white quince, but it blooms late in the season, and I consider earliness the great charm of this genus.

There are any number of good red-flowering quinces in all sizes and shapes. The colors range from spectrum red to orange. Many of the red ones are English hybrids. Two dwarf ones, 'Knaphill' and 'Rowallane', offered by Wayside Gardens, are less than two feet tall. I remember a beautiful double-flowered quince of a good clear pink in Mrs. Royster's garden in Raleigh. This was twenty-five years ago, and it was considered a very rare shrub. Now there are several double-flowered forms in the trade. The Clarkes list 'Cameo', low, spreading and thornless, with an apricot flower with more than twenty petals.

The way the quinces grow, thick and thorny and close to the ground, makes for a good hedge plant. As V. Sackville-West advised in *The Garden*, "for your hedges plant the tossing quince":

In sentimental Apple-Bloom, full blown,
Or Knaphill Scarlet . . . flown
Startling against a sky as gray as stone;
Or, deep as a Venetian robe outspread
Against a cottage wall, the veteran Red.

February 18, 1962

Wearing the Leek

In *High Rising* there is a conversation about the saints of spring and their flowers. Mrs. Morland says, "'You can send me some [leeks] on St. David's Day, and I'll wear them in my bonnet.'

"'Are you Welsh, then?' asked Amy Birkett.

"'Oh, no, but it's nice to wear things on the right day. Only the right day . . . and the right flower never seem to come together. One can't possibly expect roses to be out on St. George's Day, at least not if St. George's Day comes on the twenty-third of April. . . . And as for St. Patrick's Day, shamrock may be in season then, I don't know. . . . Luckily one doesn't have to wear thistles for St. Andrew.'"

Perhaps there are no roses in Barsetshire at the end of April, but there are in North Carolina if you are not too particular as to kind, and there is almost always a yellow crocus to greet Saint Valentine on the first day of spring. And the leeks come up in time to provide a green shoot for Saint David on the first of March—they do not need to be in bloom.

St. David, the patron saint of Wales, was a sixth-century hermit who told the Welsh soldiers to stick leeks in their caps as they went into battle against the Saxons, so that they could tell friend from foe. As the Welshmen were victorious, they took the leek for their national emblem, but later on they thought it was not good enough, and substituted the daffodil.

I can't blame them for not wanting to wear leeks, but Mrs. Morland's friend George Knox did: "'St. David, dear Mrs. Birkett,' he said, 'had no nonsense about him, and knew that a leek was about all his countrymen were fit for . . . for a nation, despicable enough to try to change the leek to a daffodil, words fail me to express my contempt.'"

In *Henry V*, Shakespeare refers frequently to wearing the leek. The King, having been born at Monmouth, a town celebrated for its caps much worn by soldiers, finds a great bond between him and the gallant captain Fluellen, who says, "If your majesties is remembered of it, the Welshmen did good service in a garden where leeks did grow, wearing leeks in their Monmouth caps; which your majesty know to this hour is an honourable badge of the service. And I do believe your majesty takes no scorn to wear the leek upon St. Tavy's day." And the King answers, "I wear it for a memorable honour; for I am Welsh, you know, good countryman."

In another scene, Fluellen makes the bully, Pistol, eat the leek, which means eat humble pie. Pistol says he is "qualmish at the smell," but Fluellen takes the leek from his cap and forces his victim to swallow every bit, with blows for sauce. "If you can mock a leek, you can eat a leek," he says.

It seems to have been customary for royalty to wear the leek, and for it to be worn in their presence, for the *London Gazette*, in 1722, described the company as wearing it in honor of the Princess of Wales; and in 1882 London papers, announcing a drawing-room held by the queen on the first of March, said, "Her Royal Highness the Princess of Wales wore a dress of a new shade of green velvet, with broad revers of palest blue and gold brocade, over a petticoat of fine Irish lace, fastened up with a bunch of Shamrock leaves and forget-me-nots. Being St. David's Day, Her Royal Highness also wore the Leek."

In *The Useful Herbs*, Eleanor Chalfin says that the leek, *Allium porrum*, the mildest of the onion tribe, is valuable as a cut flower (both fresh and dried), as well as for salads, soups, and as a vegetable. It is easily and quickly grown from seed, which can be sown in either spring or fall in rich soil. Leeks have been valued as pot herbs since the days of the Pharaohs. They were probably brought to England by Roman soldiers and have been grown in cottage gardens ever since. In his instructions to sixteenth-century gardeners for March, Thomas Tusser wrote:

Now leekes are in season, for pottage full good,
And spareth the milchcow, and purgeth the blood.

February 25, 1962

Mount Vernon

As George Washington's birthday comes around again, I have been thinking of the view from Mount Vernon, and wondering how the plans for the park along the Potomac are progressing. I wrote to Robert Fisher, horticulturist of the Ladies Association, to ask about it. So far, Mr. Fisher says, only part of the land for the park authorized by Congress in 1961 has been acquired, and the support of the public is needed to see that we get the rest. He says, "We must keep the public advised that they must ask their congressmen and their senators why this park is not now an entity." George Washington's birthday is a good day to do it.

In 1798 Julian Niemcewicz visited Mount Vernon, and wrote in his diary: "The whole plantation, the garden, and the rest prove well that a man born with natural taste may guess a beauty without ever having seen its model. The general never left America; but when one sees his house and garden it seems as if he had copied the best sample of the grand old homesteads of England."

Washington's plans for Mount Vernon are not only of the high order his Polish guest granted them, they are also unique in the way they combine the geometric patterns of Elizabethan gardens with the flowing curves of the English landscape school of the eighteenth century. The pair of walled gardens, placed symmetrically on either side of the bowling green, are laid out in formal box-bordered beds, and between the gardens and the bell-shaped lawn of the bowling green there are matching serpentine avenues.

The kitchen garden, the first to be planted (in 1760), had "all the vegetables, indispensable for the kitchen," Niemcewicz said, and "different kinds of berries—currants, raspberries, strawberries, gooseberries—and a great quantity of peaches and cherries." He was also impressed with the beauty of the trees, especially the tulip trees. He thought the scent of the magnolias less pleasing than that of orange blossoms, and said the small flowers of the "sweter scent" had the pleasantest smell he had ever noticed, "a mixture of strawberries and pineapple." This must have been the sweet-Betsy, *Calycanthus floridus*, sometimes called the sweet-scented shrub, planted by Washington at Mount Vernon.

There was a splendid catalpa, but it was not in bloom when Niemcewicz was there, and a new Scotland spruce of beautiful dark green, and "many other trees and shrubs, covered with flowers of different hues, planted so as to produce the best of color-effects," and weeping willows. Two of the original tulip trees are still standing (or were in 1960), as well as two ash trees, three buckeyes, one hemlock, three American hollies, two box trees (the weeping form) and one Kentucky coffee tree.

The box trees are now 20 feet tall. Washington's plans for his shrubberies adjoining the Serpentine were published by *Harper's* magazine in March 1859. Among the flowering trees and shrubs were red bud and dogwood, crab apples, lilacs, fringe trees, mock orange, and altheas. Shrubberies were typical of eighteenth-century gardens and so was the ha-ha, a retaining wall with a ditch beyond it to divide the pleasure grounds from the fields, and the wilderness. These are all features of Mount Vernon, as well as boxwood parterres though these were out of fashion by the time they were planted. A young English visitor, Benjamin Latrobe, wrote in 1796 that he hoped the parterres, "clipped and trimmed with infinite care into the form of a richly flourished Fleur-de-lis," were "the expiring groans of our grandfather's pedantry."

Since it acquired Mount Vernon in 1858 the Ladies Association has been gradually collecting the scattered possessions of the Washingtons. One that has come home to the garden is the fine old dial-face that is pictured in Alice Morse Earle's *Old Time Gardens*. It had been given to a friend of the last of the Washington owners, and had gone through several hands before it was bought for the association by Miss Annie Burr Jennings, vice-regent for Connecticut. It is now on a new post in its old place in the courtyard. Mrs. Earle loved to visit Mount Vernon. "Whenever I walk in the gardens," she said, "I am deeply grateful to the devoted women who keep it in such perfection." They have done it for more than a hundred years.

February 20, 1966

Annual Vines

It is a comfort to me in a changing world to open *Park's Flower Book* for 1967, and find inside the same picture of George W. Park, founder, along with his creed and his favorite prayer (by John Henry Jowett) which have been in the catalogue as long as I can remember. This is the ninety-ninth year that the flower book has been sent out to gardeners. The seeds come in new metal-foil, hermetically-sealed packages, but they still bear the old trade mark of a little girl holding an umbrella over a wheelbarrow full of flowers trundled by a small boy in a sailor hat. Now George B. Park, president, son of the founder, goes about in the company plane, and on the cover of the catalogue there is a photograph of a combo (or some such) in full swing in front of Impatiens À Go-Go, but inside I find the old-fashioned flowers that have always been there—Jewels of Opar, Bells of Ireland, Job's Tears, Fountain Plant, and Joseph's Coat—along with Missile Series, Giant F-1 Hybrid gloxinias, Tryosomic stocks, and Rocket snapdragons.

I had annual vines in mind, and when I turned to the page I found the same ones I had been growing, or trying to grow as long as I have been gardening: cathedral bells, black-eyed susan, cardinal climber, glory flower, and the perennial flag of Spain. Flag of Spain is a Mexican vine, and I am not sure whether it is perennial here, but it can be grown as an annual, and I once saw it in bloom at the fall flower show. The leaves are three-lobed, and the scarlet flowers change as they age to creamy yellow. It is *Quamoclit lobata*; the cardinal climber is *Q. sloteri*, a vine with finely slashed leaves and scarlet flowers.

Cathedral bells, *Cobaea scandens*, is also a perennial from Mexico that will bloom from the seed the first year, but the seed should be planted indoors for early bloom, though I have known them to produce flowering plants by September when sown the first of June. The seeds are flat; they germinate best when they are put in the soil sidewise with the edge showing. The plants need plenty of water, and I think full sun, though they are said to bloom in shade. The long-stemmed flowers, something like Canterbury bells, are very frost proof. They bloom on into November. The slender vine will cling to a rough surface, or can be trained on a thin string. It is not thick enough for a screen.

Park is probably the only American source for *Eccremocarpus scaber*, the glory flower, which is perennial in Chile, but annual with us. I am pretty sure that I have planted seeds at some time, but I have no record of it. If I did, they didn't come up; and this reminds me to try again. The scarlet flowers are said to be as showy as their name is impressive; seeds planted inside are supposed to produce blooming plants by midsummer.

The gourd list in the flower book is one of the best in the country, with the ornamental kinds listed individually and in collections: miniatures (orange, hedgehog, spoon, striped pear), giant bottle gourd, Hercules' club, penguin, dolphin, serpent and dishrag. Along with these several other members of the gourd family are listed. There are two momordicas, the balsam apple and the balsam pear. I once grew them to see what they were like. Both have very pretty yellow flowers, and leaves like those of the wild grape. The warty golden yellow fruits burst open when ripe, showing the scarlet seed.

Fruits of the balsam pear are long and narrow and tapered at both ends; those of the balsam apple are small and more oval—not at all like apples, as I remember. I planted seeds of both in late May. The plants clambered over a low wall, bloomed in July and fruited in the fall. They are easy to grow, and so is *Cucumis melo* variety 'Dudaim', which grows in country gardens as pomegranate, and is sometimes called Queen Anne's pocket melon because the small fragrant fruits are carried about, like sweet-Betsys for their perfume.

February 12, 1967

The Robin and the Earthworm

When Caroline Dormon wrote to me about the "slaughter wrought by pesticides," I thought of E. B. White's poem in *The New Yorker* (October 8, 1966) and asked his permission to quote it:

The Deserted Nation
(In 53 eagle's nests examined in Maine in 1965, only four eaglets were found. Charles M. Brookfield, ornithologist, ascribes the depletion of the eagle crop to sterility of one or both parent birds. Undeveloped eagles' eggs were examined and found to contain DDT, DDE, and other poisons.)

Ill fares the land to hastening ills a prey,
Where wealth accumulates along with spray.
Chemists and farmers flourish at their peril:
The bird of freedom, thanks to them, is sterile.
And a Bald Eagle, still its country's pride,
When once destroyed, can never be supplied.
—E. B. White
(Reprinted by permission; copyright 1966 The New Yorker Magazine, Inc.)

In *Fish, Wildlife and Pesticides*, a bulletin of the U.S. Department of the Interior, I found further discussion of the subject:

All fish and wildlife are part of nature's food chain. One chain may start with small fish concentrating persistent pesticides within their bodies. A higher dose of chemicals thus is passed on to larger fish that eat them. When the fish are eaten by the birds at the top of the aquatic food chains, such as the osprey or bald eagle, these birds may get highly concentrated doses of poison. . . . The young bald eagle, among species at top of both water and land food chains, has become rare in certain areas. Conservationists are concerned.

Another food chain begins with the leaf that falls from a spayed tree. A worm eats the leaf. A bird eats the worm. Many robins have been killed by DDT used to control the beetle that carries the Dutch elm disease. Their brain tissues have contained as much as 240 p.p.m. of DDT residue.

The robin and the earthworm come within the experience of the gardener. As I read the arguments for and against chemical pesticides, I sometimes think—as my grandmother used to say—that truth is at the bottom of the well. But when I see the birds in my garden flying away from the DDT mist as the truck comes up the alley at dawn, and later in the morning find dead and dying birds around the birdbath, I don't need any literature to help me make up my mind that the spraying is harmful. As to the earthworms, when Elizabeth Clarkson found dead fledglings of the great crested flycatcher in a nest in her garden, and upon sending them to North Carolina State College to be analyzed, found that the bodies contained lethal doses of DDT, she was convinced that they had been fed on poisoned earthworms.

"Science knows much about synthetic pesticides," my bulletin says, "but little about the ways they act in a living organism. The fate and the effects of many pesticides in soil, water, air, and particularly in animal tissue remains, in large part, a mystery. For this reason their ultimate impact on man and nature cannot be accurately appraised."

February 26, 1967

Ice Storms

The ice storm in early January was the worst I have ever seen. Now I know why Caroline Dormon writes from Louisiana that she is praying that rain will not freeze on the pines at Briarwood, her hundred-acre woodland. The ice storms I have seen before have always been brief and beautiful and not very destructive. This time it rained and froze, and snowed and sleeted, and rained and froze.

I sat in my studio window trying to write, but mostly listening for the sickening crack and crash as great limbs broke away from the pines in the garden, and on either side, and all the way up and down the alley behind it. When the sun finally came out and the glittering prisms melted from the trees I found much less damage than had seemed possible. If the air had not been so still all that time, things would have been different.

In the midst of the storm I wrote a letter to a Durham gardener, Mrs. Joseph Spengler, and when it was over she wrote: "How did your pine trees fare? Our 'primeval forest' was like a battlefield. We were bombarded by huge daggers of ice crashing from unearthly heights to the glacial entombment below. Perhaps this is a case where glass houses protected, providing a sheet of armor against the icy dive bombers, for the camellia leaves were not torn as they were in other storms, and we were in luck that there was no sun to burn through the ice, no wind to add catastrophic breakage.

"We have witnessed ice storms in these woods for 27 years. This is said to be the worst in 37, so what happened is all the more astounding. Plants, shrubs and trees that had lain prostrate, encased in ice for five days and five nights, began their magical ascent at noon on the thirteenth and by five o'clock—in only five hours—they had risen to erect positions, so that no one just arriving on the scene would believe they had ever been down."

In my garden the storm did a good deal of much-needed pruning. Dead limbs came down along with live ones, and trunks of overgrown pyracanthas were broken six or eight feet from the ground. Now I won't have to make up my mind about cutting them back severely. And the storm taught me a reason: shrubs that have been regularly pruned are not apt to be broken by the weight of ice.

On the day the rain began to freeze on the pine needles, I went out to see what flowers I could rescue from the cold. I didn't find much. Although this has been a rather mild winter, there has been less bloom than usual. I came back in with cold fingers, a Lenten rose, the last few flowers of the winter clematis, some lavender-tipped sprigs of heath, and a branch of the flowering quince, 'Pink Lady', with coral buds ready to open. The open flowers of *Crocus imperati* had been spoiled by the rain.

When I went out again, after the storm was over, I found that the hellebores had held up very well, and so had the lingering flowers of the clematis; the heath never seems to be hurt by anything. The tiny bells continue to glow. But there was nothing new. It was not until several days later, when I was raking up twigs and trash and pine needles, that I found the first snowdrop, and saw the fragrant golden flowers of the Chinese witch-hazel beginning to uncurl.

Snowdrops have been neglected in the South, because for a long time the only one imported by bulb dealers was the English species, *Galanthus nivalis*, a creature of cold damp climates. By far the best kind for us is *G. elwesii*, a larger flower with broader petals of glistening white and broader, grayer leaves. It is a variable species in size and performance and time of bloom, so it is a good plan to get stock from various sources. This one that I found in bloom after the storm has not increased—probably because it is in a shady place, and it likes sun—but it has bloomed for me faithfully since 1950, usually in January but some years not until February.

As soon as the ice melted on the southern side of the house more buds of the little violet crocus were opening, and now, as I am writing on the twenty-fourth of January, they are blanketed again. Before it was light I heard sleet rattling on the window pane, and by the time breakfast was over the snow was beginning to stick.

February 4, 1968

More Winter Blooms

I love being asked to identify plants, and I don't know which gives me more pleasure: to know what they are or not to know what they are.

On that suddenly spring-like day at the end of January, Mrs. Dan Beckham called to ask the name of a yellow-flowered shrub in bloom in her great-aunt's yard on Elizabeth Avenue. "My aunt calls it the Japanese Christmas tree," she said. I told her it must be the Chinese witch-hazel, as I don't know of any other yellow flowering shrub—except the January jessamine, which everyone knows—that would be in bloom at that time.

But she then said that her aunt had had it for 70 years, so I knew it couldn't be the witch-hazel for that was not growing in southern gardens that long ago, and it is still uncommon.

In that case, I said, it must be the winter-sweet, only the flowers of winter-sweet aren't yellow. They are a very pale straw color. When she insisted that her aunt's flowers are dark yellow, I decided she must be color blind, but I told her she could easily settle the matter by coming to my garden.

She arrived in a few minutes with a branch of her aunt's shrub, and the flowers are yellow, a deep, golden, wax yellow with wine-red centers. And so I was pleased to be wrong, as I had never seen the yellow-flowered form before, and did not know that it was in North Carolina gardens.

My winter-sweet came from an old garden in Raleigh, and its parent came from a still-older one. Miss Janet Badger gave it to me, and I thought she rooted it, but that is said to be difficult. It is best to layer the lower branches in early fall.

Winter-sweet (*Chimonanthus praecox*) comes from China, not Japan. It is listed among the authentic shrubs for the gardens of Colonial Williamsburg, but the date given, 1768, is for its introduction into England, and I have not found any very early reference to it in this country.

I spoke too soon when I wrote that this is not a flowery winter. By

January 16, the small and fragile flowers of *Iris vartanii* were open, and the winter heath was coloring, and the first snowdrops had appeared. Then on the 20th, the Algerian iris began to bloom. Slugs got the first two buds, but I found the third before they did, and it opened in the house. The flowers last longer, and are more perfect, when they are picked before the buds unfurl. On the 24th I cut a branch of Chinese witch-hazel just as the narrow petals of the jonquil-colored and jonquil-scented flower began to uncurl. At the same time more little florets smelling of heliotrope opened on the twigs of *Viburnum fragrans*.

The next day I found the fawn-colored buds of *Crocus imperati* opened wide in the sunshine, showing themselves to be bright violet within. They stayed closed on the snowy and sleety days that followed, but when spring-like weather returned they were as gay as ever. The flowers are described as fragrant, and they do have a fresh springtime scent, but it is rather faint.

On the 29th, the small golden flowers of *Crocus ancyrensis*, a Turkish species, appeared in the stone steps. When I planted it 10 years ago I found a chipmunk munching the corms and thought he had eaten them all. But he left one or two, and there are still a few flowers early in the year.

Sternbergia fischerana bloomed the same day. The flower is like a large lemon-colored crocus with a buttercup sheen, but you can tell by the daffodil foliage that it belongs to the amaryllis family. This is the species that William Lanier Hunt grows in quantity in Chapel Hill, where it usually blooms before Christmas, and sometimes by Thanksgiving. But when I talked to him at the end of December no buds had opened. The bulbs are expensive and not often available. Last fall I bought one from Dr. T. M. Howard, and next fall I'm going to get half a dozen, even if I have to do without something else.

On the last day of January I found the first flowers of *Iris histrio* (an early form), *Helleborus atrorubens*, *Adonis amurensis*, and *Vinca minor*. And the birds began to sing.

February 23, 1969

Ornamental Grasses

Few people who write about their gardens have much to say about ornamental grasses, but in *My Garden in Summer* E. A. Bowles devotes a chapter to them. "One often sees well-filled gardens where about the only grasses are those that form the turf of the lawns, and a clump of Pampas Grass," he says, "but I think many of our summer flowers look all the better when they have clumps of grassy foliage or feathery flowering heads growing among them to soften their effect." Unfortunately, many of the grasses that Bowles delights in are not in the American trade, but I did find the great quaking grass, *Briza maxima*, in *Park's Flower Book* for 1970.

Briza is a hardy annual from the Mediterranean region. In Bowles's garden it was self-sown "and left where needed in patches, or isolated plants which of course are the finest, but not so effective as a clump a yard across. Its pendant heads are as lovely as any green thing in the garden in early June; their light yellow-green goes so well with their own rich green leaves, and also contrasts with the deeper shade of an edging of *Saxifraga cordifolia*. . . . Later on the heads turn yellow, then buff, and still later the stalks ripen to a rich foxy burnt-sienna red, and especially just before sunset a large patch lights up and looks wonderfully brilliant even among the flaming colours of a July border."

"Shakers, or Quaking Grasse" was growing in English gardens at the end of the sixteenth century. By means of small hairy strings which they hang on, Gerard says, "the knaps which are the floures do continually tremble and shake, in such sort that it is not possible with the most stedfast hand to hold it from shaking." And Park's catalogue writer says, "Airy spikelets tremble in the slightest breeze."

Bowles considered *Festuca glauca*, "the grass with imitation hoar frost eternally on its leaves, one of the best blue-grey plants in existence." As the flowers are not effective he pulled them out as soon as they appeared, and that made the tufts grow thicker. Blue fescue is one grass that is plentiful in local nurseries, and I can give a mail order address to anyone who cannot find it nearby. A frosty-blue six-inch clump is one of the things still worth going in the garden to look at in the dreariest parts of winter when even the epimediums are bedraggled and the yuccas are droopy.

Vetiver is another thing that comes through severe weather unscathed. It is a tall grass, to six feet or more, a fountain of green all summer, and a fountain of ivory all winter. It is really a year-around plant, as the bleached foliage stays in good condition almost until new green appears in spring. Vetiver doesn't seem to be in the trade. Mine came from Mrs. Walter Hobbs who brought it from a garden in New Orleans to put in her herb garden. She uses the aromatic roots as a sachet, and as a fixative in pot pourri. They smell of mignonette and myrrh.

Lyme grass (*Elymus arenarius*) is another one that is not in the trade. After a long search I found it at last in Marion Becker's garden in Cincinnati. She gave me a root which is holding its own and even spreading a little. I hope in time it will make a thick patch of blue green, as it did in Gertrude Jekyll's garden where it grew in poor sandy soil with sea-holly and santolina. "I believe I may truly say," she wrote in *Home and Garden*, "that of all groups of plants in my garden there is none that attracts so much notice and admiration."

Seeds of *Coix lacryma-jobi*, a perennial grass grown as a half-hardy annual, are listed in *Park's Flower Book*, and are advertised as Indian beads in the *Mississippi Market Bulletin*. Last spring I got some from my old friend Mrs. W. L. Null who sells them for necklaces. They are too beautiful to bury in the ground, but I did plant a few (the rest I kept on my desk to look at), and they produced bright green stalks like miniature corn, and I had more beads by the end of summer. The beads are small and oval, and seem to be made of porcelain in tints and tones of nearly grey. They are called Job's-Tears.

February 22, 1970

𝒮 MARCH

. . . .

"Cameelias" and Such

When C. M. McKimmon of Hartsville called me to account for saying that camellian is pronounced "chameleon," I hastened to assure him that it was not pronounced that way by me, and that I spent many years pointing out to others that the "e" is short.

Those years were spent in vain. I don't think I made a single convert. But he says that ever since Dr. Hume told them in a lecture at Coker College that the genus is named for Father Kamel, and pronounced the same way, "everyone in this section follows his advice."

I am afraid Dr. Hume didn't make such an impression on us, when he talked to the Charlotte Garden Club, for I still hear much of "cameelias." When I was young, and a crusader, I set out to reform the garden clubs, but now I am perfectly willing to allow them to call a crinum a lily, a trumpet daffodil a jonquil, a snow flake a snow drop, a camellia a "cameelia"—or even a japonica, though that does get rather confusing if Japan quinces are called japonicas, too. I even like the flavor of this local usage.

For myself, although I try to pronounce the names of plants correctly, I find it very hard to be consistent. Why make a point of "kamelia" when you say "dootsia"? Doesn't Johan van der Deutz deserve as much honor as Father Kamel, and if he does we must say "doytsia." And if we love and honor Dr. Dahl we must call his namesake a "dall'-ya"—but I can't ever remember having heard anyone do it.

Many eyebrows were raised when an airy flower-arranger talked to the Charlotte Garden Club about "Gerbeerias," but when I got home and looked it up, I found that it was originally spelled and pronounced that way, and that spelling and pronunciation is still given preference in *Hortus Second*, though not in *Standardized Plant Names*.

Once you start trying to do the right thing by plant names, you find that there are a great many that you have mispronounced all your life. Then your lot is not a happy one. For you must choose between continuing in the wrong and feeling very foolish. Having always said "ox-alice" and "pitt'-osporum," I cannot now change to "ox'-alis" and "pittos'-porum" without a blush or a stammer.

When talking to Lady Whitby I managed to say "siklamen" twice, but when it came into the conversation for a third time, I broke down completely and went back to "sighclamen." I often wonder why you must say "siklamen" when you say "sighdonia," but that's the way of it. I do my best, but "gladeye'-olus" I cannot say. Occasionally there is a choice between the correct and the accepted, but I have never found any justification for Amy Lowell's rhyming clematis with window lattice.

The "ch" in a plant name is another trap for the unwary. It seems natural to call the wintersweet "kimonanthus," but it is hard for me to call the turtlehead "kelone"; and I was undone when I discovered that all these years I should have been saying "ankusa." Once I heard a three-year-old correct a visitor who said she admired our lilies: "They are not lilies," he said. "They are 'col-ki-cum'." I was about to correct him, but thought better of it, and when I looked it up I found that "colkicum" is correct, though "colchicum" is accepted—at least it is accepted in America.

Usage differs when a plant is named for a person. One may say "Golden'-eye," and another "Goldeen'-ee." I say "Golden'-ee." Once when I admired a daylily in Miss Nanny Holding's garden in Wake Forest, she said it was *Hemerocallis* "Golden-eye." I looked at the wide-eyed golden flower, and thought that a delightful and appropriate name. It never occurred to me to check it, and so *Hemerocallis goldenii* went into *A Southern Garden* as Golden Eye. And as I described it in glowing terms, I expect a lot of gardeners are still searching for it.

Changes in the spelling of plant names distress me very much. *Hortus Second* clings to wisteria because it was originally spelled that way. *Standardized Plant Names* holds out for wistaria because it was named for Dr. Caspar Wistar. And as for camellias, if they were named for Father Kamel, why aren't they spelled with a "k"? And why should crepe myrtle be changed to crape myrtle?

I used to have a collection of picturesque pronunciations. The only ones I remember now are the "wiggly rose," which turned out to be *Weigela rosea* (and by the way, if you are going to make a fuss about "camell'-ia" you should call it vigela); and the "paleeda delmeetisha," which proved to be *Iris pallida dalmatica*. And of course we commonly meet "cotton-easter" for "Coton'-e-aster." It is all very confusing, and sometimes I feel for the woman who asked if I could tell her the difference between an arborvitae and an evergreen.

March 30, 1965

Altars in the Fields

For a long time I have had it in mind to write something about garden prayers, and now, the beginning of Lent, seems an appropriate time to do so.

Like Coleridge, men of all ages have built their altars in the fields; and like Emerson, they have found healing by digging in the ground: "All my hurts my garden spade can heal." Sir Thomas Browne said that he "collected his Divinity" from two books, one written of God, and the other of His servant Nature; the Bible and "that universal and public manuscript that lies expansed unto the eyes of all; those that never saw Him in the one, have discovered Him in the other."

As long as I can remember, the Parks (those devout descendants of John Knox) have printed a prayer of John Henry Jowett's at the top of the first page of their spring catalogue, and have reminded their "Dear Patron Friends" that in planting seed they "join the Great Creator in the miracle of life." This is in the best gardening tradition, for Richard Gardiner of Shrewsbury, who published the earliest known seed catalogue (in 1597), compares the owners of gardens to stewards:

This is the total sum of thy Stewardship, whatsoever thou bee, and if thou careless omit to doe thy office heerein, thou makest a hard accompt for thy selfe, which God forbid, if it bee his good pleasure therein.

In the early days the Christians made use of pagan customs by giving them a new significance. One of the Roman festivals was dedicated to the god Robigus who was asked to preserve the young corn from blight. On the day of the Robigolia the Christians, of the time of Saint Gregory and Saint Augustine, taking very much the same route that the pagans had taken (as described by Ovid), went in procession, asking God's blessings upon the fruits of the earth.

Later on, the three days before Ascension were set aside for special prayers for the newly planted crops. There are two collects for this season, one begins, "Almighty God, Lord of Heaven and earth; we beseech thee to pour forth thy blessing upon this land, and to give us a fruitful season. . . ." The other is, "Almighty God who hast blessed the earth that it should be fruitful and bring forth whatsoever is needful for the life of man, and has commanded us to work with quietness, and eat our own bread; Bless the labours of the husbandman, and grant such seasonable weather that we may gather in the fruits of the earth, and ever rejoice in thy goodness, to the praise of thy holy Name; through Jesus Christ our Lord. Amen."

On Thanksgiving Day, the collect is, "O most merciful Father, who hast blessed the labours of the husbandman in the returns of the fruits of the earth; We give thee humble and hearty thanks for this thy bounty; beseeching thee to continue thy loving-kindness to us, that our land may still yield her increase, to thy glory and our comfort; through Jesus Christ our Lord. Amen."

One of the most beautiful of garden prayers comes from Leonard Mascall, clerk-of-the-kitchen to Archbishop Parker, who wrote *A Book of the Arte and maner howe to plant and graffe all sorts of trees* (1572).

> A note for all Graffers and Planters! And whensoever ye shall plant or graffe it shall be meete and good for you to saye as foloweth, In the name of God the Father, the Sonne and the holy Ghost, Amen. Increase and multiplye, and replenishe the earth: and saye the Lordes prayer, then say: Lord God heare my prayer, and let this my desire of thee be hearde. The holy spirite of God which hath created all things for man and hath given them for our comfort, in thy name O Lorde we set, plant, and graffe, desiring that by thy mighty power they maye encrease, and multiplye uppon the earth, in bearing plenty of fruite, to the profite, and comfort of all thy faithfull people, thorow Christe our Lorde—Amen.

March 6, 1960

Ground Covers

I have had to eat my words so often, they are getting to be almost palatable.

Mr. Parker had just asked me to name an evergreen ground cover that can be walked on, and I had just told him that I had never found one that is satisfactory, when I went into a charming garden where all the paths were solidly covered with *Mazus reptans* in full bloom.

I have known this little creeper for at least a quarter of a century, but it has never grown like that for me. I think it wants some shade. In Raleigh we grew it in a flagged walk in very poor, dry soil and in baking sun. In Charlotte I have had a hard time getting it started and I still have only a small patch. But once started, and in the right place, it is evidently a plant that takes care of itself, and may even go where it is not wanted, although it is not one of the things that given an inch will take an ell.

When it takes over, mazus is a perfect carpet, flat, smooth and thick, that wears well even in an outdoor sitting room. The color is light green in the spring, but cold weather burnishes the foliage, and winter sun may burn it, though it recovers quickly. The flowers are white with lavender spots, or perhaps they are lavender with white spots—I can never tell.

Mazus is not an uncommon plant in gardens, but when I looked for it in the trade I found only one source, the Sky-cleft Gardens, which is also the only nursery that lists *Veronica filiformis*, another very useful carpeter.

The veronica can also be grown from seeds, and Mr. Saier has them. It is called *filiformis* because the stems are as fine as thread. They take root at the nodes, and spread quickly to make thick, shallow-rooted mats that come up whole if they get to be too much of a blanket. The blue and white flowers are as small and round as the tiny pale green leaves. They bloom very early, sometimes in late winter. The leaves keep their bright color in all but the most severe weather.

Tempe Franklin has used this veronica very successfully to replace grass in a green panel between two paths. It can be cut over with a hand mower, if grass or weeds come through, and it makes a nice lawn, though it will not stand hard wear. *Veronica filiformis* is a good creeper to use between flagstones.

I have also seen ajuga used to carpet paths. I had heard that it could be walked on, but I did not believe it. However, it can, at least where the traffic is not heavy.

I am not as enthusiastic about ajuga as I used to be. It looks shabby even in the shade in severe weather, and in exposed places the leaves shrivel whenever it is very hot or very cold.

When Dr. Meyer, from the Department of Agriculture, was here last spring he identified the tiny evergreen creeper that threads its way through cracks between the bricks in Elizabeth Clarkson's garden as *Hydrocotyle rotundifolia*, one of the water pennyworts. It is a tropical plant that has escaped from the greenhouse, and grows in lawns from Pennsylvania southward. It is particularly useful to cover wet spots, but is also very drought resistant. The round, bright green, highly polished and shallowly scalloped leaves are even smaller than those of dichondra. I know of no commercial source for this little plant, which is probably considered a weed, and I would like to hear from anyone who knows where to find it.

In my Raleigh garden I used to grow the pretty barren strawberry, a much coarser plant than any of these that I have mentioned, but less coarse than periwinkle and Japanese spurge. The leaves are like those of the wild strawberry, but daintier, glossier and more evergreen. Sprays of lemon-colored flowers bloom in March. This is a northern plant that comes down into our southern mountains. In the Piedmont it needs shade and plenty of leaf mold to keep its roots cool and damp in hot weather.

March 13, 1960

Viburnums

I like the books of E. A. Bowles because, in spite of the fact that the gardens at Myddleton Place were very large and very celebrated, Mr. Bowles seemed to garden just about the way I do. He would never have enough room, no matter how big his garden, and was always stuffing some shrub into a place too small for it. In *My Garden in Summer*, he says, "A fine old bush of *Viburnum plicatum tomentosum*, its horizontally spreading boughs clad from stern to tip with large white snowballs, is as good a sight as anything in the gardens. It is a pity it is so shut in here, for it grows just where the vine pergola and the main pergola join, and has not sufficient space to sprawl out as far as it might."

Space to sprawl is needed (though sprawl is not the right word for an erect and symmetrical shrub), as this viburnum, the Japanese snowball, grows to a height of ten feet and is equally wide. It is a common shrub in gardens, and a beautiful one, though not so beautiful as the variety 'Mariesii', which was brought to the Veitch nursery from Japan by Charles Maries, and first flowered in England in 1875.

The variety 'Mariesii' has been available in this country only a few years. It bloomed the first year after it was planted in my garden, and has bloomed better every year since then, in spite of being in rather deep shade. In five years it grew to almost its full height, but was very slender, as it had no room to sprawl.

The flowers are lacy clusters four inches wide, with a center of perfect flowers, like little stars, encircled with flat sterile flowers an inch and a half across. The flowers are lovely in themselves, and so well presented that they lie on top of the branches like snow. It looked so pretty, even when the branches were bare, and I hope that it will fruit when it has enough sun, and room to spread. It never fruited in my garden, and I did not realize that large clusters of bright red berries (which turn black as they mature) are considered one of the shrub's best features.

Viburnum plicatum tomentosum is an easily grown and vigorous shrub, not susceptible to disease and not attractive to insects; it grows well in sun or part shade in any soil rich in humus and not too dry. It is called the doublefile viburnum because the flower clusters are in two rows. All forms bloom in April. Victorian gardeners preferred the sterile globes of the Japanese snowball, even though they bore no fruit, to the lacy heads of the variety 'Mariesii', so the latter is just beginning to be known.

March 20, 1960

Lenten Flowers

When Lent comes, and the days lengthen, the Lenten rose and the Lent-lily are in bloom.

The Lenten rose is like the Christmas rose, but the flowers vary in color from pure white to violet to deep purple; and there are several flowers to a stem; and the leaves are taller, wider and more upright. It begins to bloom early in the year, and lasts until April or even into May. It is much easier to grow than the Christmas rose, requiring only shade and a soil in which there is a good amount of humus.

The Lent-lily is the wild English daffodil. It came to this country with the early colonists, and has become naturalized in Virginia and all through the South. The bunches of golden trumpets sold on the street corners are our first sign of spring; but it must bloom later in England. Shakespeare describes it as taking the winds of March with beauty, and the *Calendar of Flowers* says:

> Then comes the Daffodil beside
> Our Lady's Smock at our Lady-tide.

Lady-tide is the Annunciation, the twenty-fifth of March, when "lady-smocks all silver-white, Do paint the meadows with delight." It seems odd that Mother's Day, coming so near this time, should have no connection (as far as I know) with Our Lady.

The fourth Sunday in Lent is the traditional time for visiting parents, giving them presents, and receiving their blessings. I have never known why this Sunday was chosen, but having read that the Scriptures appointed for the day might have given rise to the custom, I looked them up, expecting, of course, that I would find something about obedience to parents. But mothers are not mentioned; the lessons are all about bread; manna from heaven, the loaves and fishes, and a verse from Isaiah that should always be read in spring: "The rain cometh down, and the snow from heaven, and returneth not thither, but watereth the earth, and maketh it bring forth and bud, that it may give seed to the sower, and bread to the eater." The custom that arose from this was making a present of bread, or a fruit cake called a simnel. Herrick wrote to Dianeme:

> Ile to thee a Simnell bring'
> 'Gainst thou go'st a mothering.

In England the flowers to take home were violets: "He who goes a mothering finds violets in the lane"; but in this country the flower connected with Mother's Day is the rose.

In England, sprigs of pussy willow take the place of palms on Palm Sunday, which explains lines that Housman wrote for March:

Afield for palms the girls repair,
And sure enough the palms are there,
And each will find by hedge or pond
Her waving silver-tufted wand.

The Easter flowers are the wood-sorrel, whose pale and delicate flowers are called Alleluias; and the Pasque-flower, *Anemone pulsatilla*. V. Sackville-West says that the anemone

> ignores
> A date the moon ordained, but takes its rule
> From sun and rain, as both by chance occur;
> Yet some years by a nice coincidence
> Opens upon our very Easter day.

The anemone was originally associated with the Passover, and also called Pass flower.

The traditional Easter dish, a cake or pudding flavored with tansy, is a symbol of the bitter herbs of the Paschal Feast. Perhaps, too, it was considered an appropriate herb for the resurrection, as its name comes from the Greek word meaning immortality. Tansies were looked upon as a sort of spring tonic to purify the system after the Lenten fasts. On the twentieth of April Pepys wrote in his *Diary* that he had spent a pleasant hour with a friend, and had eaten a tansy. Tansy is the flower of Saint Athanasius, also immortal, whose feast is the second of May. He was the defender of the doctrine of the Trinity and of the divinity of Christ.

March 5, 1961

Buxus

Box is the proper evergreen for decorating the house and the church in Lent: holly at Christmas, box at Candlemas, yew at Easter. In ceremonies for Candlemasse eve (February 1) Herrick says

> The Holly hitherto did sway;
>   Let Box now domineere;
> Untill the dancing Easter-day,
>   Or Easter's Eve appeare.
>
> Then youthfull box which now hath grace,
>   Your houses to renew;
> Grown old, surrender must his place,
>   Unto the crisped Yew.

Thus times do shift; each thing his turne do's hold;
New things succeed, as former things grow old.

Sprigs of box have sometimes been substituted for palms on Palm Sunday, and in parts of France it is the custom on Palm Sunday to decorate the graves with box. A poem of Wordsworth's refers to the custom of putting a basin of box sprigs at the door of a house where someone has died. On the way to the church each friend takes a sprig, and later throws it in the grave:

The basin of Boxwood, just six weeks before
Had stood on the table at Timothy's door.

In the language of flowers box stands for constancy and stoicism, I suppose because the wood is hard and enduring, but I don't know why it was chosen as one of the four woods of the cross: cypress, cedar, pine and box.

Before the Christian era, box belonged to Pluto, the protector of all evergreens as symbols of life that endure through the winter. Earlier still it was sacred to Cybele. Because it lives to be so old, boxwood is said to breathe the fragrance of eternity. Some mysterious quality in the scent of box is supposed to have a strong effect on memory.

In writing about its power to recall the past, Mrs. Earle (in *Old Time Gardens*) tells a story of a young girl who returned from abroad to her mother's old home in Massachusetts, and walking in the garden with her aunts, suddenly cried, "The dog, he will kill me!" Her aunts assured her that no dog was there; but once under that very box bush now grown taller, a vicious dog had bitten her mother. "The box told her," Mrs. Earle says. She tells another story of a man of middle years to whom the scent of box so vividly recalled an old love that he travelled thousands of miles in search of her. "I ought to be able to add that the twain were married as a result of this sentimental memory-awakening through the old box," Mrs. Earle adds. But the truth was that they found they had nothing in common.

March 3, 1963

Shamrocks

Today, the seventeenth of March, is the Feast of Saint Patrick, on which (an eighteenth-century writer says) "the vulgar superstitiously wear shamroges, 3 leaved grass." In our family, though our attitudes are Anglo-Saxon, we always wear the green for Saint Patrick, and feel for him great affection, for his feast is my mother's birthday.

As far back as I can remember I was given that day a little green gauze trefoil with a tiny clay pipe attached, and my grandmother would sing, "They're hanging men and women, now, for wearing of the green":

So take the shamrock off your hat,
   And throw it on the ground:
It will take root and flourish there,
   Though nowhere else 'tis found!

The English are forever sneering at the Irish and their emblem, the "chosen leaf of Bard and chief, Old Erin's native shamrock," and mocking Irish poverty with such expressions as "Go feed on Shamrootes as the Irish doe," and referring to toasts to Saint Patrick as "downing the shamrock."

"This plant is worn by the People . . . upon . . . St. Patrick's Day," Threlkeld wrote in 1726. "It being a current Tradition, that by this Three Leafed Grass, he emblematically set forth to them the Mystery of the Holy Trinity. However that may be, when they wer their Seamar-oge, they often commit Excess in Liquor, which is not a right keeping of a Day to the Lord."

As for Saint Patrick, although his provenance is uncertain, he was not an Irishman. As a very young boy, he was taken to Ireland as a slave, and having escaped he later returned to rescue the Irish (much against their will) from the power of the Druids and to free the island of snakes, the symbol of all evil.

The shamrock also stands for faith, hope and charity, and is "noisome to witches." Like other Christian symbols it was inherited from the Greeks, and whether with three leaves or four (the form of the cross), it protects the wearer and brings him luck.

> The person who carries a leaf of the four-leaved or cruciform Clover about with him will be successful at play, and have the power of detecting the presence of evil spirits. The lover may put it under his pillow, and he will dream of his beloved, or the maiden may, by slipping a leaf into her lover's shoe without his knowledge, as he is about to set out on a journey, secure his sure and safe return to her embrace. It may be employed to prevent the wearer being drawn into military service and is said to cure diseases and lunacy. Shakspere says:

I will enchant the old Andronicus
With words more sweet and yet more dangerous
Than baits to fish or Honeystalks to sheep. . . .

It is generally supposed that the Honeystalks on which the sheep delight to feed are Clover flowers. The Shamrock, or at least the plant which now usually bears that name, is a species of Clover or Trefoil, and among the Irish is still regarded as a magical, one might almost say a sacred, plant.—The Rev. Hilderic Friend, *Flowers and Flower Lore*

There are many contenders to the title of shamrock: "The white clover, *Trifolium repens*, the red clover, *T. pratense*, the black medic, *Medicago lupulina*, the wood-sorrel, *Oxalis Acetosella*, and the water cress. The name is now most commonly applied to the lesser yellow trefoil, *Trifolium minus*, which is the plant most frequently worn as an emblem on St. Patrick's Day" (*Oxford English Dictionary*).

Having always worn the artificial shamrocks, I was interested to see that Saier lists seed of "the True Irish strain," which he says will produce sturdy plants for Saint Patrick's Day if they are sown in January or February and kept in a sunny window.

March 17, 1963

Planting the Highways

In the British *Gardeners' Chronicle*, December 7, 1963, Richard C. Ward complains, in a letter to the editor, of the lack of anti-dazzle planting on dual-carriageway roads. "In Germany," he says, "many of us must have seen mile upon mile of young cypressus, berberis, privet, beech, and so on, which serve their purpose admirably when planted in double-staggered rows or in groups of three at about twenty-foot intervals." In the same issue there is a photograph of a planting of box and yew in a grass strip dividing carriageways in Surrey. With these are planted cherry trees and whitebeam to reduce glare from headlights. Whitebeam is *Sorbus aria*, a small tree, beautiful in foliage and fruit, and native to the British Isles.

I thought of this letter when I was driving back to Charlotte with Carolina Tillett, on Highway 85, with the setting sun in our eyes—it seemed to me—all the way from Greensboro to Salisbury. And then we faced the glare of the headlights for the rest of the way. It does seem to me that shrubs and trees, planted in the central grass strips, and trees at strategic spots on the right-of-way, could do away with at least part of the strain and hazard of driving in fast traffic with eyes blinded by light. Where planting or central strips is not possible, the Europeans use anti-dazzle fences or screens.

In this country it is not considered desirable to plant highways for beauty. They say that a striking form in a tree or shrub, or conspicuous flowers or fruit, might distract the driver. But it seems to me that people accustomed to driving along roads lined with billboards are unlikely to be startled by the color of flower and fruit. It is much more likely that beauty and variety in wayside planting will make travel more safe by relieving the monotony of long straight stretches of road. I can see no objection to planting trees for bloom at all seasons: *Cornus mas* for earliest spring; shadblow, dogwood, *Prunus americana*, viburnum, and silver bell, to carry on the season; the golden-rain tree for early summer; and witch hazel for fall and early winter.

The qualities wanted in trees for highway planting are quick growth, long life, freedom from disease, and resistance to heat, drought and gasoline fumes. Often trees, like the poplars, that grow very fast do not live very long, but some of those that grow quickly, last for a reasonable length of time. *Populus alba* is reasonably long-lived, is immune to diseases and pests, and tolerant of both wet and dry soils. The type is wide spreading, but Bolle's poplar is a beautiful columnar form. Short-lived but fast-growing poplars can be used to fill in while more permanent and desirable trees are getting started.

Ulmus alata, the winged elm, though not long-lived, is pest free and quick growing, and has the added virtue of tolerating poor soils. It is one of the few trees that lightning does not kill. The ashes grow quickly, are easily transplanted, and not often hurt by storms, but they are not untroubled by pests. The cucumber tree, *Magnolia acuminata*, and its relative the tulip poplar, *Liriodendron tulipifera*, grow fast in good soil and with sufficient moisture, but they are difficult to transplant unless set out when small, and in the spring. These are on the pest-free list, and so is the sweet gum, but I have known the sweet gum to be attacked by borers.

The pin oak, *Quercus palustris*, and the willow oak, *Q. phellos*, are easily transplanted, long-lived, comparatively fast growing, but not free from pests.

The ginkgo is a tree of first magnitude, and has all of the virtues except that it usually does not grow very fast. It adapts itself to unfavorable conditions, is not bothered by pests, and is tolerant of fumes and smoke. Its one fault, the fetid fruit, can be overcome by planting only male trees. Edward Scanlon offers four male forms: pyramidal, fastigiate, spreading, and umbrella.

In spite of the borers, the loblolly pine (*Pinus taeda*) is a useful evergreen for poor, dry soil. Although it cannot be transplanted when more than a foot tall, it grows fast enough to make up for this draw-back.

March 22, 1964

Anemone Pulsatilla

In English-speaking countries, the great festival of the Church is called Easter, from Eastre, the Anglo-Saxon goddess of dawn (that is of the East), to whom April, the dawn of the year, was dedicated.

April is also, Bede says, the same as the "mensis paschalis," when the Passover is celebrated. The European names for Easter come from the Latin "pascha," which in turn comes from "Pesach," the Hebrew name of the Passover. The old festival is celebrated with the "gladness of a new solemnity": "Christ our Passover is sacrificed for us; therefore let us keep the feast."

The Pasque or Pass flower, *Anemone pulsatilla*, was given that name by Gerard, who was moved to do so, he says, because it blooms for the most part about Easter.

> The first of these Pasque floures hath many small leaves finely cut or jagged, like those of Carrots: among which rise up naked stalkes, rough and hairie; whereupon doe grow beautifull floures bell fashion, of a bright delaied purple colour. . . . The white Passe floures hath many fine jagged leaves, closely couched or thrust together, which resemble an Holi-water sprinckle, agreeing with the others in rootes, seedes and shape of floures, saving that these are of a white colour. . . . The Passe floure groweth in France in untoiled places: in Germanie they grow in rough and stonie places, and oftentimes on rockes. Those with purple floures do grow verie plentifully in the pasture or close, belonging to the parsonage house of a small village six miles from Cambridge, called Hildersham: the Parsons name that lived at the impression hereof was Mr. Fuller, a very kind and loving man, and willing to shew unto any man the said close.

V. Sackville-West says the Pasque-flower ignores the date the moon ordains, and takes its rule from sun and rain. It sometimes

Opens upon our very Easterday . . .
Lavender petals sheathed in silver floss
Soft as the suffle of a kitten's fur;
That pulsatilla, 'shaken by the wind,'
That fragile native of the chalky Downs.
—*The Garden*

In Tudor times the juice of the purple sepals of the Pasque-flower was used to dye Easter eggs a beautiful green color, but Gerard said nothing had been written of the flowers as having any peculiar virtue, but "they serve onely for the adorning of gardens and garlands, being floures of great beautie." "In Cambridge-shire where they grow, they are named Conventrie bels."

In *A Modern Herbal*, Mrs. Grieve says:

> The drug Pulsatilla is highly valuable in modern curative uses as an herbal simple. . . . The tincture of Pulsatilla is beneficial in disorders of the mucous membrane of the respiratory and of the digestive passages. Doses of two to three drops in a spoonful of water will allay the spasmodic cough of asthma, whooping-cough and bronchitis. For catarrhal affection of the eyes, the tincture is serviceable. It is also available in the relief of headaches and neuralgia, and as a remedy for nerve exhaustion in women. It is specially recommended for fair, blue-eyed women. . . . It is included in the *British Pharmacopoeia* and was formerly included in the *United States Pharmacopoeia*. In homoeopathy it is considered very efficacious, and even a specific, in measles.

A seventeenth-century quotation from the *Oxford English Dictionary* adds a sinister note: "Poisonous things delight in the Plant called Pas-flower."

Anemone pulsatilla is a field flower that likes rather poor, dry soil, full sun, and some lime. It is supposed to be easily grown in the border or rock garden, but has never done well with me. I would like to try it again, especially—if I could find them—some of the forms that Reginald Farrer describes, one called 'White Swan', and one that he says is by far the loveliest, 'Mrs. van der Elst'. The latter is "indistinguishable from the type, except that its chalices are of a soft rosy shell-pink, absolutely clean and true, without the slightest tint of mauve or magenta."

March 29, 1964

Mulching

On one thing all gardeners—organic and inorganic alike—are agreed, and that is the value of mulching.

Some think mulching is all there is to gardening. One of these is Ruth Stout. She advocates keeping a six-inch mulch of hay over the whole garden at all times. Then, she says, no plowing is needed, no hoeing, no cultivating, no weeding, no watering, no spraying. The only thing the gardener has to do, is to bury the garbage under the hay, and plant and pick the flowers and vegetables. All this is explained in her books: *Gardening Without Work*, and *How to Have a Green Thumb without an Aching Back*. For her, it works. Earthworms carry on underground while she sows and reaps.

Mrs. Stout's garden is in sandy soil in Connecticut. In other parts of the country, and in different soils, J. I. Rodale says (in *How to Landscape Your Own Home*), the no-digging, permanent mulch system has been tried with varying degrees of success. "In one Pennsylvania garden where the soil is well-drained but clay, no appreciable difference (that is improvement of the soil) can be seen after five years of permanent mulch, except in rows which have been stirred deeply each year. But even the stirring is not enough to control white grubs. The soil noticeably suffers from lack of aeration and, though the earthworm population is greatly increased, it is not sufficient to do the job of churning such heavy soil."

I believe in mulching, but in my garden it has not only failed to solve all problems, but has added some extra ones. In mulching camellias, for example: dead leaves and dead flowers fall into the mulch, and if they are left to disintegrate I cannot but think that diseases and insects are encouraged. My sasanquas have had a good deal of scale this year.

In the American Rose Society's official book, *What Every Rose Grower Should Know*, the authors say that a two-inch mulch should be applied in the spring before the plants bloom; and that it may be worked into the soil in the fall. But I think this is a doubtful practice, and I notice that other rose growers advocate taking off the old mulch when winter is over, cleaning up the ground thoroughly, fertilizing, and then applying the new mulch. One grower that I read about puts on such a thick mulch of straw that it is four inches or more deep when it packs down. Between mulches the ground is left bare to the sun and air, and when the roses begin to put new shoots, the new mulch is put on.

It has been my experience that peat moss is not satisfactory as a mulch. It is better to dig it into the soil, and put some other material on top of it. For the flower borders I have never found any satisfactory mulch, and I still think the best plan is to put the plants close together and weed by hand, and cultivate the soil.

Under trees and shrubs I think pine straw looks best and is most satisfactory. I use my own, raked from the paths, but I have an idea that the commercial kind is more sanitary. In Raleigh I always mulched with oak leaves because we had so many, and had room to keep them. I kept them in pits, though that is not considered a good thing to do, and never turned them at all. When they began to crumble I distributed them around the shrubs. For lime-loving plants, maple leaves should be used. But oak leaves certainly suited most of the wide variety of shrubs that I grew in Raleigh.

One of the chief benefits of mulching is supposed to be keeping down the weeds. It takes a very deep mulch to do this. It also takes a deep mulch to keep the soil moist and cool in summer, and to keep it warm in winter.

March 27, 1966

Mountain Wildflowers

This spring the earliest wildflower of the season was bloodroot. On the fourth of March I found the first white bud curled tightly in its protecting grey-green leaf, and on the fifth there was a gleaming flower. My stock came from the mountains. A single root, tucked in with some mountain plant that has long since perished, has been slowly spreading ever since, and the 12-petaled flowers are nearly three inches across, much larger than any I have ever seen, though nothing new to gardeners.

In 1737 Peter Collinson wrote that he had "three sorts of pecoone" in his garden in London, one with a very small flower, one with a large single flower, and one with a double flower. So far as I know, the variety *grandiflora* is not in the trade, but the variety *plena* is, and I once had a so-called pink form, though it was not pink at all. The only color on the petals was a faint wine stain on the reverse. Pocoon is the Indian name for bloodroot. The Indians used the red juice to stain themselves and their possessions. The old Negroes called it coon root. There are a number of other country names. One is sweet-slumber.

There are some violets that bloom earlier than bloodroot—they even flower from time to time all through the winter—but I have no idea what they are, probably hybrids, so I consider *Viola walteri* the first species of this season. This year it bloomed on March 12, rather earlier than usual, though it is sometimes earlier, and once I found a flower on New Year's Day. *V. walteri* is called the running violet because its spreading stems take root, and form thick mats in shady woods. In my garden it never ran. It seeds itself, and the seedlings come up and make neat evergreen rosettes in the brick pavement around the pool. This is a southern species, native but rare in piedmont North Carolina; it is named for the South Carolina botanist Thomas Walter, who wrote *Flora Caroliniana*. He grew most of the thousand plants he describes in his book, and he was buried among them, in 1788, in his garden on the Santee River.

Chrysogonum and hepatica are among the earliest wildflowers, sometimes blooming ahead of spring, and I have a record of the small pink-striped flowers of spring beauty on the first of March. Spring beauty, *Claytonia virginica*, is plentiful in piedmont North Carolina, and occurs in the high mountains, but it is not native in Mecklenburg county.

Although arbutus is called Mayflower in Massachusetts, Thoreau wrote on the ninth of April, 1859: "The epigaea is not quite out. The earliest peculiarly woodland herbaceous flowers are epigaea, anemone, thalictrum, and (by the first of May) viola pedata." With us arbutus blooms in mid-March. There are few counties in which it is not found, Mecklenburg being one of them—we must make a pilgrimage to Gaston or Lincoln to see it in its habitat. Yet it grows from the mountains to the coast in the most diverse situations, from shady broadleaved and conifer forests to sunny places in the sandhills, but always in very acid soil. In spite of this it is almost impossible to transplant arbutus from the woods.

Those who have cultivated it successfully say it is readily propagated from cuttings, taken as soon as the bloom is over, and rooted in a mixture of equal parts of granulated peat moss and sand. If the soil is not acid, half a pound of ammonium sulphate to a square yard will make it sufficiently so.

Last fall I brought back from Ohio, and planted in my garden, two clumps of the false rue-anemone, *Isopyrum biternatum*. They bloomed in mid-March. The tiny white flowers that bedew the small plants are not so pretty as those of the rue-anemone (which bloom at the same time), but the foliage is more effective because it is almost evergreen. The prettily cut, twice ternate leaves kept their freshness all winter. At some time in early spring the old leaves disappeared and new ones unfurled, but whenever I looked some leaves were there.

Bringing isopyrum to North Carolina was scarcely coals to New Castle. Although it is native to three counties around Raleigh (but not Wake) it is rare. I never saw it before, or even heard of it. It seems too bad that such a splendid groundcover, and a plant native from Canada to Florida, should not be in the trade. The only source I know of is Henderson's Botanic Garden.

March 26, 1967

Fritillaria

From time to time Lawrence Johnson sends me notes from his garden in Middlebury, Indiana. In his last letter he wrote about the crown imperial. "Every spring," he said, "I meet a number of people who describe *Fritillaria imperialis*, which they have just seen in bloom, and I ask them if they live near Constantine, Michigan, and the answer is always yes. Late this fall a visitor told me of a place where the fritillaria bloom, not by dozens but by hundreds, and I asked the same question, and got the same answer.

"They grow near a highway in the historic village of Constantine. All I know of their origin is that the property on which they grow was once the home of an enthusiastic gardener, long departed. He has left an interesting monument."

Fritillaria imperialis, the "lily of the turbaned countries," comes from Persia where it has an ancient history. "This plant likewise hath been brought from Constantinople amongst other bulbous roots," Gerard says, "and made Denizons in our London gardens, whereof I Have great plenty. It floureth in Aprill, and sometimes in March, when as the weather is warme and pleasant."

Since it blooms on their feast days, it is the emblem of three spring saints. March 18 is the feast of Saint Edward the Martyr, who was murdered on that day in A.D. 978 by his stepmother, who wanted her own son to be king of the West Saxons. The red-flowered crown imperial is dedicated to Saint Isadore, Bishop of Seville, who died in 636; the yellow form is dedicated to Saint Vincent Ferrer, who died in 1419. Saint Vincent was considered one of the greatest orators who ever lived. His theme was death and hell.

Two legends arose from the teardrops at the base of the petals of the crown imperial. One is connected with the Passion. In the Garden of Gethsemane the crown imperial was the only flower that failed to bow before Jesus, and ever afterward it hung its head in tearful remorse. The other is about a Persian queen who was unjustly accused of infidelity. She was turned into a flower, and her tears will remain until she is forgiven.

Gerard describes the teardrops in detail: "In the bottome of each of these bells there is placed six drops of most cleere shining sweet water, in tast like sugar, resembling in shew faire Orient pearles; the which drops if you take away, there do immediately appeare the like: notwithstanding if they may be suffered to stand still in the floure according to his owne nature, they will never fall away, no not if you strike the plant untill it be broken."

In the seventeenth century, *Fritillaria imperialis* was in every garden of note. "The Crowne Imperiall for all his stately beautifulness," Parkinson said, "deserveth first place in this our Garden of delight, to be entreated before all other Lillies."

Before the nineteenth century was over it had gone out of fashion. "It is still in cottage gardens chiefly that the Crown Imperial hangs its royal head," Juliana Horatia Ewing said. "One may buy sheaves of it in the Taunton market-place on early summer Saturdays. What a stately flower it is! and in the paler variety of what an exquisite yellow!"

The yellow form is generally preferred. "The orange Crown Imperials do best here, so of course I feel proudest of the pale yellow," Mrs. C. W. Earle wrote in her garden notes when she left London for Surrey on the first day of April, and found them in full bloom in her Victorian garden.

Last fall I bought a bulb of the yellow variety from De Jager. It came in a package of tulips and squills and crocuses, packed in sawdust in a separate box, and I could smell the bulb even before the box was opened—a strong foxy odor British gardeners say, but it reminds others of the skunk cabbage, only worse. They call it the stink lily.

The flowers are supposed to be foetid too, but I don't remember any unpleasant odor, and once when I picked a stalk and brought it indoors for James Dumbell to photograph, I don't remember his complaining either.

March 1, 1970

❧ A P R I L

. . . .

Spring Planting

Spring planting is as important as fall planting—really more so, for permanent trees and shrubs and bulbs bring spring bloom year after year, even if annuals and biennials have not been put out the fall before to reinforce them; but the fall garden, with less bloom from permanent plants, is very dependent upon annuals sown the spring before.

The first spring in our new garden, Mr. Barringer gave me a quantity of seeds of *Crotalaria spectabilis*. I scattered them everywhere that the soil was bare, and the garden has never again been as colorful as it was that first fall. There was a lot of the common perennial ageratum (really eupatorium) that had spilled over from a nearby garden, masses of a pale yellow single chrysanthemum that had been given to me by a neighbor, and along the path the dazzling white *Chrysanthemum coreanum*, which I had brought from my garden in Raleigh. In the background tall Mexican sunflowers were covered with large flame-colored flowers, like single dahlias.

Mr. Barringer still sends me the crotalaria seeds in the spring, but I have never had the same success with them. They must be planted late—toward the end of May—and by that time the plants in the now well-filled borders give the seedlings little room or light. With plenty of room, and full sun, this crotalaria grows to four or five feet, and flowers from early September until frost, lifting long spikes of flowers that look like golden sweet peas. It is sold as a green manure crop at the seed store, and it is important to get scarified seeds.

With an early start, the Mexican sunflower (*Tithonia*) begins to bloom by the end of July, and goes on until frost. The type is an enormous plant to ten or twelve feet tall, which I was glad to have when shrubs were scarce, but there is a dwarf and more compact form called 'Torch' that is less than half that height. It is considered a drought resistant plant, but I find that it looks very bedraggled if it does not get plenty of water.

Another good hot-weather annual from Mexico is *Zinnia linearis*, a low, spreading plant for the edge of the borders. Plants from seeds sown among the pansies in April begin to bloom late in June, and if the spent flower heads are clipped, may bloom until the end of November. The small lemon and orange striped flowers are not at all like any other zinnia. I have grown them off and on for twenty years, but have never seen them in any garden other than my own.

Chrysanthemum coreanum is one of the most satisfactory perennials that I know. Its only fault is that it grows too well and has to be kept from taking over entirely; the only attention it needs is an occasional soaking in dry weather. All summer there is a mat of fresh green foliage, and at the end of September or early in October a cascade of white daisies that lasts for a month.

The mainstay of my summer and fall garden has always been *Cosmos* 'Orange Flare', which has reseeded itself lavishly for years. Lately, I found myself without any seedlings, and, turning to the catalogue, discovered that it is no longer offered. In its stead I find a double flowered kind called 'Mandarin', described as "bushy three foot densely foliaged plants adorned with strongly double, brilliant orange flowers." For those that like double flowers there it is, but fortunately I have two strings to my bow, and I have found another source of 'Orange Flare', one of the most heat and drought and everything-else resistant annuals that I know.

Looking through the spring seed catalogues, I found a new series of dwarf marigolds, called the Petites, said to be earlier, dwarfer, and more uniform than the 'Yellow Pigmy' which I have always planted. 'Petite Harmony' is mahogany and yellow like the well-known 'Spry', and others are gold, yellow and orange. I was delighted to find that plants of these are available locally, for I know I shall never get around to ordering the seed, planting and transplanting.

The only annuals I grow from seed are those that can be sown where they are to flower. 'Limelight' is my favorite of the Giant-flowered marigolds, but everyone wants to grow the even paler 'Man in the Moon' in hope of finding a white flower in the lot, and winning a prize. For the new 'Cracker Jack' gigantea the catalogue promises "about the ultimate in Giant Marigolds. Earliest to bloom, bearing 100 per cent full double five inch flowers even under adverse conditions." The bushy, two and a half foot plants seldom need staking, and the colors are primrose, yellow, gold and orange, "blended to a formula"—whatever that means.

I always buy petunia plants to replace the pansies when hot weather drys them up. I like to have a lot of one kind, the unpretentious 'Balcony White', because it blooms long and well and looks fresh even under summer suns. For those who like the fancy kinds, 'Blue Lustre', 'White Magic', and the salmon pink 'Maytime' are giant-flowered, ruffed and fringed. Among the multiflora hybrids 'Peach Satin' has been added to the already popular 'Red Satin' and 'Pink Satin'. Last year an army of slugs came along just as I planted dozens of marigolds and petunias, and ate up every one of them. I had to go back for more plants, and put out snail bait. What is poison to snails is poison to birds, so this must be put under a board.

April 13, 1958

Flowering Cherries

When the cherry trees bloomed, the first spring we were in Charlotte, I thought I had never seen so many in one place; but when I looked for them in the nurseries, few were to be found. Now, many more varieties are at hand, and those that are not can easily be gotten elsewhere, for small trees transplant readily and grow quickly.

The first to bloom is *Prunus campanulata*, the bell-flowered cherry, with rose-red bells in February—and once, in my garden, on the twenty-second of January. It makes a slender tree to something like twenty-five feet, is said to grow quickly (though it did not with me) and is the best species for the South, as it endures more heat and drought, but the precocious flowers may be nipped by frost.

The rosebud cherry, *P. subhirtella*, blooms in March. Some forms are earlier than others. I always watch for the first flowers of one on Chelsea Drive that blooms a week or more ahead of those in the Clarkson's garden. I have found them as early as the first day of March, but this year there were none before the twentieth.

The weeping form with deep pink flowers is the one common in gardens. For a long time the awkward parasol standard was the only kind available, but now the ground grafts that grow into graceful pyramidal trees, can be found in a few nurseries.

Seedlings are lovely, too. They vary greatly in form and color. One that Miss Nooe planted at Queens College is a slender, upright tree with almost pure white flowers. I wish people with red brick houses would favor the pale ones.

'Yoshino' comes on the heels of the rosebud cherry, and their flowering overlaps. These two are the most ethereal, because their flowers bloom on bare branches. 'Yoshino' is the tree of the Japanese Cherry Festival, held when it is in bloom in the parks and streets and temple gardens of Tokyo. The city of Tokyo gave well on to a thousand trees to the City of Washington for the planting in the Tidal Basin in Potomac Park.

The one that I watch for is at Mrs. Church's front door. I have found it in bloom on the ninth of March, but this year it was not out until the second of April. Mrs. Church likes her tree because the flowers are a delicate sea-shell pink instead of the usual white. 'Yoshino' is a spreading tree that needs plenty of room. Forty feet is not too much. It grows fast, and blooms when very young.

The flowers of the various forms of *Prunus serrulata* open just as the new leaves come out. The variety 'Lannesiana', an early one, is usually in bloom by the middle of March. The single white flowers hang in little bunches. The large snowy flowers of 'Shirotae', the Mount Fuji cherry, open toward the end of the month or early in April, and the deep rose pink ones of 'Kwanzan' come about the same time. Kwanzan means Gateway to the Mountain. These two double-flowered cherries grow more slowly than the single-flowered forms, and make small, dense, spreading trees.

Some years ago, Mrs. Church gave me a volunteer that came up from the base of her 'Amandagawa', another cherry of the serrulata group. She says she has given away about fifteen. Some sucker, like the parent. Some don't. One that was left to its own devices made a thicket. Mine grew quickly into a tree of fifteen or twenty feet, as slender as a poplar, with gleaming silver trunk. It has never suckered. I really think this is the loveliest cherry of all.

Along with the late double cherries comes a very different one, *Prunus sargentii*. Unlike the others, it is extremely slow-growing, though it gets to be an enormous tree in time. A small one planted in front of our house five years ago is little over six feet now. Last year it bloomed for the first time, with a scattering of pale pink single flowers early in April. The trunk and branches of this species are dark and shiny, and the new leaves are bronze when they first come out, but they turn green very soon.

The last to bloom is the English bird cherry, *Prunus avium*. I have the beautiful double-flowering form, which is not as large as the type, but will grow to about thirty feet. Like the other doubles, the flowers last longer than those of the single-flowering cherries.

April 20, 1958

Shortia

Shortia, like everything else, is blooming late this season. It was in full bloom in Mrs. Charles Stone's garden on April 8. In other years I have found the bank above Mr. Forbis's spring covered with flowers on March 26, and in Elizabeth Clarkson's garden I have found it as early as March 10. It is a great accomplishment to be able to get a sizable patch of shortia established in a garden. Even in the mountain woods it is found only in small colonies.

I laughed when I heard that a speaker at the Williamsburg symposium had said that southerners do not make use of their native wild flowers. He said he wondered why they never use shortia as a ground cover. I guess he had not spent years, as I have, getting a single clump to grow. I could never get it to grow at all in Raleigh, and I have managed it here only after repeated trials. I feel guilty whenever I think of the shining evergreen mats that came from the mountains looking cool and fresh, and melted away in the hot weather, even though I planted them carefully in the sweet-smelling leaf mould, and watered them faithfully. The partridge-berry, wild ginger and galax that are its companions in the mountain woods are much more readily transferred to gardens.

On December 5, 1788, André Michaux, "Botanist to His Most Christian Majesty Louis XIV of France," discovered shortia in the North Carolina mountains. Knowing the exact date makes the discovery seem so much more real. I can imagine the little Frenchman kneeling on the mountainside to examine the round, shining, wine-tinted leaves—so like galax that the species was afterward called galacifolia, but so much smaller that he must have seen at once that this was something new.

It seems odd that a botanist should choose the dead of winter for collecting in the high mountains. Just think how he would have felt if he had come upon the shortia on April 5, and found the finely fringed white or pink flowers that the mountain people call Oconee bells.

Michaux took his specimen back to Paris, but it was not described, because there were no flowers—only leaves and a single seed pod. And it was not until Asa Gray found it, when he went to France to study collections of American plants, that the search for flowers was renewed. Even with all of the botanists hunting, it could not be found. It was not until 1877, when a young schoolteacher, George Hyams, came upon it, accidentally—not in the high mountains, but in McDowell county, on the banks of the Catawba River.

In the end, shortia proved not so rare as local, but even so there are now more plants in nurseries and gardens than in the woods. Gray named Michaux's plant for the Kentucky botanist, Dr. Short, which seems rather a pity.

One of the most interesting things about shortia is that it is found only in our mountains and in the mountains of Japan and Formosa. Two Japanese species are, or were, available in this country. *Shortia uniflora*, called Nippon bells, came to me in the fall from Mr. Starker (who seems to be able to grow it very well in Oregon), and seemed to flourish throughout the winter, but, as is the way with alpines, it disintegrated in the muggy days of August. Although it never bloomed, at least I had a chance to compare the foliage with that of our species, and to me they looked just alike.

April 27, 1958

Fragrant Plants

Perfume is an essential element of gardens in warm countries. I have read that the Persians understand the art of combining fragrant plants, but this is a thing too subtle for me to appreciate. I like one fragrance at a time, with never a time when there is not some sweet-smelling plant in bloom to perfume the garden, and let its fragrance drift into the house.

In *The Country Companion*, Mrs. Loudon gives her young friend, Annie, some good advice on this subject. "I think nothing can be more delightful," she says, "than to throw open your windows, and to inhale a refreshing odor from growing flowers when they are swept over by a balmy breeze, particularly after a slight shower; and, for this purpose, I would strongly recommend you to plant flowers near your windows which have a refreshing, but not a heavy, scent. The flowers of the evergreen magnolia, and those of the orange, have an oppressive fragrance, as have those of the heliotrope and the tuberose; but those of the mignonette, the lemon-scented verbena, the rose and the violet are refreshing, at the same time that they yield a delicious perfume."

For winter fragrance she says winter-sweet (*Meratia praecox*) should be planted against walls between windows; and *Lonicera flexuosa* trained over every window for its delicious fragrance in summer. The lonicera is an especially sweet-scented variety of the common honeysuckle. Mr. Loudon said that, when the wind was in the west, he could smell it for a quarter of a mile away as he came home from London.

Mrs. Loudon does not mention the sweet olive (*Osmanthus fragrans*) as a shrub to be planted near a window, for in her day it was considered a stove-plant. I always know when mine is in bloom, though it is nearly hidden by other shrubs. On mild days in winter, again in spring, sometimes in summer, and especially in the fall, its sweetness suddenly fills the garden. No matter how small my garden, it is an evergreen that I could never be without.

Although the hedges and vines are thick between us, often, when I smell something nice that I cannot account for, I find that it has blown over from my neighbor's. I always know, in January or February, when Mrs. Dooley's sweet-breath-of-spring comes out, even if I cannot see it. This summer, late in August, I noticed a spicy sweetness—like that of pinks—which seemed to be especially strong in the afternoon. I thought it came from the clerodendron, which had the same sort of fragrance earlier in the month, but when I sniffed in that direction I found that the small white flowers had faded. It took me several days to trace the odor to Mrs. Dooley's Japanese clematis.

Another spicy summer smell comes from the summer-sweet (*Clethra alnifolia*). I find the variety *paniculata* much finer and more fragrant than the type, and it may be my fancy but it seems to me that its fragrance is more intense at noon.

One hot summer evening when I had gone to bed early and could not get to sleep, I slowly became aware of the most intoxicating of all odors, of lemon and honey and something else that is strong but evasive. The next morning I parted the ivy on the fence, and saw that it was the great white trumpets of Mrs. Dooley's datura that had been pouring elixir into the night. In the morning they are scentless.

Other exotic odors of summer nights are nicotine and tuberose. Mrs. Loudon says that if tuberoses are "distributed over pleasure-grounds of limited extent, at distances of fifty or one hundred yards plant from plant, they will diffuse a most delightful fragrance in the summer and autumnal evenings; a circumstance well understood in the public gardens in the vicinity of Paris." Scents must have been more powerful, or noses more appreciative in the Victorian era. I should plant them at much closer intervals.

The sweet smells of spring are many, but none is more delicious than that of our Carolina jessamine (*Gelsemium sempervirens*).

This list nearly covers the seasons, except for fall, when the tea olives, *Osmanthus x Fortunei* in October and *O. ilicifolius* in November, fill the cool days with brief but intensive sweetness.

April 24, 1960

Lycoris

It is time to be ordering lycorises for summer bloom, so that they can be dug as soon as the leaves die down, and then they should be put out right away, as the bulbs are never really dormant. Some will be available at the seed stores and the five-and-ten, but others must be sought from Mr. Hayward, Mr. Houdyshel and Mr. Giridlian. They overlap very little. Each species seems to know exactly when the one before it is about to fade, and sends up a scape just in time to carry on.

Lycoris squamigera is the first to bloom. It is called the surprise lily because it rises from the ground suddenly and unexpectedly without any foliage. By dividing a clump every now and then, and replanting the bulbs wherever space is available, I have scattered them about so that the whole garden seems to be in bloom when the pink flowers come out. The surprise lilies bloom for a month. Before they are gone, the first scapes of incarnata appear. These are surprise lilies, too; in fact all of the species might be called that, for all come up and bloom without any foliage. The flesh-colored flowers of *L. incarnata* are followed by the pink and blue (more blue than pink) of *L. haywardii* and *L. sprengeri*. I don't know why the latter is still so expensive, for in the twelve years I have had it it has increased very fast. The flowers are dull, and I keep it only because it fills in the gap between the other species. The flowers of *L. sanguinea* are dragon's blood red. I love the color, but it must be kept far, far away from the pink-and-blue flowers, for it blooms about the same time. *Lycoris caldwellii* usually blooms the last week in August. Flowers pinkish in bud come out creamy yellow, and turn creamy white.

The foliage of all these species comes up in the spring. At the end of August or early in September the white spider lilies begin to bloom and these, like the red spider lilies, have foliage that follows the flowers. Before the white ones have withered, the red ones come into bloom, and between them carry the bloom from August to October. I have had white spider lilies from a number of sources, and I have never had one that is really white. They are all pinkish in bud, all creamy, all tinted with peach or apricot, all beautiful. They bloom well and increase very fast.

This fall after all the other lycorises had come and gone, I had for the first time a single scape of deep yellow flowers. It came into bloom on the ninth of October, and lasted for over a week. The flowers were large, frilly, and pure gold, with a deeper stripe down the center of the petal. They withered without fading. I think this is one of half a dozen bulbs that came to me without a name from a Texas importer that Miss Willie May Kell told me about. I have had them for several years and none of the others has bloomed.

Miss Kell calls them *L. traubii*, and writes in *Herbertia* (59) that the bulbs she had from the same source varied widely in form, size and depth of color. The first of the season bloomed in her garden, in northern Texas, on the twenty-second of September, and the last on October tenth. Now I must get *L. traubii* from Mr. Hayward for comparison. It is said to be hardier than *L. aurea*, which has never bloomed for me though I have grown it for years.

And I must try to persuade Mr. Hayward to part with at least one bulb of *L. houdyshelii*, which is very scarce because it increases so slowly. Miss Kell says that in beauty of grace and form and color it is far superior to any other species. She says that when mature it is an "absolutely pure white flower."

Few gardeners, perhaps, will want all of these but I consider *L. squamigera*, *L. caldwelli*, *L. albiflora*, *L. radiata*, and the late yellow if it flourishes, indispensable to continuous bloom in this climate. They are also among the easiest bulbs that can be grown. They are not particular as to soil, and most of them bloom well in sun or shade. They bloom for years without being dug, and seem to have no troubles.

April 29, 1962

Medlars

One of the plants I most regret having left behind in Raleigh is my medlar. Although it had been in the garden only four years it had bloomed for two springs, and was well on the way to becoming a graceful little tree. By now, it would have been in its prime. But the garden's present owner is not fond of medlars. They are, I think, an acquired taste. "Our common medlers do flower in April and May," a sixteenth-century gardener wrote, and that is the time mine bloomed for me. The flowers are single, white, two inches across, and not fragrant, though poets called them "sweet":

> And as I stood and cast asyde myn y
> I was ware of the fairest medle-tree,
> That ever yet in al my lyf I sy,
> As full of blossomes as it might be.
> Therin a goldfinch leping pretily
> Fro bough to bough, and, as him list, he eet
> Here and there, of buddes and floures sweet.
> —"The Flower and the Leaf"

The medlar, *Mespilus germanica*, is a member of the rose family. It is kin to the hawthorns, and is the same sort of wayward little tree. It is native to southern Europe, and was probably introduced to England, where it now grows wild in the hedgerows, in Roman times. In the early English garden books medlars are mentioned, along with apples, peaches, plums and pears, as "homely trees" for the orchard, and they were common in monastery gardens in England and on the continent. The fruits (called medlars) are like small brown apples. They must have been grown in these parts in the nineteenth century, for they are mentioned in the *Ladies' Southern Florist*, published in Columbia in 1860, and are described as the size of walnuts.

When first ripened (in November in England) the fruits are not palatable, but if they are picked and stored they become bletted in two or three weeks, and when they are soft and pleasantly acid they are eaten just so, or made into jelly. English literature is full of references to the fact that medlars are eaten when rotten—though they aren't really rotten. Bletted means "sleepy," and it describes a state when the medlar is overripe, but has not begun to decay. Chaucer said:

> ilke fruyt is ever lenger wers,
> Til it be rotten in mullok* or in street†—
> We olde men, I drede, so fare we:
> Til we be roten kan we nat be rype.

—The Reeve's Tale
* mullok = rubbish
† stree = straw

And in *As You Like It*, Rosalind says to Touchstone, "You'll be rotten ere you be half-ripe, and that's the right virtue of the medlar."

In Saki's story "The Boar-pig," it was in a medlar tree that Matilda, Mrs. Cuvering's precocious niece, was hiding when she saw two ladies trying to crash her aunt's garden party. They meant to go in the back way, and join the guests on the lawn, but Matilda knew that the gate was locked, so she waited until the ladies had crossed the paddock and gone into the gooseberry garden, and then she climbed down and let Tarquinus superbus out of his stye.

She was back in her tree when the retreating ladies found themselves confronted by a ferocious looking boar-pig. After letting them stew for a while, she made her presence known, and offered to help them—for a price. When they had met her terms, she climbed down from the tree and gathering a handful of over-ripe medlars, she went into the paddock. "Come, Tarquin, dear old boy," she said affectionately, "you know you can't resist medlars when they are rotten and squashy," and dropping them before him, one by one, she lured him back into his stye.

Medlars like moisture and good soil, but they are not particular, and will grow anywhere. Though they are not much grown in this country, one or two nurseries still list them. Tingle offers sizes up to five or six feet. In England a number of horticultural forms have been developed, the best of them being 'Nottingham'.

April 12, 1964

Shakespeare's Flowers

As so many celebrations will be taking place this coming week in honor of the four hundredth anniversary of Shakespeare's birth, I thought I would celebrate, too, by re-reading the poet who, above all others, loved flowers and gardens, and told his love in such a direct and simple way that his pleasure is as fresh and lovely today as it was when he shared it with the Elizabethans.

He takes his readers with him to pleasant places where flowers bloom:

A bank where the wild thyme blows,
Where Oxlips and the nodding Violet grows,
Quite over canopied with luscious woodbine,
with sweet musk-roses, and with eglantine. . .

Leontes's garden, and

> the pleached bower,
> Where honey-suckles, ripened by the sun,
> Forbid the sun to enter
> . . . .
> The even mead that erst brought sweetly forth
> The freckled Cowslip, Burnet, and Sweet Clover.

Where

> Daisies pied, and Violets blue,
> And Lady-smocks, all silver white,
> And Cuckoo-buds of yellow hue
> Do paint the meadows with delight. . .

To "turfy mountains, where live nibbling sheep, And flat meads thatched with stover, them to keep"; and to "banks with Peonied and twilled brims," and "Broom-groves whose shadow the dismissed bachelor loves." (None of the commentators has ever told why the dismissed bachelor seeks the shadow of the broom.)

Perdita wished for the flowers that Proserpina had let fall, to make "a bank for love to lie and play on": daffodils that come before the swallow, dim violets, and

> pale primroses,
> That die unmarried, ere they can behold
> Bright Phoebus in his strength, a malady
> Most incident to maids; bold oxlips, and
> The crown imperial; lilies of all kinds,
> The flower-de-luce being one!

The names of the primulas are confused, but according to Canon Ellacombe, Shakespeare's cowslip is *Primula veris*; the primrose, *P. vulgaris*; and the oxlip, *P. elatior*. Cowslips are associated with fairies. "In a cowslip's bell I lie," Ariel sang, and cowslips were the tall pensioners of Queen Titania,

> In their gold coats spots you see;
> Those be rubies, fairy favors;
> In those freckles live their savors.
> I must go seek some dewdrops here,
> And hang a pearl in every cowslip's ear.

Lady-smocks, probably called Our-Lady's smock because they bloom at Lady-tide, are *Cardamine pratensis*, which is also called cuckoo flower, but

Shakespeare's "Cuckoo-buds of yellow hue" are generally thought to be buttercups. The daisies that bloom with violets and lady-smocks are the little *Bellis perennis* of English meadows, but Esther Singleton, in *The Shakespeare Garden*, says the daisies that Ophelia wove into her garlands must have been the moon daisy, *Chrysanthemum leucanthemum*, which blooms in mid-summer, the time when she drowned herself.

Perdita's "Marigold, that goes to bed with the sun, and with him rises, weeping," is not (as Burpee would have you think) the modern marigold (*Tagetes*), but *Calendula officinalis*, which has a long season, and so is usually in bloom for all of the festivals of the Virgin. Perdita's carnations, "fairest flowers of the season," were originally called "coronations" because they were used for crowns and garlands. They were so popular in the Roman festivals that they were, and still are, called dianthus, or flower of Jove.

Ophelia's pansies (for thoughts) are *Viola tricolor*, and so is Oberon's "little western flower," milk-white before Cupid's bolt fell upon it,

> now purple with love's wound,
> And maidens call it Love-in-idleness.

But the flower that Shakespeare loved most of all, for he refers to it in nearly a hundred passages, is the rose.

It seems to me that the best way to celebrate his Centennial is to read Shakespeare's plays, and to plant his flowers.

May 24, 1964

Crawling

Early in April, Mittie Wellford and I went to walk in Mary Horsley's woods. Mary says that before she found Mittie and me she thought she was the only grown woman who likes to crawl over the floor of the woods. She says it is more fun when you have company.

We took a basket. I had thought to "touch a hundred flowers and not pick one," but Mary is not going to have her woods all to herself much longer. There is, even now, a faraway sound of a bulldozer, though still so far away that we could forget it as we crossed the creek, and climbed the steep bluff, and went along an overgrown access road, where mosses grow in the ruts, and bluets grow in the mosses.

It was a hot, still, dreamy afternoon when redbud was in bloom, and dogwood just beginning to turn white. Looking down, all sorts of green things were coming out among the early wild flowers; but looking up, the branches of the forest trees were as bare as winter. The trees seemed to be mostly oaks and enormously tall tulip poplars with clean, straight boles. And ironwood, Mittie said.

The bloodroot had finished blooming, but its prettily cut, pale green leaves were everywhere. I dug a clump to bring home with me, for I have never had this early and easily grown wild flower in my present garden, though I had sheets of it in Raleigh. When I cut one of the underground stems, and it bled, I suddenly remembered the first time I brought blood-root from the woods, when I was a child.

There were lots of violets in bloom, and I did not know the names of any of them. One has large flowers of Bradley's violet, and deeply cut purplish leaves. I ran it through the key when I got home, and came to the conclusion that it is *Viola palmata*. I was stumped by another, a pale blue one, on very short stems, with small round leaves. This comes up, here and there, in the tiny wood sorrel that carpets the forest floor.

Rue anemones were in full bloom, chrysogonum just coming out, and the little crested iris still in bud. The leaves of later wild flowers were coming up among the early ones. We had some argument over these, for it is one thing to know the common wild flowers when they are in bloom, and quite another to be able to distinguish the new foliage of Solomon's seal from that of the sessile-leaved bellwort. We found something we took to be a lily, and some oval leaves that Mary thinks will prove to belong to the devil's bit.

This is Mary's first season in her woods, so she doesn't know yet what the later flowers will be. She hopes for another spring before the bulldozer gets there, but she's bringing things into her rock garden as fast as she can. In the midst of new spring green I recognized the solitary winter leaf of the crane's-fly orchid, because it is purple on the underside; and I thought some tufts of grassy foliage might be the bunchflower, *Melanthium virginicum*.

When we came back to the bluff, Mittie walked out on a rocky ledge over the creek, and found the unfurled fronds and curled croziers of a little filigree lip-fern. I think it is *Cheilanthes lanosa*. There were also some clumps of *Zephyranthes atamasco*, and one was in bloom. I have never found the atamasco lily in such a dry place before. It usually grows in low woods and meadows. There used to be a lot of it along Sugaw Creek when we first came here to live, and it came up in the lawns of some houses on Westfield. It likes to be cut over.

There were patches of golden buttercups on the bluff, but I thought they were the common kind, and did not dig any up, though they seemed to be a neat and cheerful ground cover. Now I wish I had, for I find on looking them up that there are eighteen species of buttercups in North Carolina, and I should like to see *Ranunculus fascicularis*, the tufted buttercup.

The basket got heavier and heavier as we returned to the creek, and I thought of some doggerel I once saw in a garden magazine:

Oh, treat the wild flowers gently,
And call them as they're named.
For everything that's wild, dear child,
Is anxious to be tamed.

But that, unfortunately, is not altogether true.

April 18, 1965

Chervil

A few of the perennial herbs stay green all winter, providing fresh flavors for the kitchen. Rosemary and sage are always with us. French thyme is almost as dependable, although the leaves are pretty tough and tasteless by the time new growth begins. All herbs seem to me to have less of the essential oils in cold weather. More than the usual amount is needed for flavor.

Burnet is called evergreen, and is nearly so. Lacy volunteer seedlings make early rosettes. Chives usually last until the end of the year, and new foliage begins to come up in February.

In the interim I can always find some sort of onion foliage to snip for salad. I never know what they are, as I have planted so many kinds: leeks, scallions, shallots, rocambole and any others that I hear about. All are tasty. And there are always bay leaves. The bay tree gets killed back in very severe weather, but some branches will still be green.

Two annuals stay green all winter: chervil and parsley. Chervil must be one of the oldest plants in the herb garden, and certainly one of the most valued. Its name comes from two Greek words, meaning leaf and rejoice. It came to England with the Romans, and quotations in the Oxford dictionary begin with 750, when it was called cerfelle. Thomas Tusser (1573) considered it one of the "Necessairie herbs to grow in the garden for Physick," and the herbalists recommended it for any number of things, including the plague. "It is so harmless you cannot use it amiss."

"The leaves of sweet Chervill," Gerard said, "are exceeding good, wholesome, and pleasant, among other sallad herbs, giving the taste of Anise seed unto the rest. . . . The seeds eaten as a sallad whilest they are yet greene, with oyle, vineger, and pepper, exceed all other sallads by many degrees, both in pleasantnesse of taste, sweetnesse of smell, and wholesomenesse for the cold and feeble stomacke. The roots are likewise most excellent in a sallad, if they be boyled and after dressed as the cunning Cooke knoweth how better than my selfe: notwithstanding I doe use to eate them with oile and vineger, being first boyled; which is very good for old people that are dull and without courage; it rejoiceth and comforteth the heart and increaseth their lust and strength."

Having copied this, and feeling old, dull and without courage, I went out and picked a bunch of chervil and cut it up very fine, and added it with oil, vinegar and pepper to a bowl of lettuce. It was good, but I got a little too much flavor of anise, though the flavor is so delicate it is apt to be lost with other herbs.

Chervil is one of the *fines herbes* French cooks use in omelets. They use it as a garnish with chicken and veal, and consider it essential in Béarnaise sauce and French dressing. If used at all, chervil must be picked fresh from the garden, as dried leaves lose their flavor very quickly. It likes a cool, moist soil, light but well drained, and I have read that it needs lime. Seeds should be sown in the fall or very early spring. I have always sown them in late spring, and the spindling seedlings became more spindling and soon dried up in the heat. They cannot abide hot weather.

Last fall I acquired from Elizabeth Price two handsome plants in pots. When I planted them by the kitchen door, I did not suppose they would live through the winter. But they did. Their beautiful, finely cut leaves stayed green even under all of that snow and provided a fresh flavor of salads and seasoning. The plants were by far the prettiest thing in the herb bed.

In Holland chervil is much used in soups. Eleanour Sinclair Rohde gives a recipe from the cook book of the chief cook to the Prince of Orange (1774) of a pottage to be eaten in March or April, for it has more virtue in the spring to sweeten and purify the blood. It is made with a knuckle of veal, three or four handfuls of chervil, two or three leeks, and a good handful of beet leaves. On fish days the broth is made with eels cut in pieces, and you may put a handful of sorrel among the other herbs.

April 27, 1969

Something to Saw

This spring I was asked if I am bored. How can anyone ask that of a gardener? No gardener could ever be bored, for as Andrew Fairservice says, "There's aye something to saw that I would like to see sawn,—or something to maw that I would like to see mawn,—or something to ripe that I would like to see ripen."

Every season is new and different from all those that went before. There always is something new in bloom, something expected and something unexpected, something lost that is found; and there is always disappointment, but being sad is not the same as being bored.

"It acts like spring, but I dare not hope," Caroline Dormon wrote on Saint Valentine's Day. "It was about this time in 1899 that the temperature here in northern Louisiana was 20 degrees below. . . . God spare us, Daffodils are beginning now, and *Magnolia alba superba* will soon be in bloom." It is the white form of *M. x soulangiana* that Caroline calls "alba superba." She thinks it more beautiful than the Yulan.

In my garden the Yulan (*Magnolia denudata*) and two of its hybrids, *M. x soulangiana* and *M. x veitchii*, came into bloom together on March 8. I can't think when, if ever before, all three have bloomed at once when the weather was warm but not hot, when there was no frost and no rain, and when only a few petals were whipped off by wind.

I noticed for the first time the fragrance of *M. x veitchii*. Mr. Morrison used to write about it. He said it filled his whole garden at Pass Christian. It doesn't do that for me, but I did get a whiff of its strange intangible perfume when I stood on a bench and pulled down one of the lower branches.

The weather held for several days, and then, when the trees were almost in full bloom, the frost came back, and the magnolias were hung with black rags. But does it really matter, when you consider "every thing that grows holds in perfection but a little moment," how long the perfection lasts? It does matter, however, that the disfigured flowers hang on so long. It was not until the first days of April that they dried up, or were covered by the new leaves.

Pears, cherries and crabapples, on the other hand, are seldom if ever touched by frost—frost may hold the flowers back, but whenever they open they are perfect if rain doesn't hurt them, and the cherries are even more beautiful when their slender branches are dark and wet and shining. Bloom of the single-flowered kinds is often brief, but this spring the cool weather made their season unusually long. A bud or two of the autumn cherry opened on the first day of March, and the tree was still a pink cloud (with a pale green lining) on the first day of April.

Even if all that goes on in my own garden could not keep me from being bored, there are still telephone calls and correspondence. Someone called to ask me to identify a double daffodil she found in the yard of a deserted house. It looks pale yellow, but there are short orange petals hidden between the yellow ones. I told her it is called butter-and-eggs. She said, "But what is it?" I said it is the double trumpet found in old gardens. "But what is its name?" I said, it might be the one known as 'Von Sion'. She wanted to know if I could tell her the name of anyone in Charlotte who could positively identify it. I said I couldn't, but why not send it to Katherine Heath at the Daffodil Mart. She said that was just what she was thinking.

While this Alice-in-Wonderland conversation was going on, I had been skimming E. A. Bowles on *The Narcissus*. "Some double forms of 'Ajax' vary greatly from season to season," he says, "and no bulb can be relied upon to present a similar form in two consecutive years. . . . Bulbs selected for the sake of an especially pleasing form may never again produce it, and are quite likely to bear flowers of the worst possible shape in some seasons." Or in my garden even more likely not to bear any flowers at all. I wish my caller luck (I forgot to write down her name) and would like to hear from her next spring.

The best thing that happened to me this spring is that *Narcissus* 'J. T. Bennett-Poe' suddenly reappeared after having disappeared a number of years ago. It is now some feet away from the spot where it was originally planted, and of course the label was lost long ago, but the pale, trim, clean-cut flower is unmistakable.

April 26, 1970

Spring Foliage

One morning early in March I came in from weeding the borders and admiring the uncurling leaves of *Thalictrum glaucum*, silvery on top, lavender beneath, and found the January *Journal of the Royal Horticultural Society* in the mailbox. In it was an article by David Wright on "The beauty of spring foliage in the garden."

In particular he writes of the new leaves of certain roses: "Of the species, *Rosa rubrifolia* has young foliage of smoky violet green, combining subtly with the purplish brown stems, and *R. webbiana* has silvery green young foliage and young shoots of pinkish grey."

The new leaves of paeonies, he says (spelling them the British way), are known for their beauty, "*Paeonia emodi* having rich bronze-green young foliage, *P. mlokosewitschii* with bronze-red young shoots changing to soft apple-green foliage with pinky red veins and petioles, and *P. obovata alba* having perhaps the most beautiful foliage of all paeonies, a sort of cobalt-violet covered with a glaucous bloom. . . . The Aconitums (Monkshoods) emerge from the ground as rich bronzy green parsley-like fronds."

I remember vividly the wonderful celadon green of the new growth of a tree peony I used to have, but I had never noticed the emerging monkshoods except to be pleased to see them back again. So I went out to look them over, and found them not at all like parsley, but with a family resemblance to delphinium.

Members of the buttercup family seem to be especially given to early leaf beauty: aconite, adonis, aquilegia, eranthis, isopyrum, paeonia and thalictrum. Adonis is one of the earliest and brightest greens, finely dissected fern fronds coming in February with the buttercup flowers. The aquilegias in my garden are a mixture of the old granny bonnets and wild columbine; the spring leaves are in tones of rose and wine and thunder-cloud purple.

There is praise also for the soft bronze of the new leaves of *Viburnum fragrans*, but I could not remember it so I went out to look. I found tiny pale green ovals with faintly burnished edges and the little tree was full of blooms, after furnishing a few fragrant pink-tinted bouquets in every mild interval since the first of December.

The buckeyes are not mentioned, but three native ones in my garden unfurl in subdued splendor over a period of several weeks, beginning with *Aesculus sylvestris* early in March. The slender leaflets are Etruscan red at first, then bronze, and then green. In April *Ae. parviflora* and *Ae. pavia* leaf out, *Ae. parviflora* in tender spring green. *Ae. pavia* is the most colorful. First the branches are tipped with rosy bracts, and then the Eugenia red buds and blossoms and the burnished leaves come out altogether.

The early rosettes of some of the Asiatic alliums are as spectacular as their flowers. The wide, tapered leaves of *Allium giganteum* are sea-green with fine margins of hellebore red. They come up early in March with the lavender and grey of *Thalictrum glaucum* and the fine bright green plumes of fennel, when hyacinths and early daffodils are in bloom. The "white and wooly" leaves of *A. albopilosum* are edged with white hairs, and are almost as handsome. E. A. Bowles singles out the wonderful leaves of *Allium karataviense*, var. 'Ellisii': "Their wonder consists in the extraordinary metallic colouring they show when young, purple-violet on the under side and steel blue above with a deep red edge. They are especially lovely when a few raindrops are caught in their pleated folds."

The prettily marked, finely toothed oval leaves of the yellow archangel, *Lamium galeobdolon*, are with us all winter, but toward the end of it they are somewhat tarnished, and the silver of the new leaves seems all the more brightly polished. I wonder why no one ever mentions this pretty and useful plant.

April 4, 1971

The Old Daffodils

Many years ago Carl Krippendorf lent me William Baylor Hartland's *Original Little Book of Daffodils* (1887), the first catalogue ever to be devoted entirely to daffodils. Hartland, an Irish nurseryman, said white trumpets were a specialty at Temple Hill, his place near Cork, and he listed nine varieties. One of these was 'Colleen Bawn'. "No daffodil is more pure white," he said, "or so easily recognized by its broad twisted propeller-like perianth segments, and long cylinder-like trumpet." It is described in A. M. Kirby's *Daffodils* (1907) as "a gem among white daffodils, silvery-white, drooping, nodding flowers; gracefully twisted petals. Best when grown in shade and grass."

'Colleen Bawn' is still with us, though extremely rare. I had it last fall from the Daffodil Mart, and it bloomed in my garden on March 23. It is very like the other small trumpets of its day, the silvery swan's neck daffodil, *Narcissus cernuus* (now called *N. moschatus*), and the silver bells of old gardens, but the very narrow, very long trumpet distinguishes it from the others. The trumpet is distinctly yellow, though very pale, at first, and the segments are fawn color. The second day it lifts its bowed head to a horizontal position, and both trumpet and perianth become silver white. It has a delicate fragrance.

In *One Man's Garden*, Miles Hadfield quotes from a letter that George Herbert Engleheart wrote about these old trumpets: "Away back in the 1880's and 1890's I was collecting old forms of white daffodil, chiefly from Ireland. Miss Curry—some years dead—used to hunt them up from old Irish gardens, and a small club of three or four of us used to share them. They were all white things of the 'Colleen Bawn' (I gave the name) type, but varying in size and form. They didn't take kindly to cultivation, and are mostly, I think, lost. I made some attempt to discover their history, and came to the conclusion that Irish religious houses must have had some connection with Spain and Portugal—the focus of the white species."

Hartland must have been one of the small club that Miss Curry scouted for, and from these beginnings Engleheart developed 'Beersheba' (1923), still to me the most beautiful of all white trumpets, and very early, usually blooming the first week in March. Engleheart described it as a "miracle of stately loveliness," and was vexed when P. D. Williams criticized the trumpet as ¼ inch too long.

Engleheart named a cross between 'Emperor' and *Narcissus triandrus albus* (1904) for his friend and fellow clergyman J. T. Bennett-Poe. Kirby described it as "A beautiful new hybrid of robust constitution: perianth petals of cream colour; trumpet of canary yellow—straight and elegantly outlined." In 1907 a single bulb cost $25.

'Bennett-Poe' proved to be vigorous and prolific in Carl Krippendorf's woods in southern Ohio, and he prized it for its substance and its clean lines, but the clump he sent me dwindled. I thought I had lost it, but last spring, after a rest of several years, the lovely thing bloomed again.

He also sent me 'Little Dirk' (1889), an old Barri that he had grown since the turn of the century. This has prospered and increased in the 20 years I have had it. When I came across a description of it, in Barr's 1910 catalogue, as "a dainty flower no larger than a penny piece, borne on a long slender stalk," I began to wonder if I had put the right name to it, for the flowers are more than two inches across. So I sent one to Carl's daughter, Rosan Adams, and she said it is indeed 'Little Dirk'. Then I remembered that English penny pieces are bigger than ours.

April 11, 1971

 # MAY

· · · · · · · · · · · · · · · · · ·

The Painter of the World

O gallant flowering May,
Which month is painter of the world,
As some great clerks do say.

I think of May as the last month of spring, but the old writers divided the year in two, with May Day marking the passing of winter and the coming of summer. The day begins at dawn, for "May loves no sluggard":

It fil ones, in a morwe of May,
That Emelye, that fairer was to sene
Than is the lylie upon his stalke grene,
And fressher than the May with floures newe
· ·
Er it were day, as was hir wone to do,
She was arisen, and al redy dight;
For May wole have no slogardie anyght.
The sesoun priketh every gentil herte,
And maketh it out of his sleap to sterte,
And seith, "Arys, and do thyn observaunce."

And the "bisy larke, the messager of day," had scarcely saluted the grey dawn, when Arcite, too,

Is risen, and looketh on the myrie day.
And for to doon his observaunce to May
· ·
Is riden into the feldes him to pleye,
Out of the court, were it a myle or tweye;
And to the grove of which that I you tolde
By aventure his way he gan to holde
To maken hym a gerland of the greves,
Were it of wodebynde or of hawethorn leves,
And loude he song ageyn the sonne shene:

"May, with alle thy floures and thy grene,
Welcome be thou, faire, fresshe May!"
—*The Knight's Tale*

In the seventeenth century the writers of the early garden calendars made much of the May Day observances. "Now Comes that merry Mayday, so long expected, hoped and prayed for," Stevenson says in *The Twelve Months*. "Now gentle Zephyr fans sweet Buds, and Dripping Clouds water fair Flora's great Garden; the sunbeams bring forth fair Blossoms, and the perfumed Ayre refresheth every spirit: the Flowery Queen now brings forth her Wardrobe, and richly embroydereth her green Apron. . . . The tall young oak is cut down for a May-pole, the frolick Fry of the Town prevent the rising Sun, and with joy in their faces and boughs in their hands they march before it to the place of Erection. . . . It is the month wherein Nature hath her full of mirth, and the senses are stored with delights; It is therefore from the Heavens a grace, and to the garth a gladness; I hold it a sweet and delicate season, the Variety of Pleasures, and the Paradice of Love."

Getting down to practical matters, Stevenson says May is the month to sow all tender seeds such as melons and cucumbers, and all sweet smelling herbs and flowers. "Now cut and set and plant all herbes and seedes, for it is sayd of olde, Set or cut in May, and grow all day."

Another old saying is, "Set sage in May, and it will grow alway." Another, "He that would live for Aye, must eat Sage in May"; and another still older saying, "Why should a man die while sage grows in his garden." The reason for eating sage in May is that the leaves are at their best before the flower stalks come up. It is sometimes called "Sage the Saviour," and Chaucer calls it "save," an old name derived from salvia, the Latin name for the genus. Salvia comes from *salvere*: to save or heal, or to be in good health. Chaucer considered sage a wound herb:

To othere woundes, and, to broken armes,
Some hadden salves, and some hadden charmes;
Fermacies of herbes, and eek save
They dronken, for they wold their limbs have.
—*The Knight's Tale*

May is the time to weed the garden and watch the bees. "Now good Gentlewomen will distill May dewe," and washing in the dew of the hawthorn tree will make anyone beautiful:

Beauty come
Freckles go
Dewdrops make me
White as snow.

Although May is the month of lovers, it is not kind to brides:

Marry in the month of May
And you will surely rue the day.

But it is a good month to be born in:

Who first beholds the light of day
In spring's sweet flowery month of May,
And wears an emerald all her life
Shall be a loved and happy wife.

May 9, 1965

Old Roses

May is the month of old roses. I spend it with catalogues spread out on my desk, several tables and the floor; with *Parsons on the Rose* open before me; and vases of quaint and curious flowers breathing cinnamon and musk. I spend it with Hannah Withers, living in the past.

Hannah has a cousin who frequents old cemeteries, stops to chat in country gardens, and comes home with slips to be rooted in her garden-house and added to her collection at The Borough, her plantation at Stateburg, South Carolina. Once she found a musk rose growing by the wayside of a deserted house. She gave Hannah one of the slips, which is now growing on the wall of her house, and will soon cover the whole gable end, for it grows to a height of forty feet.

The musk rose is the oldest of all. Native to the Far East, it is the rose of the Persian poets, that bursts into bloom at the song of the nightingale. Brought to England at the end of the sixteenth century, it became the rose of Shakespeare. The mysterious perfume of the single milk-white flowers is more intense after dark, when

each inconstant breeze that blows
Steals essence from the musky rose.

Another rare and rampant climber is the Seven Sisters (1817). I have seen this in Mrs. George Capart's garden in Windsor, but Parsons describes it better than I can: "White, light blush, deeper blush, light red, darker red, scarlet and purple flowers, all appear in the same corymb: and the production of these seven colors at once is said to be the reason why this plant is called the Seven Sisters Rose."

Parsons on the Rose, published in 1869, came to me from the library of Miss Emily Bridgers in Wilmington, but its first owner was C. Johnston of Tarboro. If either he or Miss Emily grew all of the varieties that have been checked, roses were well represented in the eastern part of the state at the turn of the century. Even their names seem fragrant: 'Ophire', 'Devoniensis', 'Souvenir de la Malmaison'. Two of those checked in Parsons are in Mrs. Capart's garden. They are large crepe-paper Hybrid Perpetuals, like 'Paul Neyron' (1869) in form, but much more brilliant in color.

Parsons describes 'General Jacqueminot' (1853) as a scarlet crimson with a soft velvety sheen—I would call it magenta. He says that a few thousand of them in full bloom is a sight to be remembered, and that a basket of buds freshly cut in the morning is sure to be appreciated. 'Giant of Battles' (1846) has the same brilliant color, and the spiciest fragrance of any rose I know.

The tea-scented rose, *Rosa indica* variety *odoratissima*, is so-called because the semi-double red flowers have a delicious fragrance, "strongly resembling the scent of the finest green tea." The tea roses come from this, and they are the real southern roses, for they thrive with us, but are too tender for severe climates. 'Bon Silene' (1835), called Bonsaleen in these parts, is the nearest to red in this class, a deep rose, almost red in the fall. Mr. Hjort offers stock from a hundred-year-old bush in a Thomasville garden. 'Isabella Sprunt' (1865) is a North Carolina rose, from the garden of the Rev. James M. Sprunt of Kenansville, but the only place I know to find it now is in a California nursery. The shell-pink, sweet-smelling 'Duchesse de Brabant' (1857) is one I would never be without, though I have room for very few roses. I can't imagine anything nicer than 'Archduke Charles', a China rose that I saw in the garden at Windsor, but have never been able to find in any catalogue. I love all of the Daily roses too, the blush, the white and charming little 'Sanguinea', but the one I must have is 'Louis Philippe' (1837) which produces little red flowers from early April to Thanksgiving.

Hannah has a charming shrub that she calls the Bengal rose, that has always been in the garden at The Borough. It has small pale foliage and bunches of tiny, double, delicately tinted flowers on long arching stems. In time it makes an enormous bush. Hannah also has the climbing noisette, a 'Maréchal Niel' (1868) with heavy-headed, creamy yellow, fragrant flowers, always a favorite in the South. I see it advertised, from time to time, in the *Mississippi Market Bulletin*, only the farm women spell it Marshal Neal. I used to have 'Solfaterre', another favorite yellow noisette, in my Raleigh garden. Hannah favors the moss roses, especially 'Crested Moss' from The Borough, with a delicate fringed calyx that rises above pink bud, which opens into a delightfully crimped pink flower.

June 22, 1958

Dictamnus Albus

Katherine White's article in *The New Yorker* (March 14), "Onward and Upward in the Garden," in which she said she "could hardly wait to get a gas-plant, and set off its eerie fires," brought to light three cases of people who have been badly poisoned by handling *Dictamnus albus*, an old favorite of the perennial border. I have never heard of this before (and I hope it won't keep Mrs. White from planting it). But if anyone has broken out with a rash after being too familiar with a gas-plant, do, pray, let me know. And if anyone has seen the eerie fires, please let me know.

It seems odd to me that a plant cherished and petted in gardens for over four hundred years should be so very poisonous, so I looked it up in all of the books available at the moment (including *The Standard Cyclopedia of Horticulture*, three plant dictionaries and *The Oxford English Dictionary*) and found not a single reference to its having poisoned anyone at any time, and this in spite of the fact that it is chiefly valued as a nose herb. In old-fashioned gardens the gas-plant was placed near a path, where people would brush against it, and could conveniently pick a leaf to rub between the fingers in order to enjoy its strong refreshing odor. Some say it smells of lemon-peel, some of sweet-clover, anise or lavender, and others say its perfume is a blend of all of these.

Although cherished in gardens for its scent, its pretty flowers, and its decorative seed pods, the gas-plant is best known for the essential oil that it gives off. The books say that at dusk, on a very still, hot summer evening, the "phosphoric vapour" (Mrs. Loudon's phrase) is easily ignited by a candle. Most books stress the ease with which this is done, but people who have told me about it usually have it secondhand. Marion Cannon is the only person I know who claims to have actually seen the brief and bluish flame. Mrs. Wilder says in *The Fragrant Path* that repeated experiments on her part "failed of any spectacular results," and my own gas-plants (planted hopefully every fall for a number of years) never survived long enough for the evenings to be hot and still. So I am just as eager as Mrs. White for hers to light up, and I think Maine is a good place for it.

Although the gas-plant is so hard to establish, once it settles down it is celebrated for its longevity. According to the *Cyclopedia of Horticulture*, plants have been known to outlive the planter, his son and his grandson; and in *Old Time Gardens*, Mrs. Earle tells of one that outlived the planter's great-grandson. She also says it was the daughter of Linnaeus who first claimed to have set fire to the gas. "This assertion was met with open scoffing and disbelief, which has never wholly ceased; yet the popular name of Gas Plant indicates a wide-spread confidence in this quality of Fraxinella and it is easily proved true."

Mrs. Earle says Linnaeus's daughter also saw (in the year 1762) "strange flashes of light which sparkled out of the Nasturtium one sultry night"; that Goethe saw and wrote of flashes of light around Oriental poppies; and "soon other folk saw them also—naturalists and everyday folk. Usually yellow flowers were found to display this light—Marigolds, orange lilies, and Sunflowers."

According to the *Oxford English Dictionary*, *Dictamnus albus* is called gas-plant only in America. In England it is known as fraxinella, burning bush or dittany. It is usually called white or bastard dittany to distinguish it from the right dittany of Crete, *Origanum dictamnus*.

May 10, 1959

The Mississippi Market Bulletin

In April my favorite garden literature, the *Mississippi Market Bulletin*, is at its best, and as usual I find in it plants that pass from garden to garden but never get into the catalogues. One of these is the Japanese climbing fern, *Lygodium japonicum*, which the farm women call climbing lace fern, and another is the Easter rose.

I first saw the Easter Rose in Shreveport, Louisiana, but later I found that it is rather common in North Carolina, especially along the coast, where it is called Mother's Day rose. No one knew its Latin name, but finally Mr. Morrison came along one spring when it was in bloom, and identified it as *Rubus coronarius*, the brier-rose.

A contributor to *Home Gardening for the South* (November 1949) wrote that she had gotten it as the brier-rose from Bobbink and Atkins in 1897, so it must have come to this country through New Jersey, where it is hardy, as well as through New Orleans, where it is supposed to have come along with the Casquette-Brides whom the nuns brought over to marry Frenchmen. In New Orleans, it is called Nun's rose or Confirmation rose.

The Easter rose blooms freely in deep shade, but in my garden it does as well in blazing sun, and sometimes in very mild winters it is almost evergreen. It is a scandent shrub to about fifteen feet, with arching canes that should be trained on a wall or fence. The old canes must be cut out after blooming, and new ones trained in their places. I always put this painful work off as long as possible, but, if it is not done, the dead canes become very unsightly, and the new ones lie on the ground, and root at all the nodes so that they soon make a brier patch. Properly trained, the tall canes, furnished with dark, shining rose leaves and white, crinkled rose flowers (to three inches across), are as beautiful as anything in the garden.

I am gradually learning some of the country names that flowers go by in the market bulletins. I feel sure that the red magnolia is *Illicium floridanum*; the candle tree is *Cassia alata*; English dogwood is mock orange; but I don't know what "tame dogwood" is. My mother once sent for grandfather's whiskers and got some little plants of *Cleome spinosa*, the spider-flower.

The *Market Bulletin* is particularly rich in vines. There is the vine peach, which turned out to be a gourd, and the old-timey love tangle vine, or Kettleworth ivy, which I take to be *Cymbalaria muralis*. In the last issue I found listed, and sent for (ten cents and a stamped envelope), seeds of the Chinese pink morning glory, the "soft thorny kind, large green leaves eight inches across; make a quick shade and very pretty." I want very much to get a redwood vine, whatever that is. Gourd vine seeds are for sale too, twenty bushel-gourd seeds, and seeds of four kinds of ornamental pepper for twenty-five cents; and gourd seeds for martin and bluebird houses. Someday I am going to sit down and order all of the oldtime roses, and see what comes: the red velvet rose, the pink saucer, the white summer rose, and the old-timey climbing red.

The *Market Bulletin* is a good source for bulbs not easily found elsewhere, *Amaryllis x johnsonii*, which is called Saint Joseph's lily; the lovely white spider lilies, which are not often listed; yellow rain lilies; and the late-blooming *Narcissus x biflorus*, called April white narcissus. In the last issue someone wanted a red crocus. I can't think what this would be unless it is the ox-blood lily, *Amaryllis advena*.

Some of the swaps are the best of all: one gardener wants to exchange a jungle potato vine (kudzu, I guess) for a rooted rosebud begonia; and another will give a lady-of-the-lake for a bird-of-paradise.

May 8, 1960

Brooms

May is the month of the Spanish broom, *Spartium junceum*, called weaver's broom because in southern Europe a coarse cloth is woven from the tough fibers. It was introduced in England in 1548, probably as a medicinal plant, and seeds were sent to America in 1736. "Inclosed is some seed of the Spanish Broome," Peter Collinson of London wrote to his friend, John Custis, of Williamsburg. "It makes a fine large shrub and looks very pretty when full of yellow blossoms. Sow where they may stand for they are difficult to remove with safety."

With this difficulty in mind I broadcast a few seed in my Raleigh garden, and by this careless method raised a shrub that bloomed from early May to late June. It was not at its best in that garden, as I had no place in the sun for it, and sun is the one thing it demands. It thrives in poor soil, especially if it is sandy, and does not mind drought in the least, for it has very few leaves.

The lemon yellow flowers are as large as sweet peas, and as deliciously fragrant. "If one nips the tell-tale sharp-nosed keel out," Mr. Bowles says, "it is possible to excite a Sweet Pea enthusiast into the belief that you have a yellow variety of his favorite flower." I am sure that he had tried the trick, and with success. Mr. Bowles discovered that in order to make it bloom profusely, and to keep it from getting too leggy, the Spanish broom must be well sheared in spring.

I don't know what success John Custis had with his seeds, but the Spanish broom is one of the shrubs that Jefferson grew at Monticello, and it has been planted in the restored garden. Nevertheless, it is now a much neglected shrub.

On the other hand, the Scotch broom, *Cytisus scoparius*, for which the household broom was named, has become naturalized in this country, and is in bloom everywhere in late April and early May. It was brought to Virginia as a food for sheep and hogs, who eat the flowers, and planted as a flowering shrub in Williamsburg gardens. When used as a hedge it seeded itself over hundreds of acres. The custom of allowing sheep to graze on broom must be an old one, for Dryden wrote:

The humble Broom and Osiers have their use,
And shade for sheep, and food for flocks produce.

I suppose he calls the broom humble because it was the symbol of humility until the Plantagenets exalted it by taking it for their emblem.

Although the flowers of the typical Scotch broom are as yellow and as bright as "bullion unalloyed," the hybrids are even more beautiful. Their glowing colors come from the variety *adreanus*, which M. Edouard André found in Normandy in 1884. There are two groups, those that come from abroad, and those that were bred in California. I had some of each in a set of eight that came to me from La Rochette Nursery when I made a new garden in Charlotte. When they came in the fall, in very small pots, the one called 'Wine' was in bloom. It had claret colored flowers. All bloomed the first spring, beginning in early April and lasting through the middle of May. 'Johnson's Crimson', an English hybrid, was the earliest, and it was in bloom for nearly six weeks. Two other English hybrids were 'George Skipwith' and 'Lord Lambourne'. There were four of the hybrids that Sidney Mitchell raised, and named for the colleges of California. 'St. Mary's' was a most beautiful mass of palest yellow when in bloom, and 'Pomona', 'Stanford' and 'California' were like domes of many-colored glass.

I say was, for they are all gone now, and some are not to be replaced, though I have tracked down a few and I hope these will be given a trial by those who have large sunny gardens. 'Pomona' lived longest, for ten years, and would probably be with me still if I had pruned them judiciously. The new wood should be cut back annually, almost to the old wood, immediately after blooming. This makes smaller, more compact and longer-lived shrubs, and gives better bloom.

May 6, 1962

Mayflowers

When I was a child, I played a game called Greenie. It was always played in spring—never at any other time. Two children would pick green leaves or blades of grass, and joining the little fingers of their right hands would solemnly repeat in unison, "Join, Join, Greenie." Then they put the leaves or grass in their shoes, and after that when one challenged the other by crying "Greenie!" the green must be shown, or a forfeit must be paid.

I wonder whether this child's game goes back to the ancient custom of wearing a sprig of elm or a bunch of hawthorn flowers in the cap or button hole on the first day of May. In some places young people would try to throw water on anyone caught without the protecting sprig.

I always think of hawthorn as the Mayflower, although more than a hundred flowers have been given that name. Even in England the name is given to a number of other things, among them the primrose, the cowslip, the marsh marigold, the lilac, the snowball, and laurustinus. The primrose, the first flower of spring, is usually connected with the earlier months of the year, but Milton says:

Now the bright morning Star, dayes harbinger,
Comes dancing from the East, and leads with her
The Flowry *May*, who from her green lap throws
The yellow Cowslip, and the pale Primrose
—"Song: On May Morn"

In England, the custom of making enormous cowslip balls for May Day is an old one. Children throw and catch the balls in a game called Tisty-tosty. As the flower heads of the snowball or Guelder rose (*Viburnum opulus sterile*) look something like the cowslip balls, they are called May balls or May-tosties. Marsh marigolds have had a prominent place in May Day celebrations. They are fastened on doors, and along with Roman and lady's smocks (both called Mayflower) were woven into garlands.

In France, the lily of the valley is the Mayflower. "Its cult," Colette says (in *For a Flower Album*), "excites the entire populace of a capital city to a pitch of effervescence. . . . Come to Paris on May Day and watch the flower sellers' frontal attack in the streets, twenty francs the sprig, a thousand francs the bunch. . . . Go to Rambouillet and pay a visit to the market alongside the President's Palace, when lilies of the valley are in season. The tight bunched lilies brim and foam over the trestle tables. Their long pale-green leaves are always arranged as a coronal round the flowers; a tradition no one dreams of abolishing." Nosegays are exchanged between friends and lovers, and are worn by both men and women.

In Italy the rose is known as the Mayflower because it is the emblem of the Virgin, and May is the month of Mary. In England eglantine is called Mayflower, but any rose that blooms then is called a May rose. Laertes calls Ophelia "O Rose of May, Dear maid, kind sister." In Alsace a girl dressed in white goes from door to door on May Day carrying a small decorated tree. Her companions sing:

Little May Rose turn round three times,
Let us look at you round and round!
Rose of May, come to the greenwood away,
We will be merry all.

In other parts of Europe, the dandelion, the buttercup and the daffodil are called Mayflower, and bunches of sweet violets are worn on May Day.

Each section of America has its Mayflower, but the best known is the trailing arbutus, *Epigaea repens*, chosen by the Pilgrims as the emblem of spring. They celebrated the day by setting up a maypole and dancing around it. Arbutus is the state flower of Massachusetts, and it is my choice for the national flower.

May 5, 1963

Botany Hill

Just before Easter Catchy Tanner sent me seeds of the pale blue gentian that grows on Botany Hill, and blooms in October. The seeds reminded me that she had promised to take Mittie Wellford, Misty Stunz and me to the hill to see the spring flowers, and I thought Easter Tuesday would be a good time to go. Botany Hill is in Polk County.

We went to Catchy's house first, and she drove us the rest of the way in her jeep along a very steep ridge. The rough road that winds along its side is impassable to cars. We rode and walked and climbed.

There were not so many kinds of wildflowers in bloom, but there were such quantities of the ones that were: so many stars of bloodroot, such drifts of rue anemone, such patches of hepatica. I had never seen masses of hepaticas before, and had never realized the variation in the color forms.

On the hillside there were flowers all the way from white with a faint wash of lilac, to those in tones of the deepest blue violet.

Though there were puffs of shadblow along the road, the dogwood was still in bud and all the trees were leafless. The soft air had an elusive fragrance that was like the scent of a sweet-Betsy warm in the hand. There were sweet-Betsys about, but they were not even in bud.

Catchy said the fragrance came from the trilliums. There were thousands of them with handsomely marbled leaves and oxblood red flowers. The flowers were much the color of a sweet-Betsy, and had a sweet-Betsy scent, but so faint that it was scarcely noticeable in the individual plant. I think they must be the whippoorwill flower, *Trillium hugeri*, a rare southern species; but the keys to the trilliums were uncertain, and they might be *T. sessile*. Catchy calls them skunk trilliums, a name I never heard, and certainly a very inappropriate one.

Among the spring flowers we found the foliage of those of other seasons—the round, silver-veined leaves of rattlesnake plantain, and the single, tapered, pin-striped leaf and dried stalk of *Amplectrum spicatum*, a little orchid called Adam-and-Eve. Amplectrum is also called putty-root, because the roots contain a cement. We identified it by a paperback Misty brought along, *A Pictorial Guide to the Wild Flowers of the Smokies*, by J. L. Caton, one of the best books to take to the woods.

As we went on down the hill we came to buckeyes with their leaves about to unfurl and silverbells in bud, and some tufts of toothwort, *Dentaria laciniata*, in full bloom. The flowers are pink-tinted bells, something like spring beauty. The spicy roots are edible. At the foot of the hill we crossed a creek, and bounced over a very large rough meadow carpeted with field pansies (*Viola rafinesquii*), tiny lilac tinted flowers which are the only American relative of the Johnny-jump-up.

We had our lunch on the edge of the meadow beside the Green River, and then bounced across the rough grass to the even rougher road and up an almost perpendicular incline to another and very different plant community from the one we had just seen on the northern side of Botany Hill.

On a sheer wall of rock *Phlox stolonifera* was basking in the sun, at its foot the roadside was fringed with blue spring daisies, whose name "poor Robin's plantain" sounds like the Old World, but belongs to the New. And there was a single fire pink, the very first of the season; later, when I recorded it in my files, I found it by far the earliest date that I had known. The others are late May and June.

On the way back, Catchy said we must come again to see the laurel in bloom on the north bank of the Green River, and to explore the rocky creek at the bottom of the ravine.

May 8, 1966

In Virginia

When Mittie Wellford and I were tracking down daffodils in the Tidewater Country, we found silver bells in bloom both at Sabine Hall and Mount Airy. No one knows them as silver bells or by any other name; they love them, but they don't think them anything special because like the early trumpets they have always been there.

At Mount Airy, fields of daffodils come up and bloom spring after spring, and generation after generation, in spite of wars and rumors of wars; and the fall brings forth rank upon rank of British soldiers (the Virginia name for *Lycoris radiata*) and golden seas of sternbergias. The garden at Mount Airy is surrounded by a ha-ha. Its wall is built of large stones skillfully laid without mortar, or at least it looks that way, and it is covered with ferns and mosses. One side is very high, with a shaded alley along the top, and a lovers' seat in a bower at the end. It is called the Cherished Walk.

It was too early for *Narcissus x biflorus*, but I found it in bud at Brooksbank, and learned a new name for it. Barbara Richardson calls it lords and ladies, which reminds me that one of its many country names is husband and wife. I don't know where I got my name, twin sisters, and the flowers are not always twins; occasionally there is only one, and occasionally there are three.

The old name, given to it by the sixteenth-century herbalists, is primrose peerless. *Narcissus x biflorus* is one of the oldest daffodils in cultivation, and along with the early trumpet it has been naturalized in Virginia for more than 200 years. I expect it has been in North Carolina as long, for it has been naturalized in all parts of the state, and as I rode along the highways in mid-April I saw it everywhere in country gardens. Rose Wharton says hers came from her mother who brought them from a garden in Edgecombe County, and her mother had brought them there from Warren County; and they had probably moved with her family long before that.

I had expected Brooksbank to be beside a stream, but I found it on a hilltop overlooking the Rappahannock. It took its name from Sarah Brook, who built it in 1731. The old flower garden is gone, though you can see where it was laid out on terraces between the house and the river, but there is a large new one full of old and new plants. In it I found in bloom the little blue violet that Mrs. Alexander Gibbes gave me. It came from the old LeConte garden in South Carolina, and Mittie says it has always been in the garden at Montrose. I think it must be a form of *Viola odorata* for the small rather pale flowers are like those of the variety *rosina* in form, and they are deliciously scented. Mrs. Gibbes calls them English violets. For her they bloom freely in January, and this year I found one frosted flower on the fifth. Perhaps this is the small early flowering variety *praecox* mentioned in E. S. Gregory's *English Violets*.

In Mrs. Richardson's garden I also found cupidone and the Yorktown onion, though of course these were not in bloom in early April. Cupidone is *Catananche caerulea*, an ancient perennial that Greek women used in love philtres. It is called Cupid's dart. It was in English gardens by the end of the sixteenth century, when Gerard wrote that seeds had been sent to him from Padua. I grew it once in Raleigh, but not for long. I must try again, as George Park lists seed of the typical blue kind and also a rarity with white flowers. They bloom the first year from spring-sown seeds.

The Yorktown onion is naturalized on the battlefield, and is much used in flower arrangements at Williamsburg, though I never heard that it was in Colonial gardens. Years ago I read in *Garden Gossip* that it had been seen by some visitors in the Raleigh Tavern, and sent to Liberty Hyde Bailey to be identified. It is rocambole, *Allium scorodoprasum*, a valued kitchen herb as well as a very ornamental plant. I got it from Plantation Gardens, and for years it grew under the kitchen window and bloomed in May, but it finally disappeared. Now I know of no commercial source for it, but I hope it is going to prove to be the elephant garlic advertised in the *Alabama Market Bulletin* as "mild and juicy, plant now."

May 10, 1970

The Battle of Summer and Winter

This year Pentecost, commonly called Whitsunday, falls on May 17. I don't suppose many people think of it now, but in the old days it was an important festival, a sort of continuation of Mayday, and a mingling of pagan and Christian customs in celebration of spring. In 1633, Charles I decreed "That after the end of Divine Service, Our good people be not disturbed, letted, or discouraged from . . . having of May-Games, Whitson-Ales, and Morris-dances."

In some places it was the time when the battle between summer and winter took place. "At Dromling in Brunswick, down to the present time," Sir James Fraser says, "the contest between summer and winter is acted every year at Whitsuntide by a troop of boys and a troop of girls. The boys rush singing, shouting, and ringing bells from house to house to drive winter away; after them come the girls singing softly and led by a May Bride, all in bright dresses and decked with flowers and garlands to represent the genial advent of spring."

A little European stichwort (*Alsine holostea*) is sometimes called Whitsunday, but more often Easter bells—a foolish name, for the flowers are starry like those of its relative the chickweed. In parts of England children call it pixy. They say those who gather it will be pixy-led. It must have a long season for "the buds are green on the Linden-tree. And flowers are bursting on the lea," when "Stichwort with its pearly star is seen in hedgerows from afar," and Anne Pratt finds it still in bloom with golden rod and foxglove.

"May brings roses, pinks and Whitsun gilliflowers," William Coles says in *The Art of Simpling*. These were a double-flowered form of *Hesperis matronalis*. Then there is the Whitsun rose, *Rosa cinnamomea*, and the Whitsunday rose, *Viburnum opulus*, also known as Whitsun bosses. In America the wild azalea, *Rhododendron nudiflorum*, is called pinxter-flower from the German word for Pentecost, a name given to it in colonial days by Dutch settlers who gathered the flowers at Whitsuntide. Pinks are also Whitsun flowers because their name is supposed to be derived from pinkster. But the real flower of Whitsuntide is the peony, the Pentecostal rose. No one seems to know the reason for its association with the church season, though Gladys Taylor says it is "perhaps on account of its crimson hue, red being the liturgical colour for that festival."

A great deal has been written about the connection between the peony and medicine. "It is reported that these herbes tooke the name of Peionie, or Paeon," Gerard says, "of that excellent physition of the same name, who first found out and taught the knowledge of this herbe unto posteritie." "Apulius saith, that the seedes or graines of Peionie shine in the night time like a candle, and that plenty of it is in the night season found out and gathered by the shepheards." Gerard also says from Aelianus that the peony "is not plucked up without danger; and that it is reported how he that first touched it, not knowing the nature thereof, perished. Therefore a string must be fastned to it in the night, and a hungrie dog tied thereto, who being allured by the smell of rosted flesh set towards him, may plucke it up by the roots." But Gerard, himself, did not believe in "such kinds of trifles, and most superstitious and wicked ceremonies . . . found in the books of the most antient writers," "for the roote of Peionie . . . may be removed at any time of the yeare, day or houre whatsoever."

In the *Iliad* Homer tells how Paeon, the physician of the gods, cured Ares when he was wounded; and laid soothing herbs on Pluto's lacerated shoulder, "and healed him seeing that he was of no mortal substance." Perhaps one of the herbs was the peony, for it is a compassionate herb. There are two principle kinds of peony, Parkinson says, the male and the female. The first is *Paeonia corallina*, and the second *P. officinalis*. The male kind is preferred as a medicinal herb.

May 17, 1970

Cardamon

After reading Edith Bestard's notes on cardamon in the October issue of *Ozark Gardens*, I sent for a plant to grow in the kitchen window. It would have been better, I think to wait until spring and plant it directly in the garden, for Mrs. Bestard says it has wintered (well mulched, and against a south-facing wall) in her garden in northern Arkansas (Zone 6). In the Oakhurst Garden catalogue (1968) Mr. Giridlian describes a mammoth cardamon as a decorative aromatic plant for California gardens, but he says it won't flower there because the nights are too cool—which seems odd, as it comes from the mountains of southern India. In California it makes a compact clump two to four feet tall. In India it is said to grow twice as tall as a man.

Hippocrates, the father of medicine, listed cardamon among the simples; ancient Greek, Roman and Persian writers considered it an aphrodisiac; and Theophrastus mentions it—along with cinnamon, cassia, spikenard, orris, saffron and myrrh—as an ingredient in perfumes. It turns up often in the *Arabian Nights*. The seeds are called grains of paradise; they are said to be good against the falling sickness, and to chew for indigestion. "Cardamomum," John de Trevisa wrote in the fourteenth century, "helped against wambling and indygnacyon of the stomak." I had forgotten, until reminded by Rosetta Clarkson, that "Cardamus" was one of the ingredients in the tincture Mrs. Crupp, David Copperfield's housekeeper, claimed to be the best remedy for her "spazzums." As he had none on hand when she was seized (which she well knew), she said brandy was the next best remedy, and brandy was produced.

Powdered cardamon is one of the ingredients of curry; it is used in candy and cookies, and Mrs. Clarkson gives a Swedish recipe for using it in Poor Man's Pastry. I found both the whole and the powdered seeds put up in glass bottles. The very fine beige powder looks pretty through the glass. They say the seed should not be ground until they are wanted for use, but when the bottle is opened the aroma and taste are so strong I shouldn't think they would need to be any stronger. And to me they are not really pleasant. The label on the bottle recommends the powder for sliced oranges, iced melon, and fruit salad. I tried it on sliced oranges, and thought there was some affinity there, but it is difficult to get just the right amount of the powder.

There should be only a hint, just enough to make you wonder what the elusive flavor is. Having read that the Egyptians use the powder in coffee, I tried that too, but I didn't like it. Here again there is such a fine line between too little and too much. I couldn't get enough to taste at all, without its being overpowering. The powdered seeds are sometimes used for dusting pomanders, but I think I like mine best with only cinnamon and orris root—that is, if I can get the orris root. I don't know where it can be found, now that the Charlotte Drug Company has disappeared. And I don't know where to get asafetida.

Mrs. Bestard says the reason she is so fond of cardamon as a house plant "is the delightful fragrance of its foliage, which you can savor without crushing the leaves. Besides being fragrant, the foliage is beautiful—narrow, lanceolate leaves on stiff upright stalks. The flower is a brownish cone-shaped stalk." She says one stalk spreads so quickly it will soon give you a potful, and the clump is easily divided.

May 24, 1970

Savory Seeds

While looking up cardamon I reread Rosetta Clarkson's leaflets, from the *Herb Journal*, on savory seeds. She discusses celery, coriander, cumin and caraway, fennel, anise and dill—all belonging to the umbelliferae. Grow the plants in your garden, she says, or if you have no garden grow them in the house. If you can't do either, go out and buy some seeds and study them under a magnifying glass. I went out and bought some and found them as beautiful as she said they would be.

The seeds of coriander are twins. They are packed in a little round case about the size of a peppercorn and the color of café au lait. The little balls are ridged with delicate precision, a straight line alternating with a fine wavy line. As the fruit ripens it becomes aromatic, and the longer it is kept the more fragrant it becomes. The foliage is foetid. The leaves are slashed, and they look something like parsley.

Coriander seeds are coated with fondant to make candies, called comfits, for children. Alice had a box of comfits in her pocket when she followed the white rabbit down his hole. She produced it at the end of the Caucus-race, when the Dodo said, "Everybody has won, and all must have prizes." Fortunately, "there was exactly one apiece all round."

Comfits were made of caraway seeds, too; the Puritans called caraway, fennel, and dill "meeting" seeds, because women and children and even men carried them to meeting on Sunday to nibble during the sermon. I like a few caraway seeds in French dressing for a change, and a few are delicious in cottage cheese along with parsley, chives and a bit of sage. The seeds should be crushed, and a little goes a long way. Caraway is useful in love potions, as it promotes constancy, and it keeps lovers and pigeons from straying. "It is an undoubted fact," Mrs. M. Grieve says, "that tame pigeons, who are particularly fond of the seed, will never stray if they are given a piece of baked caraway in their cote." Caraway is a biennial, but seeds sown in the fall will produce fruiting plants the next season. Coriander, cumin, and dill are annuals. Coriander and cumin are sown in late spring when the ground is warm.

"I have proved the seeds [of cumin] in my garden," Gerard said, "where they have brought forth ripe seed much fairer and greater than any that comes from beyond the seas. . . . My selfe did sow it in the midst of May, which sprung up in six days after: and the seed was ripe in the end of July." Theophrastus said cumin must be sown with curses, "if the crop is to be fair and abundant." The seeds of caraway and cumin are much alike except that caraway is fawn colored and cumin the color of a nutmeg; both are delicately edged in a pale cream color, and both are slightly curved.

Dill is a hardy annual. The seeds can be sown in fall or early spring. The seedlings must be thinned, and Mrs. Clarkson says she saves every scrap that is pulled up. She uses them in potato salad, and sprinkles them over broiled lamb chops. Recipes for pickling cucumbers in dill come down from the sixteenth century, and John Evelyn (in *Acetaria*, 1699) gives one for pickling cauliflower. "Boil the colly-flowers until they fall in pieces," he says, but I think they are better raw. I added dill seed, "gross pepper, and a pretty quantity of salt" to the vinegar, and poured it over the cauliflower. I used too much dill, and I shouldn't have left the seeds in the vinegar. Next time I shall strain it before pouring it over the cauliflower. John Evelyn doesn't say whether dill seeds or foliage should be used, but I think the leaves would be better.

Dill is a European herb, but the seeds I got at the supermarket came from India. They are small ovals, the color of cumin seed, with pale edges like a frame, and pale fine ridges. Boiled in wine, or even smelled, Culpeper says, "they stay the hiccough. The seed is of more use than the leaves, and more effectual to digest raw and viscous humours."

Coriander, cumin and dill are Bible herbs. Coriander is one of the bitter herbs of the Passover, and cumin and dill were used in tithing.

May 31, 1970

Man on Earth

Again this spring the *Farmers and Consumers Market Bulletin* announced that the governor of Georgia was proclaiming the fifth week after Easter as Soil Stewardship Week, and was requesting "all citizens of the state to observe the week with appropriate ceremonies . . . and to consider their responsibilities for the care of land, water, animals, plants, and other natural resources." The observance began in 1946 through a farm magazine. The response from clergymen and lay leaders was so great that the project was turned over in 1954 to the National Association of Conservation Districts. Last year "about a million" Georgians took part in the celebration. Now that old ways are being dropped as outmoded, there seems to be at the same time a return to even older ways.

The Fifth Sunday after Easter, commonly called Rogation Sunday, from the Latin *rogare*, to beseech, is a time for asking a blessing on the fruits of the earth. In 511 the first Council of Orleans ordered that the three days before Ascension be celebrated as rogation days with fasting and rogations, the chanting of litanies in procession.

This year the fifth Sunday after Easter fell on May 16. It was celebrated in Charlotte at the Chapel of Christ the King Center by singing the Litany in procession as the red Rogation Cross was taken to the garden and planted there. The cross is a symbol of God's sovereignty over the world and the world's dependence upon him. After the Rogation Cross had been planted and blessed, the procession returned to the chapel, and seed and soil (representing the soil of the nation and the seed planted in it) were offered up and blessed, with a prayer for an abundant harvest.

The Rogation Cross is left in the garden until Thanksgiving, when it is brought back into the chapel with thanksgiving for the harvest. Last year, after it was planted, a patch of Chinaberry suckers came up at its foot. This year the fronds of prettily cut leaves are waist high. After the service I asked the priest, who is called Father Jim, why the Rogation Cross is red, thinking the color must have some significance. He said, "Because I painted it red."

On Rogation Sunday garden tools are placed by the altar as a reminder that men live by the cultivation of the soil, and that it is holy work "not to be despised nor demeaned." On the back of the leaflet for the day there is an article on pollution, taken from the Episcopal Foundation of Chicago, and consisting of quotations from Genesis alternating with dire reports of conditions of the present time—such as, "Every year 2.7 million acres of farmland decline in production quality due to poorly planned use of nitrates, pesticides, and other chemicals."

The quotations from Genesis begin with the first chapter: "In the beginning, God created the heavens and the earth . . . and God saw, that it was good. . . . And God said, Behold, I have given you every herb bearing seed, which is upon the face of all the earth, and every tree, in which the fruit of a tree yielding seed; to you it shall be for meat. . . . And God saw everything that he had made, and behold, it was very good," and ending with, "And the Lord was sorry that he had made man on the earth, and it grieved him at his heart."

May 30, 1971

 JUNE

. . . .

The Blast of a Trumpet

I love Dr. Henry Nehrling's description of seeing Johnson's amaryllis for the first time, on an April day in 1879. He had just come from the still-wintry streets of Chicago, and was wandering about in the flowery fragrance of Houston, Texas, "half dreaming, half in joyful rapture," when he saw two long, glowing strips of red in a distant garden. "In the background, surrounded by magnolias, there was a low house with roses and jasmine climbing over the veranda. On both sides of the broad path, leading to the house, there appeared broad beds with great, beautiful, trumpet-shaped flowers, which glistened and shone in the light of the southern sun as if strewn with gold dust. There was not a hundred, no, a thousand of the flowers, which rose about two feet high over the somewhat short strap-shaped leaves that came forth in thick masses. The flowers showed a broad white stripe on every flower-petal, and gave off a very lovely aromatic fragrance."

I had never noticed the fragrance of the flowers. Perhaps it takes a hundred—no, a thousand—to make it perceptible in the garden. Sniffing a cut flower, I do find it pleasantly aromatic. And I agree with Dr. Nehrling that there is nothing quite like the soft flow of the spectrum-red flower, its delicately stencilled white star set off by the faint green of the throat.

In Louisiana, Johnson's amaryllis is called Saint Joseph's lily, because it blooms for his feastday, the nineteenth of March. In my garden it blooms in the middle of May. It is a gardener's amaryllis, rarely found in the trade, but Wyndham Hayward lists it, and the farm women advertise it in the *Mississippi Market Bulletin*. Mrs. Pittman says she still has a few bulbs for sale.

Another species that I have grown in the garden for a long time, both here and in Raleigh, is *Amaryllis ambigua*, a lovely thing that came from Cecil Houdyshel. He says it is a natural hybrid from Costa Rica, introduced into California before 1875. It blooms here at the end of May or early in June. To each scape there are from five to seven white flowers, marked with Eugenia red and Pomegranate purple. To me they are lemon-scented. Mr. Houdyshel says "the exquisite spicy fragrance perfumes the whole garden."

The charming dwarf amaryllis with flame-colored flowers bloomed in Helen Mayer's garden for several years, but finally petered out. I sent a flower to Mr. Hayward, who said that it was a form of *Amaryllis striata* (formerly *A. rutila*) which in Dr. Nehrling's day was as common as *A. johnsonii*. Dr. Nehrling said it was mostly found in the country as a "room plant," and that its admirers passed the bulbs from hand to hand. My neighbor, Mrs. Reeves, had the same thing. I think she brought it from Georgia. Bulbs of *A. striata* from Mr. Hayward have never prospered, so I am still looking for the hardy form that grows in Georgia gardens. A number of amaryllis hybrids are hardy in North Carolina. In my Raleigh garden I had a hardy English strain that Mrs. Slaughter sent me from Texas. The scarlet flowers were unusually early, blooming at the end of April or early in May. They were four to a scape, and measured about eight inches across.

Several were given to me at Christmastime for pot plants. I had no way of keeping them over, so I put them all in the garden as soon as they had finished blooming. All but one vanished, but it has bloomed faithfully, at the end of May, for four or five years. The large white flowers are strikingly marked with spectrum-red, and the green in the throat is very pronounced.

Mr. Houdyshel offers a strain that has proven hardy as far north as Washington, with four inches of soil above the bulbs and a straw mulch. I got two of these last spring, and they came through the winter, but they have not bloomed yet.

In May and early June, when spring is slowly turning to summer, and there are more leaves than flowers in the borders, the bold form and bright color of an amaryllis are like the sudden blast of a trumpet when all is quiet.

June 28, 1959

Magnolias

Early in May Dr. Mayer brought me a flower of a Japanese magnolia, which was blooming in his garden for the first time though he has had it for more than ten years. Perhaps the long wait for bloom accounts for its rarity in nurseries and gardens, for the species, *Magnolia sieboldii*, has been in cultivation for well on to a hundred years, and it is considered one of the finest shrubs—unsurpassed by the rose, the rhododendron or the peony.

The charm of the flowers is in the unbelievable purity of the six white petals in contrast to the brilliance of the amaranth purple stamens. When they close at night, the white globes are as pretty as the wide saucers that they open into in the morning, and the length of their stems, from one to two and a half inches, distinguishes them from the flowers of all other species.

Their perfume is said to be another charm, but to me the strong scent is distinctly unpleasant. Like the bull bay, they flower a little all summer, once the main season is over. Although the flowers are comparatively small, about four inches across (the species is often known as *M. parvi-flora*), the leaves are wide ovals to six inches long. They are bright green on top and silvery beneath.

Aside from the Mayers', the only other times I have seen the Oyama magnolia are in the Brooklyn Botanic Garden where it was in bloom the last week in May, and where it was in bloom the last week in June. In Japan I think it is sometimes a small tree, but in this country it is a spreading shrub to about ten feet in height and width. The Mayers' is already well on its way to those proportions.

A Chinese species, *Magnolia wilsonii*, belongs to the same section, and the flowers are similar, white with red stamens, but the leaves are narrow and tapered. This is supposed to have the advantage of blooming when the plant is only four or five feet tall, and in a good form the flowers are larger than those of the Japanese species.

Magnolia x watsonii, thought to be a hybrid of *M. sieboldii* and *M. obovata*, is a small tree with large leaves, and with flowers to eight inches across. The flowers are said to be delightfully fragrant.

These three magnolias are available in nurseries that specialize in rare shrubs. All are expensive, but *M. x watsonii* is the rarest and most expensive of all.

I am very fond of our sweet bay, *Magnolia virginiana*. In my garden a small seedling picked up in a local nursery grew to six feet the first summer, and in four years had shot up to about fifteen feet. It is partly evergreen—that is, most of the leaves hang on until the new ones take their places. I love its straight grey trunk, its slender open habit, and the way the leaves turn to silver when the wind blows. It reminds me of the sudden coolness that goes before a summer storm.

Sweet bays may reach a height of fifty feet, though they are usually small, and often shrubby. Mine looks as if it were going to be a real tree, and if it outgrows the garden I shall cut it to the ground and let it come up again from the roots. The species varies a good deal in the size and form of the leaves. Those of my tree are unusually long—to nine inches—and they are rather narrow and taper at both ends. When they are crushed, they are faintly but pleasantly aromatic.

The sweet bay begins to bloom before the middle of May and stays in bloom for some time, but *Magnolia x thompsoniana* blooms over an even longer period. This magnolia, found in a London nursery about 1908 among some sweet bay seedlings, seems to be a cross between *M. virginiana* and *M. tripetala*. The flowers are large, to six inches across, lemon scented, and like a water lily in form.

I have never had any trouble with magnolias, but they are considered difficult to transplant, and spring planting is supposed to be better than fall. They need a rich, moist soil, and protection from wind.

June 11, 1961

Miss Hazel Johnstone

One afternoon at the end of May, Mittie Wellford and I went over to Belmont to see Miss Hazel Johnstone. Miss Hazel had told us that her old roses were about over, "but come on," she said, "we have plenty else." We found this to be an understatement. I don't think I ever saw so many things in one garden, and walking among them were three large grey geese and five overgrown goslings.

The garden is full of old-fashioned flowers that you never see any more—cornflowers, catnip, coreopsis, bleeding-hearts, Jacob's ladder, love-in-a-mist, evening primrose, dusty miller and peppermint verbena. And along with these, such out-of-the-way things as the foxtail lily. The foxtail lily is a dwarf one, *Eremurus bungei*, with yellow flowers, and Miss Hazel says it is about to die out, but she has had it ten years. She says it likes woods dirt.

The garden goes on and on and on—flowers, fruits and vegetables, all mixed up together; a row of roses and then one of gooseberries and blueberries—and on down the hill to a pond in a pine woods. On the bank of the pond was a mountain laurel, one of the loveliest I have ever seen with white flowers and the palest of pale pink buds. Miss Hazel said it came from a little way down the Southpoint Road. I had no idea that mountain laurel grows so near. There is also a fine collection of large-flowered clematis, and these were in full bloom: two enormous white ones, 'Mrs. Henry' and *Clematis lanuginosa* 'Alba'; the brilliant purple *C. x jackmanii*; the pale blue 'Mrs. Cholmondeley'; the double white 'Duchess of Edinburgh'; and 'Ernest Markham'. 'Ernest Markham' is described as red, but it is really a red violet.

Miss Hazel has one thing that I have read about, but have never seen before, a green rose, *Rosa chinensis* 'Viridiflora'. It doesn't look like a rose at all, but, as Mr. Bowles says, it is a distinct personality. "Like other Chinas," he said, "it seems to wish to flower all the year round, and has had many bunches of sound buds at Christmas." The green rose has been called *R. monstrosa*, which is a good name, for the curious flowers are almost repulsive, but Mr. Bowles admired its shapely emerald buds, and liked to cut them to arrange with other roses. Those who like things for the sake of their age will like this one, for it has been in cultivation since 1743. An old gardener who was asked if he had ever seen a green rose replied that he had never seen a green rose, and he had never seen a blue one. If he could have visited Miss Hazel, he would have seen both.

In Miss Hazel's garden I saw for the first time, all three of the sweetheart roses blooming together: 'Cecile Brunner' itself, which has been in gardens since 1880; 'Perle d'Or', the yellow sweetheart, which was introduced a few years later; and the red sweetheart, which is not red at all, but a true rose color. I like to see these old roses in gardens that they have grown in for so long. Miss Hazel says that she has known the pink tea, 'Papa Gontier' (1882), all her life, and that this and 'Safrano' (1839) and the 'Duchesse de Brabant' (1857) came to her from her mother.

There was a 'Burr Rose'—the double pink form of *Rosa roxburghii* (1825)—which is called the 'Chestnut Rose', but is known in southern gardens as the chinquapin rose. Although it is said to grow to eight or ten feet, I have known it always as a rather small bush.

Mittie asked about a low, spreading rose bush smothered with small, double white flowers. Miss Hazel said, "Oh, Mama always called that her Little Pet. We don't know whether that's the real name, but we have heard others call it the same thing."

There was one rose that Miss Hazel has been looking for a name for, a large, ungainly bush with numerous small, round leaflets and small, single, dark red flowers. I took it to be *Rosa moyesii*, which I once had in my garden, but had to part with for lack of room. Or perhaps it parted with me, for it is not easily established.

Miss Hazel has just come back from a meeting of the American Rose Society in San Diego. While she was there, she was so enchanted by the miniature roses that she has now started a collection of them. They look so adorable in their little pots, Mittie and I feel we shall have to go back to see them in bloom.

June 18, 1961

Midsummer and Magic

Now that the countryside is clad in "glad green midsummer beauty," I have been thinking of midsummer flowers. Most of them are magic, for this is a season of mystery and enchantment. On midsummer eve, ghosts, goblins and fairies are abroad, and anyone who stands under an elder tree at midnight will see the king of the elves and his court go by. Hulda, the Elder Mother, lives in the tree, and the elves are her children.

Midsummer eve is the only time that fernseed can be procured. Some say the little blue fern flower blooms at dusk, and exactly at midnight the seed ripens and falls. It shines like fiery gold, and must be caught in a white handkerchief. Some think that fernseed can never be had this way. They believe that it is kept by the devil, and must be gotten directly from him. However or wherever it is acquired, it is well worth the luck and fortune to the possessor, as well as making him invisible. "We steal as in a castle, cocksure; we have the receipt of fernseed; we walk invisible," one thief says to another in the first part of *King Henry the Fourth*; and the other thief replies, "Nay, by my faith, I think you are more beholden to the night, than to fernseed, for your walking invisible."

Midsummer men is an old name for *Sedum telephium*. If gathered on midsummer eve, it will indicate without fail whether one's love is true or false. It does this by turning all its leaves in one direction; but whether he is true when all turn to the right and false when they all turn to the left, or whether it is the other way about, none of the books tell.

Livelong is another name that the English cottagers give to this sedum. If it is taken from the garden and hung from the ceiling on a string, it keeps on growing. If it is hung up on midsummer day, it will stay green until Christmas, and as long as it stays green none of the household will be ill.

Midsummer silver is *Potentilla anserina*, a little herb once used for making garlands which people hung in the church and in their houses.

When the church put the pagan customs to use in teaching the new religion, some of the old superstitions hung on. One was that "an Angel did foretell John The Baptist should be born at the very instant in which fernseed, at other times invisible, did fall."

Along with fernseed, a number of flowers of midsummer magic became attached to Saint John, whose feast, the twenty-fourth of June, comes at this season. The summer solstice, the period of the longest day and the shortest night, is the time when the powers of evil and darkness came into conflict with those of goodness and light. In the days of sun worship, midsummer fires were lighted on hilltops to rekindle the sun's flame. When Saint John, the Herald of Light, took the place of the sun gods, their flowers, round and golden like the sun, became his. The hilltop fires, still lighted as a protection against witches, who congregate on midsummer eve, became Saint John's Fires, symbols of the celestial fire.

Hypericum, the most potent of all plants for making magic and averting evil, became Saint John's Wort. It was gathered on midsummer eve (but not after sunup), burned in midsummer fires, woven into garlands of green birch, fennel, wormwood and white lilies, and hung in churches and on doors as a protection against witches, thunder and all things evil:

Trefoil, vervain, John's Wort, dill
Hinder Witches from their will.

Hypericum is also called Devilfuge, for Saint John is the opponent of the devil and all the works of darkness. Wormwood, Saint John's Herb, was woven into belts called Saint John's Girdles: the belts were worn as a charm against demons and burned in midsummer fires.

Other flowers that belong to Saint John and midsummer are Asperula and Lychnis. Sweet Woodruff, *Asperula odorata*, if hung up in a hot room, cools and freshens the air. *Lychnis chalcedonica*, sometimes called Scarlet Lightning, is the Great Candlestick, lit in honor of the saint who is himself a shining light.

The Scarlet Lychnis, the garden's pride,
Flames at St. John the Baptist's tide.

June 25, 1961

Drought

Last summer's water bills unnerved me so that I can no longer bear the whine of the pipes when the hose is going. Early in May, as the borders began to get hard and dry, I gave them a good soaking and then a good weeding, and left them to their fate. It was a sad one, for the growing season is the worst possible time for plants to go without water, and I doubt whether they will recover this summer. But there are some things that prefer dry weather, and these were at their best. Before we had that cloudburst—which in some places did not even wet the ground—pinks were blooming with abandon on the terrace walls, in the rosy tones that are charming with the soft gray mounds of santolina and the silvery fountain of *Artemisia absinthium*.

Grey-leaved plants revel in drought. The large, pale pink cups of *Oenothera speciosa*—which I have been trying to get rid of because it is such a weed, but have not the heart to root out entirely—were lovelier than ever. The white sweet Williams were clean and fresh, and the dwarf kinds were a blaze of bright colors.

Last fall I planted *Achillea* x 'Coronation Gold', a hybrid between *Achillea filipendulina* and *A. clypeolata*. It came into bloom about the middle of May, looking as if heat and drought were what it likes best, and now, at the end of the month, is as fresh as ever. I used to grow *A. filipendulina*, the fern-leaved yarrow, in my Raleigh garden. It was a tall, coarse plant with large, flat, dull gold flower heads—not at all choice, but welcome in the border for bloom in June and July. 'Coronation Gold' is much prettier. The finely-cut grey leaves have the bitter but refreshing redolence of tansy, and the flower heads are a clear bright yellow. My pleasure in 'Coronation Gold' sent me back to the Wayside catalogue, where I find two other drought-resistant yarrows: 'Fire King', a garden form of *A. millefolium*, and *A. taygetea*, which has pale yellow flowers on eighteen-inch stems. I put them on my list for fall planting.

On a hot afternoon in May I saw a great golden clump of *Coreopsis lanceolata* blooming on the sidewalk on Kings Drive. It couldn't have been in a hotter spot, and yet it looked as fresh as dawn. This is a wayside flower that used to be a weed in my Raleigh garden. "Like another sun risen at noonday," is a harsh color, but gay and dependable.

The poppy mallow (*Callirhoe*) is another native that I have not had for a long time, a trailer that likes to grow on top of a dry wall, or thread its way between rocks. The flowers are called wine-cups. They are small, bright satiny poppies, the color of cyclamens, that bloom all summer—from frost to frost. They never fade or flag, and the scanty foliage never seems thirsty. Last year, Caroline Dormon sent me plants from Briarwood, and I hope they will reseed and scatter themselves in this garden as they did in Raleigh.

Along with the wine-cups, Caroline sent me another Louisiana wild flower, *Oenothera rhombipetala*. All through July and August the pale sulphur saucers open in the fresh evening air, and shine in the darkness, and are still lovely in the morning, and through most of the day unless it is very hot. I do give the roots an occasional soaking. It makes the flowers much larger.

I looked in a number of garden books (including *A Southern Garden*) for a list of drought-resistant plants. The only one I found was in Mrs. Scruggs's *Gardening in the South and West*. Among the common garden flowers she listed alyssum, ageratum, butterfly weed, gaillardia, helianthus, bergamot, lantana, portulaca, salvia, verbena and four-o-clocks. "An almost dry summer garden, with a surprising wealth of blossoms, may be yours for the asking," she says. "During the great drought of 1930 gardens everywhere suffered. . . . Yet an astonishing number of plants seemed not to have noticed the heat or the lack of moisture. They continued to blossom despite all adverse conditions."

June 3, 1962

Elizabethan Gardens

Since the Elizabethan Garden at Manteo has been awarded the Bronze Medal of the National Council of State Garden Clubs as the outstanding project of the year, many gardeners will be visiting it, and I thought some notes on the Queen and her times might be of interest. I like to think of Elizabeth at thirteen as playing with her little brother Edward in the gardens of old Hatfield house when they had finished their lessons. It must have been the only happy hours that those two children ever knew. In the park there are (or were when the eleventh edition of the *Brittanica* was written) mulberry trees that Elizabeth planted while she was living there during Bloody Mary's reign, and an oak under which she was sitting, they say, when she was brought news of her sister's death.

In *English Pleasure Gardens* Rose Standish Nichols says that the Privy Garden, an enclosure surrounded by pleached limes, was surely laid out in the time of Elizabeth, and that the Queen herself "must often have walked there, shaded beneath the broad brim of a garden hat still preserved at Hatfield. This precious relic was a gift from the queen to her Lord Treasurer Burleigh." Miss Nichols says that Elizabeth followed the ancient custom of receiving important visitors in the garden, and in her private garden at Hampton Court she had a clandestine meeting with the Earl of Arran, one of her first suitors.

I gather that there is little left of the gardens of the day, but they can be reconstructed from contemporary descriptions of Nonesuch, Hampton Court, Theobalds, and Kenilworth. During Queen Elizabeth's visit to Kenilworth, the Earl of Leicester's secretary, Robert Laneham, wrote to a friend in London describing the castle garden, which, he said, covered an acre or more:

> All along the Castle wall is reared a pleasant terrace ten feet high and twelve feet broad, even under foot and fresh of fine grass, as is also the side thereof towards the garden, in which by sundry equal distances with obelisks and spheres and white bears all of stone upon their curious bases by goodly shew were set; To these, two fine arbours redolent by sweet trees and flowers, at each end one. The garden plot under that, with fair alleys green by grass, even voided from the borders on both sides; and some (for change) with sand, smooth and firm and pleasant to walk on.

The garden was divided into four parts, "much gracified" by four fifteen-foot obelisks of porphyry, one in the center of each quarter.

The garden at Manteo follows this favorite plan, made "square without to be round within," which is found on the title page of Thomas Hyll's *Most Briefe and Pleasaunt Treatyse* (1563), the first gardening book written in English. It was the Elizabethans who first planted flower gardens for the sole purpose of enjoying them. They kept the herbaries, the orchards and the kitchen gardens for physic and food; the ponds and parks for hunting and fishing; and the bowling greens, tennis courts and terraces for exercise; but they added the enclosed garden for flowers and sweet smells. On hot days one could stroll on a sweet-shadowed terrace, and feel "the frisking wind above, or the delectable coolness of the fountain beneath; taste of delicious strawberries, cherries, and other fruits, even from their stalks; smell fragrancy of sweet odours, breathing from the plants, herbs and flowers; and hear natural melodious music and tunes of birds." The garden at Kenilworth was worthy, Robert Laneham said, "to be called Paradise; though not so goodly as Paradise for want of fair rivers, yet better a great deal by the lack of so unhappy a tree."

June 10, 1962

Gardens of Adonis

Searching *The Golden Bough* for ancient customs connected with plants, I came upon the chapters on the gardens of Adonis. Adonis was the corn god, the god of vegetation, worshipped by the Greeks hundreds of years before Christ, and by the Syrians and Babylonians long before that. As a boy he was adored by both Aphrodite and Persephone, who quarreled over him until Zeus settled the dispute by deciding that Adonis should stay above ground with the goddess of love for part of the year, and in the underworld with the goddess of death for the rest of it. When he returned to the world again, all nature would revive. And when he went back to Persephone there was great lamentation.

The prophet Ezekiel tells how the women of Jerusalem wept at the north gate when the young god (they called him Tammuz) departed for the underworld, and an ancient Babylonian dirge describes how the plant world died when he died:

Her lament is the lament for the herb that grows not in the bed,
Her lament is for the corn that grows not in the ear

. . . .

Her lament is for a great river, where no willows grow,
Her lament is for a field where corn and herbs grow not.
Her lament is for a pool where fishes swim not.
Her lament is for a thicket where no reeds grow.
Her lament is for a wilderness where no cypress grows.
Her lament is for the depth of a garden of trees,
Where wine and honey flow not, and length of life no longer grows.

Every year at the Festival of Adonis the death of the god was mourned, and his image, wrapped in grave clothes, was carried out and thrown into the sea. On the next day he was thought to come to life again, and to ascend into heaven.

In time these festivals became very elaborate, and there were great processions, with decorations of fruits and flowers. At first the whole ceremony consisted of planting wheat, barley, lettuces, and fennel seeds in earthen pots and baskets. These pots were grouped around a large statue of Adonis on the roof. The plants shot up quickly, and in the intense heat of the housetop they soon withered. After eight days the dead plants were taken out and thrown into the sea with the little image of the god.

Scenes of the gardens of Adonis were painted on Greek vases. One shows Aphrodite perched on the first rung of a ladder, receiving from Eros one of the pots of sprouting plants. The pot is very large, and with a floating scarf to add to her difficulties I doubt whether she ever got to the roof.

Another scene shows Eros watering the plants. These little plants that sprang up so quickly and withered so soon were a symbol of the short life of the god, who was killed by a wild boar while out hunting. And so a garden of Adonis has come to mean a small and short-lived pleasure.

In the Christian era the celebration of death and resurrection became identified with the seasons of the church: with Easter, the time of sowing seed; and midsummer, the time of gathering in the fruits of the earth—for in the Mediterranean countries summer, not fall, is the time of harvest. Anthropologists think that Saint John has replaced Adonis in the midsummer ceremonies of Sicily and Sardinia, and the death and resurrection of Christ the ancient celebration of spring.

June 30, 1963

Conium Maculatum

Many years ago, when we were living in Raleigh, someone brought a group of farm women to see the herb garden. I distributed bits of all divisible plants among those who wanted them, and in return many little parcels arrived in the mail. I remember particularly the winter fern that one of the visitors sent me. It grew to be a big plant, and seemed well established, but one day I looked for it and it was no longer there.

Since then I have seen it in a number of gardens, and last year I begged a start from Charlotte Trotter. She dug two large plants for me, with big balls of dirt, and they did not seem to know that they had gone from one garden to another, but just as I thought they were there for good they suddenly disappeared.

Now I have another winter fern. Mittie Wellford gave it to me. She says they have it at Sabine Hall, and that they call it Mount Airy fern in Tidewater Virginia. When I told her that I had tried in vain to find out what it really is, she said, "Have you asked Mr. Forbis? Mine came from him and I think he called it hemlock." I looked it up, and hemlock it is, *Conium maculatum*, the source of the poison that Socrates drank.

People have also been poisoned accidentally by mistaking the seed for anise, the leaves for parsley, or the roots for parsnips, for it is closely related to parsley, fennel, parsnip and carrots. Children have been poisoned by making whistles from the hollow stems, and animals have been killed from eating the leaves. Hemlock is one of the plants witches use for broths and philtres.

In *Macbeth*, "root of hemlock, digged in the dark," went into the caldron along with filet of snake, frog toes, bat's wool, lizard's leg, and many other dainties, to "make the gruel thick and slab." And some think it is the Insane Root, which Macbeth speaks of as taking the reason prisoner.

As warning against its sinister properties, hemlock is said to have a nauseous flavor and evil smell. I thought I wouldn't try tasting it, but I bruised the tip of one of the beautiful fern-like leaves, and found the odor only slightly unpleasant and somewhat aromatic. The wine-colored spots of the stem might serve as a warning, too; they are said to represent the mark of Cain. On account of its narcotic properties, hemlock is useful as a medicine, and it is still in demand.

In *My Garden in Spring*, E. A. Bowles tells about an herb gatherer who used to wander about in England sowing hemlock seed, and then telling farmers that it would poison the cattle; he said he would rid them of it at a bargain. Then, having been paid for collecting them, he sold the dried plants to the wholesale druggists. "Besides its medicinal value it is a very beautiful garden plant," Mr. Bowles said, "so in spite of Gerard (who said it is not possessed of any one good faculty) I grow it. It is unfortunately biennial but makes the most of its short life by keeping brilliantly green through the winter. The leaves are as exquisitely cut as any I know of, and wonderfully glossy."

So now I know why I have always lost my winter fern. It never bloomed, and so when its short life was over there were no seedlings to take its place. But Mittie says that if this one dies she will give me more. Perhaps the thing to do is to start with very small plants, and allow them to become established the first year in order to bloom the second. Mittie says the flowers come in midsummer, and are something like Queen Anne's lace. Once they begin to seed, they seem to perpetuate themselves indefinitely, for they seem to be fixtures in old gardens. And not the least of their virtues, Mr. Bowles says, is their "amiable habit of growing and looking happy in any waste shady corner."

They will grow in sun, too, and should be given room to develop (and I should think some good soil, in spite of their amiability) into graceful, spreading plants from two to four feet tall, or even more. Hemlock is not in the trade or at least it is not listed in the *Plant Buyer's Guide*—so it will have to be begged or bartered from another gardener.

June 14, 1964

Miss Kate McDonald

We talk about conservation, but I wonder whether we are really conserving the stands of rare and beautiful plants that grow throughout the state from the mountains to the coast. I thought of this when I came across some notes, made years ago, about a visit to the Flora MacDonald country to see *Stewartia malacodendron* in bloom. It was Mrs. R. A. McLeod of Maxton who told me about it. "If you come down soon," she wrote early in May, "Miss Kate McDonald, the old lady who has guarded it for years, will take us to the woods where it grows on their old place. If the weather is warm and bright for the next few days it will go quickly."

I went on the tenth of May, when the heat seemed to me as blistering as midsummer. I picked up Mrs. McLeod first, and then we went by for Miss Kate, who was waiting for us on the front porch. She had a wool shawl over her shoulders, and she kept it on while we drove for treeless miles along sandy roads through fields where cotton was just coming out of the ground. We came at last to some woods that looked impenetrable, but when we got out of the car, Miss Kate parted some sweetgum branches and walked into the underbrush as easily as if she had opened a door and entered a country parlor.

Without disturbing a hair of her neat grey braids, or catching a stitch of her shawl, she walked straight to the place where the stewartias were growing. I stumbled behind her, tripping over roots, ducking under branches, shedding hairpins, and muttering, "The dewberry dips for to work delay." She stopped on the edge of a deep ravine. At the bottom of it a sluggish stream, fed by an old spring, ran through a carpet of fern, and the slope between was covered with a thicket of stewartias.

Standing there above them we looked down on the flowers, and that is the way they should be seen—from above, with light coming through many leaves before it reaches the ivory cups that seem to hold the sweet mystery of the woods. Here, for two hundred years, generations of McDonalds have come to see the stewartias bloom in the stillness of the spring woods, and have gone away again leaving the flowers to fall on the forest floor.

I measured one of the flowers and found it to be four inches across. The five large petals are crimped along the edges, and the stamens lie in a flat circle, like short, fine steel needles. I measured one of the tallest trees and found it to be only about twelve feet, but this species may grow to a height of twenty feet.

Stewartia malacodendron occurs along the Coastal Plain from Virginia to Florida, and along the Gulf Coast to Louisiana. It is more common in Mississippi than in the southeast. It is difficult in cultivation, and Miss Kate says she has never been able to get it to grow in the garden of Flora MacDonald College, which is not far away, but it grows (or has grown) in the Totten's garden in Chapel Hill, at Orton, in the Coker's garden in Hartsville and in the Brookgreen gardens. I have never seen it elsewhere in cultivation, but it is probably in other gardens, for it is listed by a Maryland nursery.

Our other species, the mountain stewartia, *S. ovata*, is a little taller, and it blooms in summer. There are two forms, one with yellow stamens and one with purple stamens. This species is also difficult to establish, and I have never seen it in flower, although I have planted it in my garden, both here and in Raleigh, many times. I see that the Upper Banks Nursery offers balled and burlapped plants, and they would be worth trying, though expensive. I often find that plants that are considered difficult, do very well once they get started.

In early May I often think of those cool woods, and wonder whether Miss Kate is still guarding the stewartias, or whether the place has been cut up into building lots, or whether a superhighway runs through the ravine. It has been more than ten years since I stood there and looked down on those white flowers growing gently among the green leaves.

June 21, 1964

Horse Chestnuts

The other day, Dr. Howard Steiger asked me why horse chestnuts are not being planted and why they are not in the local nurseries. I said I thought it is because they are very slow growing. I was thinking of the correspondence (1734–1746) between John Custis of Williamsburg and Peter Collinson of London. "I have several horse chestnuts growing after their fashion," Custis wrote, "but it is so slow; a man had need to have the patience of Job and the life of Methusala to wait upon them."

Collinson replied, "That the horse chestnuts are so slow in their growth is very surprising to me for they are trees of the quickest growth and will bear in five or six years. It is one of the finest sights in the world to see our horse chestnut 50 or 60 feet high, 14 or 15 in girth, in a pyramidal form cover'd all over with long pyramidal clusters of flowers which exceed the finest hyacinth. Some of the first trees that were brought from France I have measured their girth of the above dimensions. Why this name is imposed upon this noble tree I can't say for no horse that I ever heard will eat the nuts or delights in its shade than any other tree tho' I am told in Turkey from whence they came they give the nuts in provender to horses that are troubled with coughs or are short winded."

As seeds were sent from Constantinople, in 1576, to Clusius at Vienna, and the tree was in cultivation in Paris and in England by the early seventeenth century, Collinson's trees may have been over a hundred years old.

Turning to later writers I find less enthusiasm for horse chestnuts. When E. A. Bowles took over his father's garden, he began to get rid of "coarse, garden undesirables." He had to do it gradually, for if he felled too many large trees at once, his father might notice and object. After twenty years of slow elimination Mr. Bowles wrote in *My Garden in Spring*, "One of the last of the horse chestnuts dropped several stout limbs in a row of garden seats last summer, and provided a powerful argument for the removal of the trunk that shed them."

"In the past," Brooks Wiggington says, in *Trees and Shrubs for the Southeast*, "the horse chestnut (*Aesculus hippocastanum*) was a prized ornamental because of its dense symmetrical, formal shape, its rich coarse foliage, and its June showing of garish flowers. This type of plant, for better or for worse, is out of fashion now; and this particular species is objectionable for its steady production of litter, its liability to leaf disease, and its detrimental competition with turf."

The only horse chestnut that I have ever known intimately is the one that was, when I lived in Raleigh, and I hope still is, in the corner of the Capitol Square, across from Christ Church. I used to watch for it in the spring, when it bloomed—always at the same time—the last week in April and the first week in May. There was another on the campus of Shaw University, but I did not see it in bloom so often. I don't remember any disease of the leaves.

Dr. Donald Wyman shares Mr. Wiggington's prejudice, and says, "If a horse chestnut be used, the Baumann horse chestnut should be selected, for it has double flowers and no fruits. Being double, the flowers naturally last longer than do the single flowers of the species." There is a specimen of the double-flowered form at the northwest corner of the City Hall on East Trade Street.

Dr. Steiger says very few nurseries now list *Aesculus hippocastanum*, and I find he is right, though Heinrich Rohrbach still grows them at Heatherfells. Dr. Steiger has just set out six trees that Conrad Furr found for him, and I mean to keep my eye on them. I shall report later as to how quickly they grew, and how soon they bloom. I agree that the horse chestnut is one of the most beautiful flowering trees, and that we should bring it back into favor. As to the fruits, far from thinking them a nuisance, southerners consider them treasures. Osmond Barringer used to give them away for luck at meetings of the Charlotte Garden Club, and they say you will never suffer from rheumatism if you carry one in your pocket.

June 20, 1965

Native Iris

When I was in Northampton County, early in May, I thought of the blue flags that used to grow in a cool, shady hollow where the creek crossed the road, just beyond the village where we lived when I was small. It was a sandy road then, and the clear brown waters of the creek formed a shallow pool at the crossing. We liked to splash through it in the pony cart, and take off our shoes and stockings to wade. Now the road is paved, and the creek runs under it through a culvert, and its banks are so overgrown that no water can be seen. I thought the flags would have been crowded out, or grubbed up by the road builders, but there they were and in full bloom.

It seemed miraculous to find them there, as blue as I remembered. I thought of Edna St. Vincent Millay's poem "The Blue Flag in the Bog." Many people of my generation must think of that poem in these days, and wonder whether they will wake up some morning and find themselves saying, "Now forevermore goodbye, all the gardens in the world!" But for the present it cheers me to know that my flags, like those in the poem, are still blue by the creekside. I take it as a sign that they will survive human destruction.

Our flags are the southern species, *Iris virginica*. Edna Millay's are the related northern species *Iris versicolor*. There seems to be little difference in them except that ours has one row of seeds in each cell, and theirs has two. *Iris versicolor* begins to bloom about the middle of June.

When Thoreau walked to Lupine Hill on June 12, 1852, he found the meadows golden with senecio and the blue flags in bud. "Its buds are a dark, indigo-blue tip beyond the green calyx," he said. It is rich, but hardly delicate and simple enough. "The blue flag, notwithstanding its rich furniture, its fringed, recurved parasols over its anthers, and its variously streaked and colored petals, is loose and coarse in its habit. How completely all character is expressed by flowers. This is a little too showy and gaudy, like some women's bonnets. Yet it belongs to the meadow and ornaments it much."

Thoreau calls *Iris prismatica* "the Boston Iris," but it grows as far south as Georgia, although it is not common with us, and is found only in the bogs and savannahs of the coastal plain. Its stems are more slender than those of *Iris versicolor*, its leaves narrower, and its flowers smaller.

In Raleigh we grew the blue flag in the ground that was damp from the overflow of the garden pool. It is easily grown, but it is invasive, and must not be planted near less aggressive irises. It is a variable species with flowers in pinkish and violet tints all the way to a deep blue-violet. Caroline Dormon says there is a pure white form in Louisiana, with very large flowers, sometimes to five inches across.

Iris shrevei is a related species, native to the Gulf Coast, that is sometimes considered a variety of *Iris virginica*. I once had a charming and distinctive form called 'A. H. Nichols'. It has silvery white flowers, veined with silver, and delicately and deliciously scented. The flowers were small but numerous, on slender purple stems. This species will grow in wet or dry soil, and in a less acid soil than the other swamp irises.

Iris versicolor is sometimes called the poison flag, and the related species have the same property. Mrs. Lounsberry says an old mountaineer in Tennessee told her that the roots of blue flags were gathered and were chewed to relieve indigestion, but he must have had calamus, the sweet flag, in mind. Children are said to have been made ill by mistaking the blue flag for the sweet flag.

Edna Millay is not the only New England poet who has written about the blue flag. "These pure waters and the flags know me," Emerson says, and Longfellow and William Cullen Bryant wrote of them too.

June 18, 1967

 J U L Y

Robert Vernede

There are two kinds of people in the world: those who want to get out and do things, and those who want to stay at home and garden. The first are like the soldier in the old French song, who said gardening never did appeal to him, he would rather make war:

> Jardiner ne m'amuse guère,
> Mais je voudrais faire la guerre.

The others, like Montaigne, hope death will find them planting cabbages. They are like the old Turk who told Candide that he was not concerned about the affairs of the world. "I never ask what is going on in Constantinople," he said; "I am satisfied with sending the fruits of my garden to market."

There are also those who would rather garden than fight but who believe that there are things worth fighting for. One of these was an Englishman (of French descent) who fought and died in the First World War. He lived with his wife and dogs in a remote part of Hertfordshire, where he wrote poems and novels and made a garden out of a piece of ground covered with nettles and scrap iron.

It must have been at its best by the summer of 1914 when he wrote:

> It is July in my garden and steel-blue are the globe thistles.
> And French grey the willows that bow to every breeze.
> And deep in every currant bush a robber blackbird whistles.
> I'm picking, I'm picking, I'm picking these.
>
> So off I go to rout them, and find instead I'm gazing
> At clusters of delphiniums—the seed was small and brown,
> But these are spurs that fell from heaven and caught the most
>   amazing
> Colours of the welkin's own as they came hurtling down.
>
> And then some roses caught my eye, or maybe some sweet Williams
> Or pink and white and purple peals of Canterbury bells,

Or pencilled violets that peep between the three-leaved trilliums
Or red-hot pokers all aglow or poppies that cast spells—

And while I stare at each in turn, I quite forget or pardon
The blackbirds—and the blackguards—that keep robbing me of pie;
For what do such things matter if I have so fair a garden,
And what is half so lovely as my garden in July?

He wrote this in July, and on the fourth of August England declared war against Germany.

The poet and gardener, Robert Vernede, who had not the heart to rout blackbirds out of currant bushes, offered himself to the British Army, although he was 39 years old, four years overage. He was turned down, of course, but he repeated the offer until he was accepted, and by the time another July came around Vernede had left his books and his garden and was fighting the Germans. "Then I had to get two platoons into a trench we had been hastily digging in case the Boches retaliated," he wrote to his wife on the eleventh. The Boches did retaliate.

In April he wrote from Flanders, "Horticulture has begun among the troops, and consists chiefly of digging up violets and sticking them in the roofs of their dugouts, together with a suitable inscription and a few boughs of palm or something similar." The palms, of course, were pussy willows, and the men in the trenches were keeping the custom of palm-gathering. At home the children and country people would be bringing in the branches for Palm Sunday:

Afield for palms the girls repair
And sure enough the palms are there,
And each will find by hedge or pond
Her waving silver-tufted wand.
—A. E. Housman

In Germany, at the same time, the children would be gathering willows and calling them palms. "In Germany on Palm Sunday," Goethe says, "they bear the true palms. . . . More northern climes must be content with the sad willow."

A short time before he was killed, in 1917, Vernede wrote his wife that the war would soon be over, for the Americans were coming in. And now this soldier and gardener is all but forgotten.

When I came across a quotation, in a garden magazine, from "My Garden in July," I spent some years trying to find out who its author was, and never would have found it, but for the help of Mrs. E. B. White. Then, through the kindness of my friends at the Charlotte Public Library, who borrowed books for me from Canada, I was able to see the whole poem. Always in July, when the globe thistles are steel blue in my garden, I think of that English garden reclaimed from nettles and scrap iron.

July 31, 1966

Wisteria

The most beautiful thing in our garden in Raleigh was a white wisteria on the summerhouse. In the cold April moonlight, it was like a silver fountain. When we first came to the garden, the pergola and summerhouse were covered with the climbing roses that were popular in the early nineteen hundreds—'Hiawatha', 'American Pillar', 'Dorothy Perkins', and a climbing 'American Beauty'—but the wisteria crowded them out. Creeping forward from the far end of the pergola it smothered the summerhouse, and by the time we left it had almost taken over one part of the garden. Seedlings and suckers came up everywhere.

After warring with wisteria for so many years, I said that I would never plant another, but two white ones were among the first things that went into our new garden. I meant to plant only one, but remembrance of things past was so strong that I forgot I had ordered and ordered again. I planted both to grow in pine trees, which will probably be fatal to the pines, but is the most effective way of growing them, as you can see by driving about Charlotte in early April.

Wisteria is "very effective creeping up the tall bare stem of a Pine, to hang in graceful festoons from the upper branches," a gardener writes in *Flora and Sylva*, "but in such case it is well not to allow the Wisteria to wind spirally upwards as is its wont, for on gaining strength the twisted stem tightens to such an extent as to injure its support. I have seen a great Pine so nearly killed by such strangulation that the climber had to be cut away to save it. Guided straight up the trunk, an occasional tie secures it from the wind, and once among the branches it threads its own way without doing any harm." A very pretty sentiment, as Mr. Weller used to say, but not as simple as it sounds.

The finest standard wisteria that I know of is a white one in Mrs. Jerry Huber's garden. It can be seen from the street, and every April I watch, as I go by, for it to bloom. This year, even after the severe winter, it was more beautiful than ever.

Wisterias need severe pruning in summer, cutting back the new growth to two or three buds. Early winter is the time to fertilize them, and they always need plenty of water. Some forms may not bloom for years. Root pruning and feeding with superphosphate sometimes helps, but it is better to start with plants from a nursery that sends out only those that have already bloomed. They bloom most freely in full sun, but I like the delicacy and pallor of those that grow in part shade.

There are more kinds of wisteria than you would think. In the Arnold Arboretum there is a collection of between thirty and forty varieties, and nearly as many are listed in the *Plant Buyer's Guide*. The common kind is *Wisteria sinensis*. I can't remember ever having seen the Japanese species but once, and that was in Mrs. Royster's garden in Raleigh. When I think of those long, slender, delicately colored flower-fronds, I wish that I had room for it in all of its forms—the pink, the purple, the blue-violet, the white, and even the double one, which is described as a dull color, but in the colored pictures in the catalogues it looks like a string of Parma violets. In *Aristocrats of the Garden*, Ernest Wilson says that in Japan he has measured racemes over five feet long, but they are not more than half that length in this country. I was interested to find that the Japanese wisteria was introduced into this country in 1862, about ten years before it was known in Europe, and that it came to the nursery of Samuel Parsons, who wrote *Parsons on the Rose*.

It may seem strange that an Oriental vine should be named for an American, Dr. Caspar Wistar, but the American species was known to botanists first. Nuttall, the author of the genus, spelled it wisteria, and so, according to the rules it must be spelled that way.

Our species, *W. frutescens*, is a slender vine with short racemes of pale violet flowers. It is not spectacular, but as it flowers in May and at intervals all through the summer, it is rather nice in a woodsy place. The Kentucky wisteria, *W. macrostachya*, is much handsomer, but at present I know of no source for it. West coast nurseries offer another Oriental species, *W. venusta*, the silky wisteria of the gardens of Japan. It has short, broad, long-stemmed clusters of very large white flowers that open all at once. There is a double form, the only variety with double white flowers, and a cultivar 'Violacea' is sometimes offered.

July 27, 1958

Mittie Wellford

Gardeners couldn't get along without Mittie Wellford. She will take anything you give her. Most people who are offered plants think that if you don't want them, they don't either. But Mittie welcomes things from her friends' gardens, and she has lots of room.

When a pink weigela—that had grown vigorously until crowded out by taller shrubs—began to decline, I offered it to several large landowners who said they did not want a bundle of sticks; but Mittie rescued it, and gave it a place in the sun; and I hope she will be rewarded, for where it has room to spread it is one of the most beautiful of flowering shrubs. The variety is 'Abel Carriere'; now that Kohankie has gone out of business, I doubt that there is another nursery in this country that grows it. For three weeks, or more, in late April and May, the branches of the tall shrub are covered with trumpets of daphne pink.

Mittie also accepted suckers of *Indigofera amblyantha*, a low everspreading shrub with masses of small spikes of little rose-colored flowers, and fine, cool, grey foliage. It begins to bloom at the end of April, and will continue to flower through August if the dead spikes are snipped off. Cutting it back severely improves it enormously.

I had a clump of *Iris pseudacorus*, the Japanese water iris, that had been under the shrubs for nearly 10 years without ever blooming. Mittie said it didn't matter to her if it never bloomed, as the foliage is beautiful enough; but as soon as she put it out at the edge of her pond it produced its charming yellow flowers. Along with it, and blooming at the same time (the sixth of May) were some pale blue Siberian irises, and some purple ones—all much handsomer there by the water than they are in flower beds. All along the water's edge forget-me-nots were blooming. They came from a few seedlings that had strayed into the garden path and that I hated to throw away. Beyond the pond there are great drifts of daylilies, planted the way daylilies should be planted. These were not in bloom when I was there. "I'm not sure which ones are yours," Mittie said apologetically, "but there is the sorbaria you gave me."

Sorbaria, called false spiraea, is close kin to spiraea, blooming all through June, July and August, and a dependable summer shrub. It grows to something like 15 feet in height, and will spread as far as you let it. In Raleigh I had room to let it spread, but it is no shrub for a small garden. Here it stood me in good stead when the garden was new, growing to 10 feet in two years, and blooming the first summer; but now that other things have grown up it has been crowded out. This distresses me, for the fine, bright green leaves and large plumes of creamy flowers look so cool in the hot weather. I am glad for it to find the place where it grows best, which is near water.

Below the dam, where it is properly damp, Mittie has planted the elders that wouldn't flower in the dry soil under my pine trees. I am particularly anxious for these elders to flourish, as they are the large-flowered form, *Sambuscus canadensis* cultivar 'Maxima', said to have clusters more than a foot across. This, too, came from Kohankie, and I doubt if it is now available. We used to have elders of the ordinary kind in our Raleigh garden. I think they were planted by the birds, who are very fond of the berries. I did not put them there myself, but I loved the lacy white flowers that bloom in May.

The elder is a valuable shrub as well as a beautiful one. If you stand beside it on Midsummer's Eve, with your feet on a clump of wild thyme, you will see "great experiences." Thyme and elder seem to go together:

> from the thyme upon the height
> And from the elder-blossom white.
> And pale dog-roses in the hedge.
> And from the mint-plant in the sedge,
> In puffs of balm the night-air blows
> The perfume which the day foregoes.

July 5, 1959

Practical Lore

Sometime ago, Ellen Flood bought for me a job lot of garden books at an auction. Among them was *The Flower Garden: A Handbook of Practical Garden Lore*, by Ida D. Bennett, published in 1903. It covers nearly everything that has to do with growing plants: soils; fertilizers; the hotbed, coldframe and sandbox; purchasing and sowing seeds; transplanting and repotting; house plants; vines; bulbs; aquatics; roses; lilies, and perennials; bedding-out plants; shrubs; insecticides; and rock-work. The frontispiece is a splendid example of a rockpile on the lawn. It is smothered with sweet alyssum, saxatile alyssum, thunbergia, ferns, and there is no telling what else.

The book is illustrated with photographs of Mrs. Bennett and her gardener going about their tasks in potting shed, greenhouse and garden, and amongst the hotbeds and cold frames. I thought at first that Mrs. Bennett was Miss Ida, for she has a spinsterish look, but in two of her gardening operations she forgot to take off her wedding ring. Although Mrs. Bennett is not pretty, she has a slight, graceful figure which is shown to advantage when she reaches up to tie a climbing rose, or bends beneath the weight of a heavy tray of house plants (probably it was the gardener's day off), or kneels on the lawn to "turn out ball of earth to ascertain if pot is filled with roots."

When the gardener appears, his role is usually that of spectator; but in one photograph he is holding a pot, and in another he is ready with a shovel full of soil for Mrs. Bennett to sift. He is a short, stocky, serious man (German, I think) with a big mustache. Indoors and out, he wears a cap.

For gardening, Mrs. Bennett recommends "Easy, broad, solid shoes; blue denim skirts that clear the instep, and hang comfortably; and shirtwaists with easy arm-holes and collar—denim for cool days, calico for warm." Though she emphatically states that "gardening without gloves is ruinous to the hands and a needless discomfort," she never wears them herself, even when repotting. She does wear a knotted tie with the easy collar; a large gingham apron with a bib; and, usually, when out of doors, a fetching sunbonnet. In the potting shed and around the cold frames she wears sleeve protectors.

My favorite chapter is "A Chapter of Don'ts." "Don't try to follow all of the advice that is offered you; make up your mind what you want to do and go steadily ahead. . . . Don't be cast down by adverse criticism. . . . The person who 'knows it all' is never so much at home as in some one else's flower garden, where the principal labor may be done with the tongue. . . ."

Some of the don'ts might lead you to think that Mrs. Bennett is ungenerous. She tells her readers not to be wheedled into saving cuttings for people who are perfectly able to buy their own, for "there are some people who seem to feel it is an injustice for any one to possess a plant with more than one branch so long as they are not supplied with that particular variety"; but she urges them not to be lacking in generosity of the right sort.

Don't waste your flowers, she says, on "people who spend more money on unnecessary luxuries than you do for your whole garden, and then tell you how foolish you are to spend so much time and money, and work so hard for your flowers. Save them for the tired worker who has neither time nor space to cultivate them: keep the surplus plants from flats or hotbeds for those who cannot spare the trifling amount a single plant or packet of seed would cost; above all share your flowers with the sick; the young girl who will enjoy them for her party; the young matron, for her pretty luncheon; the church service, the humble funeral, where the choicest and best should go."

Although she may be out of date as to garden clothes and insecticides, much of Mrs. Bennett's garden advice is as sound today as it was when she wrote it, for she is a real gardener, whose knowledge comes from her own experience.

July 26, 1959

Lilies of the Valley

One of the perennial garden questions is "When should you put out lilies of the valley?" I put mine out whenever they are given to me, for I have never bought any, and if my friends don't keep me supplied I shall have to do without.

The pips are usually passed over the garden fence in the spring, because gardeners think of them when they are in bloom, and forget them when they are not, but according to the books early fall, September or October, or when the leaves die down, is the best time to divide and replant. The pips should be planted six inches apart to leave room for spreading. They need a rich moist soil, a mixture of sand, leaf-mould, and rotted manure, although Mrs. Wilder claims that they thrive where the soil is not rich. She also says that they will not grow in clay. But they will.

They are woodland plants that grow best and look best under trees or on the north or west side of a building, but some say they flourish in full sun. Once planted, a bed can be left for from three to five years without being divided, or until the flowers are small and few. In old shady gardens they bloom on for years without being touched, and sometimes they run wild along the roadside. A mulch of cow manure in winter keeps them well fed.

It is not likely that the lily of the valley is the flower of the Song of Solomon or the lily of the Sermon on the Mount, for it does not grow in hot countries, though it is widely distributed in Asia and occurs in Europe from Italy to Lapland. In this country it is a rare native, found only in the high mountains from Virginia to South Carolina.

There is only one species, *Convallaria majalis*, but there are a number of forms; one with double flowers which is considered very homely; 'Fortin's Giant', the one with the largest flowers; and the varieties 'Fortunei' and 'Rosea'. All of these are listed in the *Plant Buyer's Guide*, but I don't know whether they are really available.

I saw the pink flowered kind in Mrs. French's garden this spring, the dainty bells flushed with the palest tint. This variety does not seem to spread very much, for her aunt sent it to her thirty-five years ago, and she still has only a small patch—though I am sure that it has been divided many times with other gardeners. There is also a form with gold striped leaves.

The lily of the valley has been in gardens since the latter half of the sixteenth century, when Thomas Hyll wrote in one of the first garden books in the English language, "The wood Lillie or Lillie of the Valley is a flour mervallous sweete, florishing expecially in the spring time, and growing properly in woods ... but ... of late yeares is brought and planted in gardens." All parts of the plant are poisonous, but in small doses it is used as a heart tonic, and in the old days flowers distilled in wine were supposed to strengthen the memory and "procure ease to Apo-plectic persons"; the oil of the flowers was thought to ease the pains of gout, and the Golden Water, distilled from the flowers, would renew the strength of old limbs and give new courage to the heart.

In our mountains and in England the flowers are called May lilies, because that is the month that they bloom, but in my garden they are usually making the air fragrant by the first of April, though this year there were none until after the middle of the month.

The fruit, when there is any, is a round scarlet berry. I have never seen berries, and I suppose this is because the flowers are always picked. I have read that careless picking can ruin the stock, and that the proper method is to detach the stem by giving it a sharp upward jerk. The leaves should be picked sparingly, and never more than one from each plant, as it usually has only two.

I have never known lilies of the valley to suffer from pests, but Dr. Westcott says they are subject to two, nematodes and a weevil that makes curious notches in the leaves.

July 10, 1960

July 1935 and 1960

Looking through some old garden notes I found a description of my midsummer border in 1935:

> Two good rains and some cool cloudy days have brought the garden to life again. The magnificent mauve gladiolas that Mrs. Hine gave mother for Christmas are in bloom, and there are mallows shading from pale pink to cherry, and the pale ones have cherry-colored eyes.
>
> There is a milk-and-wine lily beside a tall white phlox with a wine-colored center. I never think of these things, they just happen.
>
> The new disease-proof phlox, 'Columbia', is a clear pink, but it has both mildew and rust. The disease-proof snapdragons are dying— from excess of health, I suppose.
>
> The globe thistles (echinops) got put down happily, and entirely by accident, beside the porcelain white phlox, 'Mrs. Jenkins'. Beautiful flowers seem to me even more beautiful when they are well named, like the matronly, summer-flowering 'Mrs. Jenkins', and the slender spring-flowering 'Miss Lingard'. It might so easily have been the other way. With the phlox and the steel blue globe thistles, white verbenas, petunias and nicotine are blooming, and there are pale yellow Marguerites, and a single scarlet zinnia—a gay and fresh combination.
>
> This summer, for the first time, we have the blackberry lily; it has star-shaped yellow flowers flecked with brown, several at intervals along a tall thin stem. The color is nice with yellow daylilies.
>
> Yesterday the telephone rang, and when I answered an excited

voice said, "Elizabeth, Tong speaking, you and your mother come right away; my new hybrid hemerocallis are blooming, and 'J. A. Crawford' is the sweetest thing you ever saw!" We went, and it was.

Now it is midsummer 1960. Good rains and cloudy weather have again brought out the midsummer borders. They are fresh and green, and filled with crinums and daylilies and phlox and petunias and nicotine. 'Mrs. Jenkins' is still a favorite white phlox, but 'J. A. Crawford' was left behind in our Raleigh garden, and I doubt whether it is in the trade nowadays. This year the daylily season is so late that 'Molten Gold', 'Lemon Lustre', and 'North Star' are still pale yellow against the violet mist of the bergamot and loosestrife.

I no longer grow the old garden form of the milk-and-wine lily, *Crinum erubescens*, but the hybrid, 'Cecil Houdyshel', is a mass of rosy pink. In front of it are the large, handsome flowerheads of another old phlox, 'Graf Zeppelin'. The large florets are white with a cherry colored eye.

I remember planting echinops because I like to say with the poet Vernede, "It is July in my garden and steel-blue are the globe thistles." I thought that a deep-rooted, drought-resistant perennial from southern Europe would endure the southern summer. Although echinops was brought to England in 1750, was mentioned in Gerard's *Herbal*, and was called a "gallant bush" by Sir Thomas Browne, it seems to have been little used in gardens before Miss Jekyll recognized its value in her grey border. She planted it with tall pink hollyhocks and a great cloud of baby's-breath, where the form of the round, bristling flowerheads and the deeply cut leaves would show to advantage.

Echinops ritro is a true perennial, but it behaved as a biennial with me. It is said to be easily grown from seed, and I expect that is the way to get it established. Mr. Saier lists it as *E. exaltatus*, and lists also a taller form, *E. ruthenicus*, which is considered superior. This must be what I had, for it grew to a height of more than six feet, and the catalogues show only three or four for the type.

If the flowerheads are cut before they go to seed, they can be used with dried arrangements, and they should be cut, in order to keep down the number of volunteers. Their spiky form gives the plant its name—from the Greek—which means "resembling a hedgehog."

July 17, 1960

Beneath What Star

"The Story of a City Gardener" was sent to me by Belle Clanton King, who began to garden when she was five, and has been planting flowers and vegetables for more than sixty years. Some time ago she dug up all her flowers except some unusual jonquils with red centers, and a few of her roses—and planted enough vegetables to supply herself and her neighbors. Mrs. King believes that the seed must be sown under the proper sign if the crop is to be fruitful, and she attributes her success to the prayer that she says before planting. Both customs are in the best tradition.

"What makes the crops joyous?" Virgil asks in the opening lines of the *Georgics*. "Beneath what star is it well to turn the soil?" And a sixteenth-century gardening book has a note for all planters: "Whensoever ye shall plant, it shall be meete and good for you to say as foloweth. In the name of God the Father, the Sonne and the Holy Ghost, Amen. Increase and multiplye, and replenishe the earth."

Mrs. King follows Blum's *Farmer's and Planter's Almanac*, which, for one hundred and thirty-four years, has been telling the best days to plant by the signs and the moon. She always plants her seed in the Cancer sign if the ground is right, with the exception of cucumbers, which do well when planted in the twin sign. She has planted in Libra and Scorpio. Blum considers Cancer the best and most productive sign; under it, seeds germinate quickly; it is favorable to growth, and insures abundant yield. Scorpio is next best, then Pisces. Sagittarius and Aquarius are poor signs; Leo, Gemini and Virgo are barren. Under the barren signs, weeds are most easily destroyed. Plants from seed planted under Capricorn will grow rapidly, but will not be fruitful.

Mrs. King raises lettuce, okra, Kentucky beans, Lima and pole beans, tomatoes, cucumbers and butternut squash. She has separate patches for corn, sweet potatoes and onions. "I plant the little yellow onion sets in September," she says, "and have green onions all winter. In January I plant more sets, and have green onions until they dry. Then I pull them, and tie them in bunches, and hang them up. In this way I have onions the year around."

Her story is that of a successful city gardener who moved in from the country. She is glad she was reared on a farm—out there, she learned the essential things in life. When very small, she got up before daylight to feed and milk the cows before going to the little red school house. Then, no one else tended the cows, and now, no one else puts a hoe to her vegetables. She does her ditching herself, with a lady spade, and cuts the weeds with a power mower.

When Mrs. King wrote me about planting by the stars, I was already studying Blum's *Almanac*. It was given to me by a friend who also plants his vegetables by the signs. "You should see my little garden and the results I have had by abiding by the signs," he wrote. "You see the moon attracts the earth, consequently it attracts the ground and the dirt as it does the ocean and the tides. Why challenge that? I have planted under bad signs for evidence, and I have been borne out by the results."

I was reared in the country, too. We had a big vegetable garden that was planted by the almanac. We always bought one for Mammy, who did the planting, and put it in her stocking at Christmastime. My mother used to say, "Mammy, isn't it time to start the garden?" and Mammy would say, "Not under them Twins." Mammy's almanac was *The Black Draught*. She pronounced it "dwarf," and I thought the black dwarf must be some sort of elf who ruled the vegetable kingdom.

Mrs. King hopes her experience will be helpful to others, and she would like to tell anyone who has trouble with her feet about the kind of shoes she wears for gardening. Her advice is the same as that in the *Georgics*. "Not in vain do we watch the signs as they rise and set," Virgil told the Roman farmers: "mark the months and signs of heaven. . . . Above all, worship the gods."

July 22, 1962

To Violets

Welcome Maids of Honour,
  You doe bring
  In the Spring;
And wait upon her.

She has Virgins many,
  Fresh and faire;
  Yet you are
More sweet than any.
—Herrick

"Sweet Violets," a charming brochure of the Vista Violet Farm, brought to my mind long, fragrant views of purple flowers, but I find that Vista, in this case, refers to the town in southern California where the violets are grown by Chris and Mignon Jenkyns. It is in a frost-free district, and so they can grow out of doors the tender varieties of Parma violets that are usually green house plants, but most of their offerings are hardy.

Among the varieties of *Viola odorata* listed, I see one that I have been looking for for a long time, the 'Princess of Wales', which Miss Rohde describes as "deliciously scented, with large violet-blue flowers on foot-long stems, very hardy and vigorous." 'La France' is another desirable sweet violet that is seldom found in the trade. Other species are listed, some of them rare, but not all of them fragrant.

Detailed cultural directions (which I'll save for another time) follow the price list, and then the Jenkyns give recipes for the use of violets in tea, syrup, vinegar, candy and soup, some of them modern and some known to housewives of the sixteenth century. They give directions for using violet leaves as greens or a salad. Raw violet leaves are delicious, they say, and one of the best sources of iron and of vitamins A and C.

I went out in the garden to test the taste of the leaves and after sampling several kinds, I found some that were passable, some tasteless, and some disagreeable. But I have no forms of *Viola odorata*, and that is the kind recommended for the table. Moreover the leaves must be very young, and should be crisped in ice water.

When I looked into the books, I found that the use of *Viola odorata* as a pot herb is not a new idea. A fifteenth-century manuscript recommends it as food and medicine:

Vyolet an erbe cowth
    Is known in like manys mowthe,
As bokys seyn in here language,
    It is good to don in pottage,
In playstrys to wondrys it is comfortyf,
    With oyer erbys sanatyf.

The herbalists recommended an application of violet leaves to bruises, and thought that binding them to the temple prevented insomnia. *Viola odorata* is an herb of Venus, and therefore, Culpeper says, "of mild nature and no way hurtful." The cold, damp leaves cool the heat of the body, and "ease the pain of the head, caused through want of sleep."

In mythology violets appear in the legend of Io, who is said to have fed upon them when Jupiter changed her into a white heifer, and in the death of Attis, from whose blood the flowers first sprang. In Christian art the violet is the sign of humility, especially the humility of Christ and the Virgin. In an old altar piece Mary is represented as holding out a flower to the Holy Child, who reaches up to take it from her hand. Perhaps from its association with the Virgin, it became the flower for Mothering Sunday, when children returning home gathered violets in the lane.

In the language of the flowers, the blue violet stands for faithfulness and the white for modesty and innocence: "the violets for modesty, which weel she sets to wear." The violet was Napoleon's flower. He presented a bunch to Josephine on wedding anniversaries, and when exiled he promised to return with violets in the spring. Return he did, and there were violets to greet him. Before departing for Saint Helena, they say, he gathered violets from Josephine's grave, and the dried flowers were found in a locket that he was wearing when he died.

In smelling and handling these fragrant flowers, Gerard said, "many by these Violets receive ornament and comely grace: for there bee made of them galands for the head, nosegaies, and poesies, which are delightfull to looke on, and pleasant to smell to, speaking nothing of their appropriate vertues."

July 14, 1963

The Willow Herb

In May, the willow herb, *Epilobium angustifolium*, came into bloom in my garden. It has been a long time since I have grown it, and I had forgotten how brilliant the flowers are, and how delicate the long finely tapered spikes. As the clear red violet flowers fade, the narrow seed pods take on their violet tones, and so the color is kept for days and weeks, and more spikes continue to come.

A number of common names means that a plant has long been in gardens, and the willow herb has a long list: blooming Sally is a corruption of sallow or willow, and refers to its long narrow leaves, rose bay and purple rocket describe the flowers, and it is called fire weed because of its habit of coming up in places recently burnt over.

In the sixteenth and seventeenth centuries the willow herb was already established in gardens. Gerard described the "brave flowers of great beauty" as consisting of four petals apiece, of "an orient purple colour . . . very goodly to behold," and Parkinson said he kept it in an out-corner of his garden "to fill up the number of delightful flowers." John Hill gave directions for its cultivation, and said, "The Garden does not afford a Plant more specious and elegant than this, although it be native of our own country. It is not so common wild as to put the Vulgar in mind of calling it a weed in Gardens; and those who have Judgment despise the little Predjudices which represent everything as mean that comes easily." Perhaps Parkinson kept the willow herb in an out-corner because of its far-reaching underground runners, which led a later writer to brand it as "altogether improper for small gardens."

In *The Compleat Herbal, of the Botanical Institutions* of Mr. Tournefort, it is described as "often transplanted into Gardens, by reason of its beautiful flowers," but hated for its "licentious and ungovernable Creeping." Far from being ungovernable, in my garden it never crept at all, but disappeared completely as soon as it went out of bloom. This time I hope it will creep, for there is not a great deal of bloom in the borders in May, and the slender spikes are becoming to the few flowers that are there, the early pale yellow daylilies, the round, fluffy heads of *Allium giganteum*, and the old-fashioned pinks that edge the paths.

The willow weed is useful in the kitchen garden, too: Loudon says the young shoots, which are cooked like asparagus, and supposed to be quite as delectable, "are eatable, although an infusion of the plant stupefies; the pith when dried is boiled, and becoming sweet, is by a proper process made into ale, and thus into vinegar." He says it is "valuable in shrubberies as thriving under the drip of trees, and succeeds everywhere, even in the smoke of cities and in parks; it is a good plant to adorn pieces of water, being hardy, of rapid increase, and very showy when in flower." The dried leaves are added to tea to give it a special flavor, and in England it is considered a valuable bee plant.

In addition to its usefulness in the kitchen and flower gardens, the shrubbery, the park and the pond's edge, this versatile perennial has long been known for its medicinal properties. In his *Complete Herbal*, Nicholas Culpeper, the celebrated astrologer-physician (1616–1654), says, "All the species of Willow-Herbs have the same virtues: they are under Saturn, and are cooling and astringent. The root dried and powdered, is good against hemorrhages: the fresh juice acts the same." He does not mention its stupefying property, and the epilobium is not included in Muenscher's *Poisonous Plants of the United States*.

The willow herb has a wide range in the northern hemisphere, in Europe and Asia, and in this country, where it occurs as far south as North Carolina.

July 21, 1963

Walks

A garden, even a small one, should, if possible, have a walk—I mean a real walk with a name, not just a garden path. I know of two Charlotte gardens with dogwood walks. They are straight walks with trees planted on either side. And I know of a winding rose walk that runs from the top to the bottom of a hillside garden in Pennsylvania.

I have written before of the Alphabet Walk at Runneymede, one of the Ashley River plantations. It disappeared so long ago that no one remembers the names of the twenty-six kinds of trees that were planted, but I imagine them as beginning with apricot, and ending with ximenia, yaupon and zixyphus. Ximenia is a tallowwood, a native of Florida and a member of the olive family, that is sometimes planted for its edible fruit. At Flat Rock, an old path through the woods, used by the congregation of St. John's-in-the-Wilderness, was called the Jerusalem walk. It is gone now, which seems a pity, but no one walks to church anymore. I should like to hear from anyone who knows of other walks in these parts.

The Enoch walk, a feature of English gardens in the sixteenth and seventeenth centuries, was named for Enoch, who walked with God for three hundred years. "He that walks with God can never want a good walke, and good company," Sir William Waller wrote in his meditation "Upon the sight of a pleasant Garden": "There is no garden well contrived, but that which hath an Enoch's walk in it."

Like the Enoch walk, the hermitage walk is a quiet place for uninterrupted meditation. Early in the Renaissance, Italian noblemen introduced the custom of having a hermit in residence to lend a spiritual atmosphere to country places; as the idea spread to Northern Europe, it became the fashion to have a hermitage in the park.

In England it was difficult to get the hermit to stay, though he was given his living and paid a salary, but even when there were not hermits left, their walks were still featured. Jane Austen mentions two hermitage walks. When Lady Catherine de Bourgh pays an unexpected visit to Longbourn, Mrs. Bennet says to Elizabeth, "Go, my dear, and show her ladyship about the different walks. I think she will be pleased with the hermitage." And it was to the Hermitage Walk at Northanger Abbey that Henry Tilney retired to finish *The Mysteries of Udolpho*.

Like the shrubberies of Jane Austen's novels, the walks in Gertrude Jekyll's garden at Munstead Wood were pleasant places to wander through. To the north of the house there was a nut walk a hundred feet long, between ten pairs of hazelnuts—which the English call the nut-tree. Such plantings must have been common at the turn of the century, for Miss Jekyll speaks of fine old nut alleys with the tops arching overhead. To the south of the house the green walk (twenty feet wide), which led from the lawn to a fine old Scotch fir deep in the woods, was considered "the most precious possession of the place, the bluish distance giving a sense of some extent and the bounding woodland one of repose and security, while in slightly misty weather the illusions of distance and mystery are endless and full of charm." All through the woods there were "lesser grassy ways" such as the fern walk, which passed under oaks and birches, and was bordered with bracken, and lady fern, with intervals of Solomon's seal, and trillium, and white foxglove.

The Christmas path in Elizabeth Clarkson's garden is bordered with clumps of the Christmas rose and patches of Christmas fern. It reminds me of the winter walk that Eleanour Sinclair Rohde tells about in *Gardens of Delight*: "A comparatively narrow path bordered on either side by wonderfully varied collection of evergreens, mostly small shrubs. Even on a dull winter's day it is full of colour—and endless variety of greens. The colours range from the greenish silver of the santolinas, the curious blue-grey (unlike any other) of rue, the grey of the lavenders, the rich claret of the leptospermums, the deep green of the hollies . . . to the wonderfully varied hues of the heaths and dwarf conifers."

I have read of lavender walks, and of laburnum, apple, and pear walks (often trained over arches or arbors), but I really think a walk of flowering cherries would be the nicest of all.

July 19, 1964

Lilium Candidum

My one Madonna lily bloomed this spring at its appointed time, the middle of May. Its blooming reminded me that it is said to be the first flower ever cultivated. Whether this is true or not, it was known to artists more than a thousand years before the birth of Christ and appears on Cretan vases of the Minoan period.

Linnaeus named it *Lilium candidum*, but Virgil (in the *Georgics*) wrote of *Lilia alba* in the garden of the old Corycian, where it grew among the herbs and the verbena, and the slender poppy. Candidum means white and shining. It is still called the white lily, though it is no longer the only one known with white flowers. Early writers called it "the lily."

"The Lillie," Gerard said, "is called . . . in Latine, Lilium, and also Rosa Junonis, or Juno's Rose, because as it is reported that it came up of her milke that fell upon the ground. . . . St. Basill in the explication of the 44. Psalme saith, That no floure so lively sets forth the frailty of mans life as the Lilly." Some of Juno's milk spattered in the sky, and there (Gerard says) it formed the Milky Way. The Romans carried the white lily from camp to camp, establishing it in various parts of the Roman Empire—and probably in England, where it later appeared in portraits of the British saints. One was Queen Ethelfreda, who in the seventh century founded an abbey on the Isle of Ely where later the cathedral was built. She is depicted with a white lily in one hand and the gospel in the other.

Lilium candidum was not called the Madonna lily until fairly recent times, but it was associated with the Virgin Mary very early in the Christian era as the emblem of beauty and purity, first with her Resurrection, and later with the Annunciation and Visitation. The Venerable Bede found it a twofold symbol: white for the purity of the body, gold for the light of the soul. The Madonna lily is also called Assumption lily, although it is not in bloom for the Feast of the Assumption, August 15. It is associated with this feast because on the third day after the death of the Virgin the apostles were said to have visited her tomb and found in it nothing but roses and lilies. The lily does bloom at the Feast of the Visitation, the second of July, and is dedicated to that day.

The Virgin is often portrayed with three lilies on a stalk, two open and one in bud, in a vase beside her. These mystic flowers are said to have originated in the miraculous appearance of three lilies to confirm the faith of a master of the Dominicans. It is for this reason, I suppose, that Gentile Bellini painted Saint Dominic with the lily—two flowers and a bud on the stalk. In a painting of Saint Clare, she holds a stalk with three flowers and a bud.

The white lily is usually present in Italian and Flemish paintings of the Annunciation, though it is not of course in bloom on March 25. Sometimes the archangel Gabriel has a lily in his hand, and sometimes there is a stalk in a vase. In Simone Martini's Annunciation in the Uffizi, the archangel holds out an olive branch and there are several stalks of lilies in a vase.

The white lily appears as a symbol of purity in the Mary Garden, which was such a popular subject in the Middle Ages for woodcuts, paintings and tapestries—a charming vision of the Virgin and child in a little walled enclosure filled with flowers and fruiting trees. The lily is also an emblem of celestial joy, and the flower of Paradise. *Lilium candidum* is also called Saint Joseph's lily, but he has other flowers of his own.

In this country the Madonna lily has been in gardens since the early days. I am not sure how early, but it was in Jefferson's garden at Monticello, and at Mount Vernon, and Lady Jean Skipworth lists it among the flowers growing at Prestwould in 1793. How have we ever allowed the modern lilies to crowd it out? It still grows in country gardens, and I expect it can be had from the curb market.

July 2, 1967

Perfume after Dark

Mrs. Price, who knows how I like perfume after dark, gave me a pot of the night-scented geranium (*Pelargonium gibbosum*). It is called gouty storksbill because the nodes of the stem are curiously swollen. The flowers are nothing like those of any other geranium. They are small and lime green and in close umbels, and are more like spurge than anything I can think of. In the daytime they are as scentless as spurge, but after dark their perfume is like that of angel's trumpet, though not so pervading. The pinnately divided leaves are frosted and curled in a charming manner, and their grayness suits the subdued color of the flowers.

These night scents sent me back to my favorite books about sweet-smelling plants, and one of the most pleasant is Mrs. Gaskell's story of *My Lady Ludlow*. My lady's sitting room was "full of scent, partly from the flowers outside [the window], and partly from the great jars of potpourri inside." My lady divided scents into two classes, the delicate and the vulgar. She considered bergamot and southernwood vulgar, and when a young man came to church with a sprig of lads-love (as the cottagers called southernwood) in his pocket, "she was afraid that he liked coarse pleasures."

But she distinguished between the vulgar and the common. Violets and pinks and sweetbriar are common, and the honeysuckle of country lanes, but these are fit for a queen to wear. My lady had a beau-pot of freshly gathered pinks and roses on her worktable all summer long. Lavender reminded her of country gardens, and she liked sweet woodruff because it grows "in wild, woodland places, where the soil was fine and the air delicate." Attar of roses "reminded her of the city and of the merchants' wives, over-rich, over-heavy in its perfume. And lilies of the valley somehow fell under the same condemnation." Their smell was too strong.

Above all she was proud of being able to detect the delicate odor of decaying strawberry leaves, a quality she believed she had inherited from her aristocratic ancestors, the Hanburys. "My dear," she said to a young cousin, "if you can smell the scent of dying strawberry-leaves . . . you have some of Ursula Hanbury's blood in you." The cousin was dismayed when she couldn't smell anything at all as she stood over the strawberry bed in the fall, but the truth of the matter is that what is attributed to blue blood is merely a matter of chance. "It cannot be had for the seeking," Gertrude Jekyll says. "It comes as it will."

In her chapter "The Scents of the Garden," Miss Jekyll makes many more distinctions than the mere difference between the delicate and the vulgar. Roses, honeysuckle, primrose, cowslip, mignonette, pink, carnation, heliotrope, lily of the valley, she says "are sweet scents that are wholly delightful. . . . Then there is a class of scent that is intensely powerful and gives an impression almost of intemperance or voluptuousness, such as magnolia, tuberose, gardenia, stephanotis and jasmine."

In contrast to sensual perfumes are the wholesome scents of a clover or bean field, a buttercup meadow, and sun-baked heather. And "the most delightful of all flower scents are those whose tender and delicate quality makes one wish for just a little more. Such a scent is that of appleblossom, and of some small pansies, and of the wild rose and the honeysuckle. Among roses alone the variety and degree of sweetness seems almost infinite. I observe that when a rose exists in both single and double form the scent is increased in the double beyond the proportion that one would expect."

Miss Jekyll took the greatest pleasure in aromatic leaves. When crushing a bay leaf, brushing against rosemary or treading on thyme, she felt "that here is all that is best and purest and most refined in the range of the faculty of the sense of smell." She said she wished she had room for a large planting of aromatic bushes and herbs, all planted so close together that no one could walk through it without brushing against them.

In the last class she puts things that are neither sweet nor aromatic, but decidedly pleasing and interesting. These are ivy, box, bracken and the flowers of grape and elder.

July 7, 1968

 A U G U S T

Summer Perennials

For a long time, I have been in search of perennials that bloom in June, July and August, that stand up to the summer sun, and are reasonably free from insects and diseases. When I made a list of the half-dozen that I have found most reliable, I realized that all but one, the purple loosestrife, are native to this country, and even the loosestrife is naturalized in North America, though it is an Old World plant.

The purple loosestrife (*Lythrum*) comes as near as any plant I know to filling the requirements for a perfect perennial. Once planted, it can be left to improve with age, and I have never known it to sicken or die or be chewed in leaf or flower. In spite of this I seldom see it in gardens other than my own, and I expect this is because of the general prejudice against any flower that approaches magenta. Some of the old forms and the Tyrian pink of the variety 'Lady Sackville' are entirely pleasing in a border of pink and violet, white and pale yellow: bergamot, phlox, daylilies and petunias.

Most forms of loosestrife are four or five feet tall, or more, but there is a new dwarf one called 'Robert'. All of the loosestrifes bloom furiously from mid-May until the middle of July. Then, if the spent spikes are snipped, there will be flowers for a few more weeks. The plants are homely when the bloom is over, but they don't seem to suffer from being cut back severely, and the fall flowers soon cover them.

I have been wondering about the name. It seems that the plant was once used to ease the disordered mind, and so was called loose-strife. Pliny said that if it were fed to oxen they would be more likely to draw together.

Loosestrife is generally available, but *Heliopsis helianthoides* 'Pitcherana' has disappeared from all the catalogues that I know of. Fortunately, Mr. Saier still offers seeds, and seedlings will bloom the first year. They are not long lived, but they seed so freely that there will be plenty of volunteers for the garden and for the neighbors. This is a coarse perennial that would be five feet tall if it stood up, but no amount of staking will keep it from flopping; so I try to see that it gets behind an early-blooming daylily whose foliage will support the large branches of golden daisies.

The flowers are long-lasting and absolutely sun proof. Heliopsis is one of the best drought-resistant perennials, but it has never been so fine as it is this rainy summer. The year's volunteers begin to bloom in August when the old plants are slowing up, and so the old and the new keep a golden glow in the border from early summer until frost.

Another good thing that has been dropped from the catalogues is Bolton's aster, called *Boltonia* in honor of an eighteenth-century English botanist, James Bolton. I am glad to say that I still know of one plantsman who still provides it, for the small white daisies and the cool grey leaves are essential to the comfort of a southern summer. I keep a few of the six-foot plants in the back of the borders to bloom when the forward plants have faded. About the middle of July a few stars begin to come out, and by the middle of August they are like the Milky Way.

Monarda was named for Nicolo Monardez, a Spanish physician and botanist who wrote what was probably the first book about American plants. The English edition, published in 1577, was called *Joyfull Newes out of the newe founde worlde*. Monarda is the balm of the herb garden, to which it attracts butterflies and hummingbirds as well as bees. It has the refreshing aromatic fragrance of the mint family, and the flowers are used in tea and potpourri. For the flower border there are color forms ranging from spectrum red through pink and purple and a series of violets, with named varieties such as 'Croftway Pink', 'Cambridge Scarlet' and 'Mahogany'. Mr. Saier offers seed of new hybrids "saved from the Cabham Hall Strain" in shades of pink, red, lavender, mauve, purple and ruby; but it grows slowly from seed. Set out plants in early spring instead of fall.

I like white phlox best because it is sturdier, blooms more freely and stands up to hot sun better than the colored forms. The variety 'Mrs. Jenkins' has always been the mainstay of my summer border, but I doubt whether it is in the trade any longer. Fortunately, 'Mary Louise', a dependable variety with large sparkling white florets, is still popular. In July, my borders would be a sad sight without the very tall white seedling that I found on the place when we came here, an escape from a neighboring garden. I am afraid it has no name, but it is common in old gardens, and anyone who has it has plenty to divide.

Rose-mallows have the fault of drooping in the heat of the day, but they are the gayest flowers of summer mornings. Like everything else these days, the modern forms are super: the New Super Giant Hibiscus is advertised as having flowers ten to twelve inches in diameter. The named varieties are 'Clown', 'Crimson Wonder', 'Fresno' (silvery pink) and 'Satan' ("deep, deep velvety crimson").

I prefer those that Hannah Withers brought me from a country garden. Some are a delicate pink with a touch of white at the center, some a clear rose with a rose-red eye. They are only nine inches across, but that is enough.

August 31, 1958

A Lavender Stick

Some time ago, my cousin Harriet sent me a lavender stick from Greece. She wrote that she had bought it from a lavender-woman on the streets of Athens because it reminded her of Grandmama. Every summer, Grandmama used to weave sweet-scented sticks for us from the lavender that grew in the little garden outside of her parlor window. I wish I could remember what else grew in her garden. I do remember old roses; little pink lilies that we called sand lilies, and that I later found to be *Zephyranthes grandiflora*; and a bush of lemon-verbena which would live through the winter in Marietta, Georgia.

My mother learned to make lavender sticks, and she was working on one on a morning in June, when Anne Phillips came by. Anne was so charmed, she went off and picked lavender from her own garden and came back to learn to weave it. She has been making lavender sticks ever since.

Anne says she never cuts more lavender than is needed for one or two sticks, for it must be used immediately. If it dries out, the stems get brittle and are sure to break before you are halfway through. The lavender must not be put in water. That would dilute the aromatic oil. The time to cut the stalks is when the first flower opens; then the whole plant is at the height of its fragrance, and the stems are fresh and pliant. Cut stalks with strong stems, eight to fourteen inches long.

All that is needed for a lavender stick is some lavender stalks and four to five feet of lavender baby ribbon (a quarter of an inch wide). It doesn't matter how many stalks you use, except that you must have an even multiple of an odd number. Anne likes to use eighteen (twice nine). The Greeks must use a great many more than that, for the stick Harriet bought was large and thick, and must have had some extra flowers stuffed inside. Grandmama's were short and slender, made to fit a handkerchief case.

The stalks, however many are chosen, are laid together with the tips of some of the spikes extending beyond the others, so that the flowering end measures about six inches in length. Then one end of the baby ribbon is tied tightly around the stems, just below the lowest flower, and the stems are gently bent backward (two at a time) over the flowers. Then the ribbon is woven through the stems, under two and over two, in a basket weave around and around, drawing the stems down over the flowers until all of the flowers are covered. When the weaving is done, the end of the ribbon is tied with a bow. Anne says she thinks the bow is too fixy, but she leaves a little loop at the flower end before she begins weaving, so that the stick can be hung on a coat hanger or on a peg in the linen closet.

Although lavender needs the heat of the sun, it is a mountain plant, and is not easy to grow in our climate. Cuttings from shrubs in old gardens make the best plants. Anne's original plant is one of these. It is ten years old, and nearly dead, but in its prime it was about three feet tall and measured seven feet across. Cuttings from it now make a vigorous silvery hedge. It is a form of *Lavandula vera*, and is the most aromatic lavender I have ever sniffed.

Lavender must be planted in a sunny place, in light, well-drained soil to which lime in some form has been added. There is not much more to be done for it, except to see that some lime is added every year, that it is thoroughly clipped after flowering, and that it is not crowded by other plants.

The old herb books say that the scent of lavender is the most comforting of all odors except that of roses. It is good for headaches, and clears the eyes, and "is the odour of the domestic virtues and the symbolic perfumes of a quiet life."

August 9, 1959

Bees

The hum of bees is the voice of the garden, a sound that lends new meaning to the flowers and the silence; music that has not changed since Virgil heard it and wrote of Heaven's gift, honey from the skies.

First, Virgil says, you must choose for your bees a place where the hive will be sheltered from the wind. Water must be nearby, clear springs and mossy ponds, and a little stream threading its way through the grass. Let a palm or a wild olive shade the entrance to the hive and let shadows of willows lie on the water. Plant violet-banks all about, with carpets of savory and wild thyme; and there must be crocuses and hyacinths, arbutus from the mountains, laurustinus and linden trees.

When you see the swarm rising skyward in the clear air of a summer's day, the bees are in search of sweet water and a leafy shelter. Then, if you clash Cybele's cymbals, and scatter bruised balm and the leaves of honeywort on the place where you want them to go, of their own accord they will light on the scented spot. These customs, described in the *Georgics*, persisted until modern times. Old woodcuts show the bee-master "ringing the bees" by beating on a pan, and Miss Rohde writes in *The Scented Garden* of the ancient practice of smearing the hive with balm and sweet Cicely.

Virgil says you must have smoke at hand when you break into the treasure that the bees have hoarded, but first you must rinse out your mouth with fresh water. The smoke-pot is still a necessary part of the bee-master's equipment, and writers of all ages stress the importance of cleanliness in the person and clothes of anyone who goes near the hive. Bees are fastidious creatures. They find strong scents offensive. You must never go around them after eating strong-smelling food—especially garlic, for they dislike the odor of all members of the onion family. And never, Virgil says, "roast the reddening crab upon your hearth."

On the other hand, drinking a mug of good beer is advisable, and it is well when visiting bees to carry along a handful of sweet herbs. Rub your hands and face with rue and no bee will come near you. If, after taking all precautions, you happen to be stung, you have only to lay the crushed leaves of balm on the wound and the pain will go away.

Jack Mitchell knows an Indian bee-keeper on the Lumber River who calls him a honey-thief because he has never learned to take the harvest without mask or gloves. Mr. Mitchell says he is perfectly at home with his bees at all other times, but he doesn't like to open the hive with bare hands, even when it is overflowing with honey. I think he feels like Maeterlinck, who said, "The first time that we open a hive there comes over us an emotion akin to that we might feel at profaning some unknown tomb."

Mr. Mitchell says bees are like a lot of people. "So often the quick-tempered ones don't mean a word of what they say. When a bee stings me," he says, "I know he has mistaken me for my brother." He says he has noticed that the best bee-keepers are always mild-mannered, and so easygoing that they are almost lazy, and that they are unfailingly kind. Like Miss Rohde's old Gregory, they go about their work with calm and gentle movements. Gregory always talked to the bees when he went among them. One day Miss Rohde said, "Do the bees understand what you are saying to them, Gregory?" and he replied, "Just as much as horses and dogs and cattle; it stands to reason they do. Sometimes I think they understand more nor we do."

August 30, 1959

The Sabbath's Posy

When sermons were longer than they are now, it used to be the custom to take aromatic herbs to church to refresh the spirit and quieten the nerves. Even children carried posies made of herbs and strong-flowers.

Mrs. Ewing's little Phoebe once lost her Sabbath posy as she was going to Sunday school, and kind Jack March found her in tears. She said the flowers were only old man and marigolds, which are common enough, but when Jack offered to replace these she saw a chance to get something better. "My mother says Daddy Darwin has red bergamot in his garden," she confided. "We've none in ours. My mother always says there's nothing like red bergamot to take to church. She says it's a deal more refreshing than old man, and not so common."

Perhaps in Queen Victoria's day everyone read *Daddy Darwin's Dovecot*, for the Sabbath posies were always the same: bergamot, old man, and marigolds. Mrs. Ewing's marigolds were not our marigolds; in England that is the name for calendulas. Old man is *Artemisia abrotanum*, called lad's love, because the maidens put it in their pockets to attract the lads, and also called maiden's ruin. Another name for it is southernwood. I don't know why. If well clipped, it is one of the nicest herbs for summer, but it looks very sad in winter.

Bible leaf, *Chrysanthemum balsamita*, was sometimes added to posies, and the long markers in prayer books and Bibles. It is also called costmary maudlin in England. Some think it was named for Saint Mary Magdalen, perhaps because the delightfully aromatic foliage suggests the scented ointment. Others say it belongs to the Virgin. Another name is alecost, as it was used to flavor ale and beer. I always like to have costmary in my garden. This is easily done, for it is very persistent. A root that came to me from Elizabeth Clarkson years ago is still there, and in spite of its reputation as a spreader it has never increased more than enough to provide offsets to give away. In summer, when it gets lanky, I cut it back, and the cool, pale green basal leaves of early spring soon return.

Red bee balm, southernwood and Bible leaf were the standard herbs for churchgoers, but Mrs. Wilder, in *The Fragrant Path*, gives a list of others. Among them, these from Mary Howitt's poem, "The Poor Man's Garden":

> here, on Sabbath mornings,
> The good man comes to get
> His Sunday nosegay, moss-rose bud,
> White pink, and mignionette.

Mrs. Wilder adds that gray feathery sprigs of southernwood are "the perfect accompaniment for white Moss Rose buds." She says a man will like southernwood, nasturtiums and hot-scented marigolds.

Mrs. Earle's *Old Time Gardens* has the best chapter that I know of on the Sabbath posy in New England. The seed of dill, fennel and caraway were called "Meetin' seed," and nibbling on them was supposed to keep the congregation awake. A sprig of fennel was a "theological smelling-bottle," recommended by Peter Parsely both to men and to women who found themselves tempted to nod in church. He assured them that fennel would "exorcise the fiend that threatened their spiritual welfare."

Mrs. Earle knew a little country girl who brought the new leaves of what we called checkerberry to Sunday school. This is true wintergreen, *Gaultheria procumbens*. The Sunday school children were delighted to have the aromatic foliage to nibble in the spring, and in the fall the little girl brought the spicy scarlet berries. She also contributed roots of sassafras and sweet flag. The latter was a favorite for Sunday nibbling.

The queerest custom of all was that of Thoreau and other young men of Concord, who liked, after their Sunday morning swim, to pick a long-stemmed pond-lily to wear to church. Its odor, Thoreau said, contrasted with and atoned for that of the sermon.

Mrs. Earle comments on the fragrant things that were not carried to church, as well as those that were. She says she never heard of putting lemon verbena or rose geranium or the mints in a Sabbath posy. This seems strange, for they are the most fragrant and refreshing of all.

August 13, 1961

Rain Signs

St. Swithin's day if thou doest rain
  For forty days it will remain:
St. Swithin's day if thou be fair
  For forty days 'twill rain na mair

Saint Swithin was the ninth-century bishop of Winchester who later became the patron saint of Winchester Cathedral. It has been suggested that the ancient superstition, attached to him in the twelfth century or earlier, is the survival of a still more ancient pagan augury, and that it became connected with his feast day, July 15th, when a great downpour occurred on that day, in 971, while his body was being transferred from a forgotten grave to the cathedral. In France the weather on the feast of Saint Medard (June 8th) is said to determine whether the next weeks will be wet or dry. In Flanders the day is July 6th, the feast of Saint Godelive, and in Germany it is the Seven Sleepers' Day, June 27th.

The superstition goes even further afield. In a Chinese gardening book of the seventeenth century, the writer says if the sky is clear on the twentieth day of the fourth moon, commonly called the little day of the dragon (the rain god), it means that the dragon is tired and dry weather will follow. If it rains, the god is full of energy, and it will rain twenty days longer. Because he is an amphibian, many primitive people consider the frog the lord of the waters, and believe that he brings the rains:

Send soon, O frog, the jewel of water!
  And ripen the wheat and millet in the field.

I asked Elizabeth Russell, who often passes on the folklore she learned as a child in South Carolina, whether frogs foretell the rain, and she said of course they do: whenever you hear the tree toads at night there will be showers before morning. The same, she says, is true of the bull-bay, by which she does not mean the night-hawk, but a regular bat who hollers like a bull. Once after a long rainy spell, when the weatherman said it was going to clear, Elizabeth said it wasn't. "Don't you hear that old chipmunk up in the tree?" she asked. "Long as he hollers it's going to rain."

And of course everyone knows about the raincrow. "Never," Virgil says in the *Georgics*, "has rain brought ill to men unwarned. Either, as it gathers, in the sky cranes flee before it in the valleys' depths; or the heifer looks up to heaven, and with open nostrils sniffs the breeze, or the twittering swallow flits around the pools, and in the mud the frogs croak their old-time plaint."

Flowers, too, are weather prophets. The anemone curls its petals before a storm; if the marigold opens before seven, thunder will be heard; when chickweed flowers stay closed there will be rain; when they open wide there will be none for four hours; and if they stay open it will be fair all day. But of all the flowers the scarlet pimpernel is the most dependable. It is called the shepherd's weather glass, and, whatever the barometer may indicate, if it has its flowers "expanded fully in the morning, there will, to a certainty, be no rain of any consequence on that day." "Come tell me," the poet says,

Who gave the magical power
Of shutting the cup on the rain?

But I forgot the bees. If rain threatens, Virgil says, they do not "stray far from their stalls, or trust the sky when eastern gales are near; but round about, beneath the shelter of their city walls, draw water, and essay short flights." That a bee is never caught in a storm is proverbial: "When cautious bees forbear to roam . . . tokens are that rain is nigh."

Aratus, the Greek poet, whose writing on weather signs Virgil imitated, said no sign should be neglected. It is good, he said, to compare one with another: "If two agree have hope, but be assured still more by a third."

But the skeptics are always with us. All weather talk is foolish, the Scots say: "When it rains in the hill, the sun shines in the valley."

August 4, 1963

Ferns

One morning in July when we were having a delightful spell of "poor man's mountain weather," I asked Elizabeth Clarkson to walk through her garden with me and name the ferns. The one that grows most luxuriantly is the New York fern, *Dryopteris noveboracensis*. It spreads and spreads, and makes a thick border on both sides of a long shady path. The yellow green, once-pinnate fronds are delicately cut and tapered at both ends. In the woods the New York fern grows in moist thickets, but it will grow in dry, sunny places as well.

The other wood ferns are not all luxuriant, but they have persisted in Elizabeth's garden for years. *Dryopteris marginalis*, the evergreen wood fern, gets smaller and smaller. In my garden it has disappeared entirely. *D. spinulosa* flourished with Elizabeth for a while, but it needs a richer moist soil. *D. hexagonoptera*, the broad beech fern, comes from dry hillsides, and so it grows fairly well in Elizabeth's woods. Its triangular fronds are twice pinnate, and are usually broader than long. *D. goldiana* is the largest of the wood ferns; in good soil it grows to a height of four feet, but in the fifteen years that Elizabeth has had it, it has decreased rather than increased in size.

Athyrium filix-femina, the lady fern, has seeded itself all over the woods; although the seedlings are variable, all of them are dainty and graceful. In one clump the fronds have red stems. Lady fern will grow in wet or dry places and in sun or shade, and so will the sensitive fern, *Onoclea sensibilis*. Sensitive fern is much larger and finer when grown in moist soil, but it will grow anywhere, even where other plants fail, and its coarsely cut foliage is as decorative in the borders as in the woods. Some people think of it as a pest, but after seeing it in Mrs. George King's garden I consider it one of the best foliage plants. The sensitive fern is native to this country, but lady fern and royal fern are Old World plants.

The royal fern, or water fern, *Osmunda regalis*, is always at its best in circles, Thoreau says, and "it may be on a steep bank with half the circle in the water." Elizabeth has a fine clump growing with Jack-in-the-pulpit beside a shallow pool in the part of the garden she calls Frog Hollow. As it grows near streams, royal fern is dedicated to the saint who carried the Christ child across the river, and it is sometimes called Saint Christopher's herb. The old herbalists called it Osmun the Waterman, after a legendary boatman whose wife and daughter hid under the fern fronds during an invasion of the Danes.

In those days fern seed was used in divination, and was supposed to discover treasure hidden in the earth. Gerard wrote of water fern growing in "divers bogges . . . especially neere unto a place that some have digged to the end to find a neste or mine of gold; but the birds were over fledge, and flowne away before their wings could be clipped." The herbalists set great store by royal fern as a wound herb, effectual for "both inward and outward griefs."

Osmunda cinnamomea is called cinnamon fern because the sporanges are cinnamon-colored, and fiddle-heads from the shape of the fertile fronds as they come up in early spring. Like royal fern, it will grow even in very dry places, but is at its best in rich moist soil where it reaches a height of from three to six feet.

Like the royal fern, bracken (*Pteridium*) belongs to the Old World as well as the New and has a long history of folklore and superstition. Linnaeus named the species *aquilinum* because he thought the mark at the base of the stem was like a spread eagle; another mark—said to look like the Greek letter that is a symbol for Christ—puts witches to flight. The smoke of burning bracken is supposed to drive snakes away and to produce rain. Although bracken comes from dry hillsides, and is said to grow where other ferns fall, it is difficult to transplant; but Elizabeth Clarkson has managed to get it established in her garden.

It was already growing under our pine trees when we first came here to live, and as I have encouraged it by digging out the briers and cow-itch, it has grown into a cool sea of green. But I have a continual fight to keep it from taking over everything—even the gravel walks.

August 16, 1964

Camellias

I always like to know where the names of flowers come from, and so when Polly Anderson told me that she walked every Sunday in Descanso gardens I thought that that must be where the camellia 'Pride of Descanso' was developed. I had no idea when Polly came home with me from the Daffodil Society's meeting in Asheville that I would be talking with her the next spring, in those very gardens in La Canada, California.

'Pride of Descanso', now called by its original name 'Yoki-Botan', is an old one, introduced in 1895, but the history of the gardens is older still. The land was part of a grant from the Spanish governor, Pedro Fages, to José Maria Verdugo in 1784. It became a part of the celebrated Rancho San Rafael and was finally bought in 1937 by E. Manchester Boddy, a Los Angeles newspaper publisher. He called it Rancho del Descanso, the place of rest.

The first camellias in California arrived in 1852 on the Pacific Mail Company's steamship *Panama*, which carried "484 passengers and 40 females." They were in bloom when they arrived in Sacramento. Two years later the Golden State Nursery in San Francisco advertised seventy varieties, and soon people were going in carriages from garden to garden to see the collections, and the camellia ball became an annual affair.

But camellias had gone out of fashion by the time Mr. Boddy became interested in them in 1936, and he could find very few kinds in the California nurseries. Nevertheless, with the help of J. Howard Asper, he set about building up one of the largest collections in the world. Now I know where the names of two other varieties come from: One was named 'Berenice Boddy' for Mr. Boddy's wife, and another (now called by its Japanese name, 'Hana-Fuki') for Mrs. Howard Asper.

When Polly and I walked in the gardens the first week of April, the camellias had passed the peak of bloom, but there were still more flowers than I had ever seen at one time, for there are a hundred thousand plants in the collection, and six hundred varieties. They are planted in a thirty-acre grove of live oaks (not our live oak but *Quercus agrifolia*, native to California), and some of the original bushes have grown to a height of twenty feet.

The rare collection of varieties of *Camellia reticulata* were flown out of China just before the Communists took over. I was interested to see these in bloom in the open, as I knew them only as greenhouse plants. And I was interested in the hybrids between *Camellia japonica* and *C. saluenensis*. They are such good garden plants, so free-flowering and with the fast-growing habit of their saluenensis parent.

I think I am going to find *Camellia saluenensis* itself a valuable and delightful evergreen. A plant set out a year ago from a container has already reached a height of four feet, and last winter it bloomed from the middle of November until well into the new year. The flowers are small but finely drawn, and of a warm ivory delicately tinted with wine. They are very fragrant.

At Descanso I saw several more of the some eighty species now recognized. The flowers of *Camellia maliflora* are adorable. They are small, and semi-double with rose-edged petals. There seems to be some doubt as to its hardiness, but I should like to try it. I gather that it is smaller than the other species, with an ultimate height of only six or eight feet.

The tea plant, *Camellia sinensis* (which we always called *Thea sinensis*), has a near relative in *C. talensis*, though the flowers of the latter are larger. Both are fall blooming. I think this must have been the evergreen I used to see blooming in the snow in a garden on Park Drive in Raleigh. As with the tea plant, the buds are as decorative as the flowers.

C. cuspidata is the hardiest species. The shrubs are small but very floriferous. The small, white flowers bloom in spring. The leaves also are much smaller than those of most species. 'Cornish Snow' is a hybrid between this and *C. saluenensis*.

August 22, 1965

Bedding-Out

All summer, as I have gone up and down Westfield Road, I have enjoyed a charming bit of bedding-out at the corner of Maryland Avenue. It is a narrow border against a house, about two feet wide, and curving to make a semi-circle around the chimney. Tall, yellow French marigolds are at the back, then yellow-green caladiums, with a dark wine-red one at each end; a row of red salvia comes next, and then dwarf ageratum, and in front of that dwarf marigolds of a pale lemon yellow. The edging is sweet alyssum. This gay and fresh example of nineteenth-century design set me to rereading *The Victorian Flower Garden*, by Geoffrey Taylor.

Mr. Taylor says that bedding-out, the system of filling ribbon borders and geometric beds with annuals and exotic plants raised indoors, was practiced to some extent by Philip Miller, who published *The Gardeners' Dictionary* in 1733. But it did not become popular until a hundred years later, when it was introduced by Lady Grenville at Dropmore and by Paxton at Chatsworth. Mrs. C. W. Earle said Paxton's bedding-out "altered the gardening of the whole of England, and consequently of the world. He used the old patterns of Italy and France for designs of beds, filling them as had never been done before, with cuttings of tender exotics, which were kept under glass during the whole winter." With no limit to his expenditure, Paxton created a blaze of color on the Chatsworth terraces for the months of August and September, when the Duke of Devonshire was in residence.

The example of Chatsworth and Dropmore was followed by other great houses in England, and then by the smaller places. In time, crescents, stars, triangles, and circles were cut into every lawn, and filled with plants "marshalled in regular order, and at equal distances, like beaux and belles standing up for a quadrille."

In *My Garden in Summer*, E. A. Bowles describes the "most bedded out garden" he ever saw as having "thousands of plants in long straight lines in unbroken sequence. You begin at the gates with Blue Lobelia, Mrs. Pollock Pelargonium, Perilla, Yellow Calceolaria, and some Scarlet Perlargonium in ranks according to their relative stature, and so you continued for yards, poles, perches, furlongs, or whatever it was."

"Well," Mr. Bowles says, "I do not champion that sort of thing, but I confess to adoring Scarlet Pelargoniums, rejoicing in Blue Lobelia, and revelling in Yellow Calceolaria. But they must be certain varieties, well grown and well placed."

In this country, bedding-out must have been at its height at the turn of the century. In 1903 Ida Bennett wrote, in *The Flower Garden*, "Beds of ornamental foliage plants, Cannas, Ricinus, Coleus, and the like, appropriately placed, add much to the beauty of a well-kept lawn.

"There should be only one bed on a small lawn, and not more than three on a large one." These should be placed so they could be seen and enjoyed from the hammock while the gardener rests from her labors.

"A very good arrangement is to put a large bed of Ricinus on the most remote space of the lawn—four plants in the center of a twelve-foot bed—surrounded with a row of *Salvia splendens* edged with 'Little Gem' Sweet Alyssum.

"Nearer, an eight-foot bed of the large flowered Cannas may be introduced and edged with Coleus or the second size of Caladiums, while a six-foot bed of ornamental grasses—*Arundo donax, Erianthus ravennae, Eulalia gracillima univittata*—will make a third. Such beds are rich in tropical effects and give more distinction to the lawn than any other class of plants."

William Robinson is usually given credit for putting an end to all this and bringing back the old-fashioned perennials. But his classic, *The English Flower Garden*, was not published until 1883, and long before he ridiculed "bedding-out and carpet-bedding and mosaic culture," the characters in Disraeli's *Lothair* (1870) were doing it even better: "How I hate modern gardens," Saint Aldegonde said. "One might as well have a mosaic pavement there." And Madame Phoebus added, "The worst of these mosaic beds is, you can never get a nosegay."

August 7, 1966

Bulb Catalogues

In summer, when the bulb catalogues begin coming, I try to make up my orders right away, especially when I am getting fall-flowering kinds, for the sooner the bulbs get in the ground, the better.

If colchicums are kept out of the ground too long, they begin to flower before they are planted, and the flowers are small and thin and pale. Last year I planted *Colchicum autumnale majus* (which is the meadow saffron that has been most satisfactory) at the end of September, and it bloomed in a few days, freely and beautifully. This year the buds began coming up out of the ground on the 25th of July, which I did not expect, and did not want, for they are not at all in harmony with *Rhododendron prunifolium* which is a mass of vermillion at that point. In the 20 years I've had it, it's never done that before, and I hope it goes back to its September season.

The fall-flowering crocuses are not so impatient as the colchicums, but they lose some of their plumpness when they are kept out of the ground. They last and increase if they are not eaten up by rodents. *Crocus zonatus* and *C. speciosus* are the most dependable ones, and they are very cheap by the hundred.

This summer found *C. niveus* listed, for the first time in years, by the International Growers' Exchange. Unfortunately, it is not cheap. It is as expensive as it is rare. But I ordered one corm, as the large, pure white flowers come in November.

The Growers' Exchange issues two catalogues, spring and fall (50 cents each). These are good for three years, with "addenda, supplements and end-of-season offers" gratis. The catalogues list rare bulbs and plants from "the wide, wide world": Holland, Kashmir, Asia Minor, Italy, South America, South Africa and our West Coast. I find in it many bulbs, especially from Van Tubergen, that I cannot find locally or from other importers.

Seeing foxtail lilies in English gardens in May made me feel I must have some next spring, although they are expensive and difficult. The only one that ever bloomed for me a second season is *Eremurus robustus*, but I am going to try *E. himalaicus* this time, as it is much less expensive. As I saw it in the garden at Sissinghurst, the silvery white spikes were six feet tall. One of the difficulties with foxtail lilies is that the long fleshy roots that radiate from the crown are very brittle and must be handled gently. They should be planted on a bed of sand—some say with the crowns barely covered and some say six inches deep.

There are several decorative alliums that I like to keep going, more or less. They are not permanent, but the bulbs are cheap. *Allium albopilosum* has huge round heads (nearly a foot across) of metallic violet flowers on 12-inch stems. If they are cut and dried when every flower is in bloom, they will last for years. Mr. Riordan, of the Growers' Exchange, considers *Allium aflatunense* far superior to *A. rosenbachianum*. They are similar, with four-inch heads of violet flowers on scapes about three feet tall. All three species bloom in late April and early May when it is nice to have something to follow tulips.

While I was writing this, Mrs. H. W. McMillan called to ask where to get tanier, a kind of elephant ear, but with smaller leaves. Tanier, I found, is the common name for *Xanthosoma*. I looked it up in the *Plant Buyers' Guide* and found that *Xanthosoma violaceum* is listed in the catalogue of the Oakhurst Nurseries. I don't know whether this is the species she wants, and if anyone knows this plant, and a source for it, we'd be glad to hear. Mrs. McMillan says it is commonly grown in South Carolina, and some people eat the roots in salads.

August 11, 1968

Tidewater Virginia

At the end of July I spent a few days with the Wellfords in Tidewater, Virginia. Mittie and I drove along dirt roads where chicory and bouncing bet were in bloom. We found a wild phlox in the woods, and roamed the fields and the edges of the marshes, and went to Sabine Hall where the lawn was carpeted with wild petunias. The southern wild petunia, *Ruellia ciliosa*, is a low-growing, blue-violet flower that blooms all summer. It is a good plant for the wild or rock garden and sometimes volunteers in the flower borders, but I had never seen it in quantity before.

One morning we got up at 6 a.m. (which is really 5 a.m.) to go up the creek with Hill in search of birds and flowers. The sun came up round and red through the early fog, and puffs of white mist hung over the still, dark water. Herons flew out of the trees when they heard the sound of the boat motor, swallows skimmed, and every now and then a duck flew up out of the marshes. The mallows were not yet in bloom, but to my amazement tall, red lilies stood above the reeds and grass on the creek bank.

Hill cut the motor and paddled over to the fern-carpeted hummocks so Mittie could reach them. I don't see how they could be anything but *Lilium superbum*—nodding, green-eyed, spotted Turk's-caps, in tones from dusty gold to dark brick red—but what were they doing there in the marshes? In North Carolina they grow in the mountains. However, I looked in Mrs. Dana's *How to Know the Wild Flowers*, and she says that they grow in lowlands along the coast of New England, and can be seen from the train between New York and Boston.

On the wooded bluffs beyond the marshes, the trees come down to the water. There are oaks and beeches, sweet bays turning silver when a little breeze turns up the undersides of the leaves, and the most beautiful hollies I have ever seen. Here and there a tupelo leaf was already scarlet. Button bush was still in bloom along the edge of the water, and under the trees the slopes were covered with the slender white spires of summersweet.

In the shallow water the flowers of pickerel weed were lavender shadows. At the water's edge Mittie found a stalk of white three-petalled flowers in whorls of three. It was obviously an arrowhead, but we were puzzled by the lanceolate leaves. The photograph in *Wild Flowers of North Carolina* showed it to be the duck potato, *Sagittaria falcata*, a species of the southern coast. I have referred to this book constantly since it was published in April by the University of North Carolina Press, sponsored by the Garden Club of North Carolina and the North Carolina Botanical Garden. In it are full-color photographs by Dr. William Justice of 400 of the 2945 species of flowering plants of North Carolina with descriptive notes by Dr. Ritchie Bell.

From one of the photographs we were able to identify the beautiful swamp milkweed, *Asclepias incarnata*, which I had never seen before. The tall plant, with its round heads of rosy flowers, is beautiful in bud and is handsome enough for the border. It is listed by the Gardens of the Blue Ridge. Some of the delicate wild flowers, such as rhexias and sabattias, were wilted by the time we got them home, but Mittie revived them by putting them in hot water, and by the time we got the books out they were fresh again.

There was one viburnum that we couldn't find in the books, so we sent a twig with a bunch of pointed green berries to Lionel Melvin. Mr. Melvin says it is an unusual form of the possum haw, *Virburnum nudum*, which blooms in May. The fruits begin to color in August, turning pink and then blue so that there are three colors at one time. When they ripen in September, they are eaten by the birds. The possum haw is essentially a shrub, but sometimes gets to be a small tree.

August 18, 1968

Irises

The irises of the Evansia section are few—only seven or eight species have crests on their falls. When I started collecting iris species, years ago, I thought that this group at least could be complete, and I did eventually get them all (except *Iris speculatrix*, which does not seem to be in cultivation). Keeping them is another matter; only three are still with me.

One of these is *Iris japonica*, a native of Japan and Central China. It is perfectly hardy, but in our climate the springs are usually too cool to allow it to bloom. This year, in April, it bloomed for the second time in the six years since Mr. W. O. Freeland brought it to me from Columbia. The flowers are very like those of *Iris cristata*, but paler and fancier, and on longer, stouter stems. They are almost white with a pale lavender wash, and this makes the golden crest and the deep violet markings more conspicuous. The falls and the standards and the tips of the style branches are finely fringed.

The flowers are said to smell like clove pinks, but to me their scent is sharp and faint. Though they are flowers of a day, there are so many to a stem that they last a long time, and even a few scapes provide bloom for more than two weeks. With or without bloom, the fans of almost evergreen leaves make a shining carpet in shady places. It grows only too well, for the long runners reach out in all directions and travel fast. However, they are shallowly rooted and easily pulled up.

Iris tectorum is called the roof iris because it is grown in the thatch of Chinese and Japanese houses. E. A. Bowles says there is no truth in the story that the women (who wanted it for hair-dye, face powder, and corn plasters) grew it there in time of famine when the government had ordered that every inch of ground be used for grain, but he liked to tell it because it pleased visitors to his garden. The blue violet flowers are somewhat larger than those of *Iris japonica*. Their crests are white and the falls are marked with manganese violet. The frosted flowers of the albino form are all white except for a touch of yellow on the crest.

W. R. Dykes, in his monograph of the genus, begs us to remember to always call it *Iris tectorum alba*, rather than the *I. tectorum album* of the catalogue writer. I try to, but I find it difficult. It is the most beautiful of all white irises—I can't for the moment think of any other equal to it, except perhaps a dwarf Delta variety called 'Mac's White'. And there is a horrid and almost invisible little bug that usually eats the buds of 'Mac's White' before they open.

The roof iris does not like to be too dry. It needs some shade and is said to need dividing every three years. Mine has been in the garden for nearly twenty years without being disturbed at all except for niggardly snips to give away. Sky-Cleft Gardens, I think, still lists the type, but I don't know of any sources at present for the white one.

For me *Iris gracilipes*, a tiny Japanese alpine, is as difficult to grow as the roof iris is easy. I have tried it three times, and would try again if I knew where to get it. It has bloomed for me only once, late in April. I saw it in bloom in May in a rock garden in the Pocono Mountains. It seemed to be flourishing there, and Mrs. Wilder described it as blooming in profusion in her garden in Westchester.

Iris milesii and *I. wattii* are by far the tallest species of the group. These, too, are probably no longer in the trade. They come from the Himalayas, and are evidently not hardy in this climate, for they did not survive the winter in my garden. W. R. Dykes says *I. milesii* promises more than it fulfills. The small flowers overtopping the wide, yard-high leaves seem insignificant in comparison. "They are curiously mottled with two shades of pale and deep red-purple, and the characteristic crest of the group is conspicuous."

The other two species in this group are our native *Iris cristata* and the smaller, darker *I. lacustris* which grows on the shores of the Great Lakes and does not like summer heat.

August 31, 1969

Summer Blooms

This summer the black-berry lily, *Belamcanda chinensis*, bloomed from early June until well into August. There was scarcely a day when there were not several small, ephemeral, red-spotted flowers. They open at various times in the morning, according to the amount of light, I think, but I could never catch them at it, though the clump is right outside my studio window, and I see it every time I look up from my work.

The flowers close before dark, neatly furling themselves into a minute and almost invisible red and yellow striped barber pole, so they do not detract from the appearance of the plant even though they persist for some time. The handsome pale green seed pods form quickly, and when they burst open, early in September, the bunches of shiny seeds look like ripe blackberries. If the stalks are cut to the ground as they finish bloom-ing, the plant will bloom again in September, but most people like the fruits for winter arrangements. The fan-like foliage is pale green with a delicate silvery bloom, and the stiff, well-branched flower stalks stand well above it. Although the stalks are from three to four feet tall, I am glad I put the plant in the front of the border, for it deserves to be seen as a whole and to stand alone.

Belamcanda is the Malabar name for the black-berry lily, which grows spontaneously in India where it is considered a cure for snakebite. John Weathers, in the *Bulb Book*, says it was introduced into England from China in 1759, an earlier date than that given in the *R. H. S. Dictionary*. I haven't been able to find out when it came to this country, but I think it must have been in early times, for it has escaped from old gardens and grows in woods and along the roadsides from Connecticut to Georgia. It is advertised in the southern market bulletins, and Parks Seed Company lists both seeds and plants.

I find in my files a record of the butter-iris, *Belamcanda flabellata*, a Japanese species recognized in *Hortus Second*, though I have not found it elsewhere and the genus is considered monotypic. I got it from William Borsch, who wrote in his catalogue of that date that it was a new species and a better one than *B. chinensis*, having large yellow flowers valuable for cutting in hot dry summers, and long lasting when cut. It bloomed in Raleigh in August, 1946, but I can't remember the flowers at all, though I described them as being Indian yellow with pale flecks of primuline yel-low, and as having three small segments and three larger ones. I don't know what happened to it, as we left Raleigh soon after that, and I have never seen it listed since, though I continue to hope, for I would like to try it again.

I had better luck in replacing *Cypella herbertii* (named for the Honour-able and Reverend George Herbert by his brother the Honourable and Reverend William Herbert). I found it at the Growers' Exchange and planted it last June, and it bloomed in July. This year it bloomed in early June, and I suppose it will go back to blooming in May as it used to do in my Raleigh garden. I hope it will also keep its habit of repeating in the fall. My first bulbs came from Felicity, my dear Ruth Dormon's place on

Mooringsport Road in Shreveport. She loved it too, and she said it bloomed all summer in Louisiana. The flowers are like small golden tigridias.

Montbretia (or tritonia), another little summer-flowering iris, is found in country gardens all over the South and advertised in the market bulletins. They call the old red-flowered kind "red-flowering summer iris." It is a rather forlorn spike of drooping flowers that never open wide. There is a lovely orange-flowered montbretia with larger flowers that do open wide. In July Carrie Fultz brought me a stalk of this to identify. She said she got it from a friend's garden, and she brought me some corms. I will soon be able to pass it on again, for it multiplies rapidly.

August 23, 1970

ℐ SEPTEMBER

. . . .

Southern Lilies

On Labor Day, Laura Braswell called to say that she had a flower she wanted to show me, if I wasn't too busy. I was too busy, but I have learned that anything that Mrs. Braswell considers important enough for a telephone call is worth considering—even if the house is on fire. "It's a lily we found in a ditch near Fairmont," she said. "Harry's wife saw it as we drove by. She never misses a flower. Her children may not know the names of their grandparents, but they know the names of the wild flowers."

The lily from the roadside ditch proved to be *Lilium catesbaei*, the southern red lily, one of the rare species of the country. Although I had never seen it before, I had no trouble identifying it by comparison with the color plate in Caroline Dormon's *Flowers Native to the Deep South*. The plate shows the distinctive form of the up-facing flower. When you look down on it, the long, slender, light green claws of the petals are like the spokes of a wheel, and the tapered, long-pointed, slightly curved tips make a graceful pattern. The color is a warm, coral red—redder than the wood lily, *Lilium philadelphicum*, the only native species for which the southern red lily could be mistaken—and at the base of each petal there is a pale yellow zone dotted with dark red freckles. The leaves are alternate, slender and pointed, lying at intervals all along the stem, not in whorls like those of the wood lily. There is a single flower (or sometimes two) at the tip of the stiff stem, which grows to two or three feet.

The southern red lily grows in the savannahs and grass sedge bogs of East Carolina, where it blooms from July into September, and in low pine lands along the coast into Florida, and along the Gulf Coast as far west as Louisiana. Caroline says that it is fast vanishing, and should not be collected for gardens unless it can be given the very bad bog conditions that it demands. But Mrs. Braswell thinks the bulldozer a more formidable enemy than the gardener, and she says the roadscraper was right behind her when she found her flower in the ditch.

Lilium catesbaei was named by one distinguished botanist for another. Thomas Walter, who named it, wrote *Flora Caroliniana*, which was published in London in 1787. When he saw it on the Santee river "lit by the slanting rays of sunshine which pass through the grey tillandsia," he must have found it as Mrs. Lounsberry did, "almost mysterious in its radiance." Mark Catesby was an English botanist who made two long visits to this country, one to Virginia in 1712, and one to the Carolinas in 1722. Soon afterward his *Natural History of Carolina, Florida, and the Bahamas* was published in London.

Two rare lilies from the Southern mountains were also named for early botanists: *Lilium michauxii*, the Carolina lily (in the trade as *L. carolinianum*), for the Frenchman who so loved our mountains; and *L. grayi*, for Asa Gray, who discovered it in 1840 on Roan Mountain. Both of these are available from the Gardens of the Blue Ridge.

The Carolina lily blooms in the mountains in July and August and is like *Lilium superbum*, except that it is smaller, daintier, and has usually only one flower to a stem. The flowers have a delicate and pervasive fragrance. The color plate in *Flowers Native to the Deep South* shows the distinguishing character of the flower: the petals curve backward so sharply that the tips are interlocked. Gray's lily is so rare that it is known only from a few stations; one of these is the bald on Roan Mountain, where it comes up in a stand of the ever rarer mountain alder. The flowers of the lily are nodding and bell-like, the petals not reflexed. They are usually solitary, but there may be several to a stem. Gray's lily blooms in June and July, and must be planted in moist soil.

September 18, 1960

Scattering Seed

September is the best month for sowing hardy annuals. In late summer I sit down with the catalogues to make out my list in plenty of time, but the seeds seldom get scattered before Thanksgiving. I used to want all that the catalogues offer, but now I keep to the easy kinds.

My list always begins with sweet alyssum, larkspur and nemophila. Nemophila is a California annual that must be sown early in the fall if it is to do well in this climate, for it quickly perishes in hot weather. As the Greek name tells that it is a lover of groves, it is recommended for shade, but it blooms well for me only in sun. Tiny plants that begin to bud by the end of February, if seeds have been sown early enough, gradually spread to make a circle of blue that lasts through April. The flowers are of a tint that is as near to pure blue as any that I know, except those of the *Nigella damascena*, the forget-me-not-flowered anchusa and *Hyacinthus azureus*; they must be kept away from the blue-violet of squills and pansies.

As the plants are sprawling, I like to put them on a low wall, but they do very well for edging. *Nemophila insignis* is one of the plants that the ill-fated David Douglas discovered on his trip to the West Coast early in the nineteenth century. Aided by the horrid name of baby blue eyes, it soon became so popular that seedsmen measured their rows by the mile, and Mrs. Loudon (in *The Ladies Flower Garden of Ornamental Annuals*) pronounced it exceedingly valuable and almost a universal favorite.

Nigella is another annual that I have had in my garden, and it self-sows just enough to keep it going, but from time to time I scatter fresh seeds. There must be something a little sinister in the appearance of the flowers to have given them such names as barbe-bleu, Jack-in-prison, and devil-in-the-bush.

When Forbes Watson was a child, he felt the spell so strongly that the sight of them filled him with a sense of wonder and awe. "This must be one of the flowers, he told himself, that a young man once gathered for his sweetheart, not knowing until he had put them in her hands that their touch is the touch of death" (*Flowers and Gardens*). He had not heard of the nymph who was changed into this plant as punishment for her misdeeds and whose heart was said to have been as black as the seeds which give it the Latin name, nigella, a diminutive of niger. The early Christians called the flower Saint Catherine's wheel because it reminded them, in some far-fetched way, of the instrument of torture that was rolled over the body of the young martyr. To me their blue is the color of innocence, a color I would not be without in my garden, and I like to call them by their more common and less alarming names, fennel-flower or love-in-a-mist. *Nigella damascena*, the common fennel-flower, is supposed to have journeyed to England by way of Damascus, but it is a native of southern Europe, where it grows in cornfields.

This fall I am trying *N. hispanica*, which Mrs. Loudon considered the most beautiful species. "The flower is very large and handsome," she said, "with the carpels rising boldly like a pillar in the center. The petals are of a deep rich mazarine blue: and when they fall, the carpels are almost, if not quite, as ornamental. . . . The plant is about a foot and a half high, and is of a bushy, compact habit of growth."

Mrs. Loudon says that all nigellas can be transplanted, and sweet-alyssum can be transplanted too, but I think that the seeds of these, as well as those of nemophila and larkspur should fall where they are to grow. Just scratch the soil a little, toss out the seed, and rake the spot very lightly. But do it soon.

September 10, 1960

Midsummer Mountain Flowers

I expect most people would prefer to visit Reflection Riding and Lookout Mountain in spring when the wild azaleas are in bloom, or in the fall when the woods are red and gold, but I was content to be there in the quiet time of midsummer. I like the mountains when sourwood is in bloom and the snowy hydrangea frosts the roadside banks; when butter-flies visit the butterfly weed, and there is a honeyed scent of button bush in the meadows. A very fine button bush, about four feet tall and crowded with honey-scented balls, made me think how much we miss by not plant-ing some of the lesser shrubs such as the Virginia willow with its fragrant white spikes in May; the sweet pepperbush, which flowers so fragrantly in July; and some even more lowly.

It is a familiar complaint that there are no rock plants for the South, and no one thinks of two dwarf shrubs that bloom early and late at Reflection Riding. *Ceanothus americanus*—called New Jersey tea because during the Revolution the troops brewed their tea from its leaves—covers the rocks with snow in early summer, and at summer's end there is Saint Andrew's cross with its four golden petals in the form of an X, with the cross on which Saint Andrew was put to death.

In summer as in winter, leaf patterns are more important than in spring and fall. Summer patterns vary greatly in shape and texture and tones of green: the round grey-green wings of the twin-leaf, the dark lacy rosettes of black snake-root, the bold arching stems of giant Solomon's seal, the mottled scimitars of the green dragons, and finely divided fern fronds are all woven together in a tapestry of green. Where little springs break out from the mountainside, ferns and mosses grow among the rocks: delicate whorls of maidenhair, bold clumps of royal fern, clusters of the purple-stemmed cliff brake.

Against this green background, some plants stand out as individuals. One of these, a member of the gentian family which does not look at all like a gentian, is a six-foot pyramid of stout, sparsely furnished branches tipped with small, purple-spotted yellow flowers; it is well-named monu-ment plant, but is commonly called American columbo. I thought Ameri-can columbo an unlikely name, and had difficulty in finding out what it means, but at last discovered that columbo is a corruption of calumba, an African plant with medicinal properties. So I suppose our plant is consid-ered an American substitute. The generic name, *Frasera*, is in honor of John Fraser, who published Thomas Walter's *Flora Caroliniana*.

In the woods the most brilliant summer flowers are lilies and lobelias. The great panicles of *Lilium superbum* sometimes reach a height of eight feet, with as many as forty orange Turk's caps to a stem. These follow the Canada lilies, and are just past the height of their bloom when the lobelias are still to come.

I think red Betty is the prettiest of the local names for the cardinal flower, *Lobelia cardinalis*. Mrs. Lounsberry, who roamed the South collect-ing plant lore, was distressed to find the splendid red velvet flowers called nose-bleed, and she would probably have been horrified to learn that in some places they are called hog-physic. She says the flowers will color water if dropped into it, and that country girls use them for rouge. She says she herself has picked four-foot stalks of *Lobelia siphilitica*, and has found the blue flowers still in bloom in late October. Both species can be grown in the wild garden, and Mr. Saier offers seeds. The cardinal flower will bloom the first year from seed sown in late winter.

The Indians who used to roam the woods of Reflection Riding knew the uses of plants as medicines, and passed their lore on to the pioneers. Some of the names linger: pleurisy root, rheumatism root, fever bush, Indian physic, and rattlesnake master. As the cures for snakebites were so many and apparently so effective, Asa Gray came to the conclusion that in the cool mountain climate rattlesnake and copperhead bites are not apt to be fatal or even dangerous.

Turman's snake root, named for an Indian famous for his cures, is the starry campion, *Silene stellata*, also called king's cure-all. It is a charming plant with fringed white flowers that float like snowflakes over ladies' tresses and wayside grasses. At the same time the black snake-root lifts its tall white candle in shady places, and in deeper shade slender flower spikes stand above the white-veined leaves of rattlesnake plantain.

September 3, 1961

Butterfly Weather

Moments of summer happiness, Edith Sitwell says, come in butterfly weather. There must be many of these moments in cool English summers, but in my garden butterfly weather comes in early fall, when flowers are fewer than in summer, and the butterflies therefore all the more welcome. I don't know what flowers they come for at that time. I have read that they like Michaelmas daisies, but I haven't any of those.

Once a large, black swallowtail with blue-edged wings flitted about superciliously, and then stopped on the Florence fennel. The fennel was not in bloom, but after he had flown over the garden wall he came fluttering back and visited it again. He never lighted on anything else. Perhaps he thought the fennel was parsley, on which the swallowtail caterpillar is said to feed. I remember now that I have often found handsome striped caterpillars on the fennel. I killed them all. Perhaps that is why we have fewer butterflies than we used to. I had been blaming it on the DDT trucks.

Edith Sitwell's brother, Osbert, said he would like to have a special garden for butterflies. He thought the radiant shimmering of their wings would supply even lovelier colors than the flowers. I don't think he had much idea of how this was to be accomplished. He was more of a poet than a gardener.

The flowers most attractive to butterflies are the ones that bear their name, the butterfly bush and the butterfly weed. I have planted butterfly weed several times without success, but this year I think I have gotten a good start. I got it from Wayside Gardens, and they must have sent me good roots. However, it will be several years before they form free-flowering clumps. I like to have the flowers in bloom with the daylilies, but now that my garden has grown shady I am afraid they will never bloom as they do in the fields and along the roadsides.

I used to have a white butterfly bush in the back of the borders, but I got tired of the chore of keeping the dead flower spikes cut off, so I dug it up. I have an idea, though I never heard anyone say so, that the old summer lilac, *Buddleia davidii*, is more fragrant and therefore more appealing to butterflies. Mr. Bowles thought the variety 'Magnifica' superior to the type, but he said he always kept a few seedlings to bloom earlier or later, and so prolong the season of banquets for butterflies by day and supper parties for moths by night.

Butterflies are said to be very fond of bee balm, *Monarda didyma*, but I have never seen any visiting mine, though I have a great deal of it in the borders—too much, in fact, for it is hard to have any without having far more than is wanted. Yellow and black swallowtails—I think that's what they are, I must get a book—come to the borders when the rubrum lilies are in bloom. The rubrums (a variety of *Lilium speciosum*) are the lilies that do best for me. They last for years and bloom in August as the daylilies wane.

In a copy of *My Garden*, an invaluable little magazine that was a casualty of the war, I found an article by Walter Murray about an English butterfly sanctuary. He says he gathers in one part of his garden all of the flowers that butterflies like. Primroses attract the earliest, the brimstones, which hibernate in winter. Sweet rocket is sure to be visited by the orange tip, and if red admirals come before the first of May, they have crossed the sea to get there. The painted lady, the best known of migrant butterflies, goes to England from Spain and Africa. It is found hovering over early marigolds in June—these marigolds are probably calendulas, as the British call them marigolds. The flowers for summer butterflies are verbenas, sweet alyssum, dahlias, and most of all the butterfly bush, which Mr. Murray says need not be so untidy if it is cut back hard in winter. Perhaps I had better get another one.

September 1, 1963

Perennials

I spend my summers going through the catalogues, making notes of what I want to plant in the fall. I make lists and then tear them up and start over again. I want everything I see, and it is so hard to choose. I used to try a hundred or so new things each year, but as I grow older the days seem to get shorter—also the garden gets fuller.

My garden is more of a problem than most, because I expect it to be beautiful every day in the year, and at the same time it must make room for plants that are new to me and may grow poorly or not at all. There are always a number of these, looking very forlorn until I make up my mind that they are not going to do better and might as well be discarded.

In the catalogue of the Heatherfells Nursery I found a perennial I had never heard of before. It is *Kirengeshoma palmata*, a member of the saxifrage family, and a native of Japan, introduced into England in 1891. As most Japanese plants do well with us, I thought of succeeding with it, but I find that it likes moisture, not only in the soil but in the air.

Mr. Bowles had it in his rock garden. "It is rather dried and starved," he says, in *My Garden in Autumn and Winter*, "but, as I cannot find a more suitable spot, it must stay there. It does just manage to flower, but is never the luxuriant, two-feet high plant I have seen in Ireland. It is a curious and beautiful object when a spike of its large, flashy, yellow flowers rises above the light-green, handsome leaves."

Well, I'll try to make room for it near a spigot, and give it plenty of peat moss and some shade. I hope it will bloom in the fall, as it does in New England, but it may bloom earlier here.

At Heatherfells I also found *Adonis amurensis*. This won't be an experimental plant, for I have had it for years, but I have only one, which was given to me by Mr. Krippendorf, and I have never been able to find it in the trade since Mr. Kohankie went out of business—a sad day for me. This adonis is the earliest perennial (except the hellebores, but I think of them as belonging to winter), blooming almost always in mid-February, but occasionally later, and once on the twenty-second of January. It belongs to the buttercup family, and the glossy, golden flowers are like buttercups, only they are much larger and many-petalled. This too likes some shade and a deep, moist soil. It is easily established, but doesn't increase.

Coreopsis 'Baby Sun' is one of the nicest things I had this year. I liked the varied shapes of the golden flowers, and one had a dark red eye that made me think it had a calliopsis in its ancestry. Mrs. Price says she was disappointed because the plants were not as small and compact as she had expected, but I find them just as useful in the borders, though they are not really an edging plant. Park lists 'Baby Sun' among the annuals, but now, at the end of the summer, they look fresh and green and bushy as if they were meant to live on through the winter. I shall buy a few, in case they don't.

Coreopsis 'Baby Sun' and other late-flowering things can be put out in the spring, but October is the time to set out saxatile alyssum and hardy candytuft. The yellow of the alyssum is the brightest thing in the spring garden, and I always get new plants every fall so I will be sure to have plenty. The old ones sometimes live over, but I never have enough unless I add more in the fall.

It is important to get hardy candytuft that is propagated from cutting, and best to get ones that are grown nearby. Seedlings are often poor in quality and they are not of uniform growth. I always buy lots of pinks in the fall, because it is so much easier than dividing the old ones, and they soon peter out if this is not done. I like the old spicy clove pinks and the Grenadin carnations with flowers in tones of crimson and Tyrian rose. This spring I found at a nursery in Georgia some little old-fashioned grass pinks with white flowers that are finely fringed and delightfully scented.

September 22, 1963

Hardy Bulbs, Early Blooms

Tulips and daffodils are not the only hardy bulbs that bloom early in the new year. There are many others, and I have been making a list of the best of them. All gardeners want bulbs that, once planted, bloom happily ever afterward, and some of these do. Others are what E. A. Bowles calls buy-and-die plants, but they are so beautiful that we should be willing to replant every fall.

One that must be replanted annually is the lovely poppy anemone, *Anemone coronaria*, called coronaria because it was a favorite garland flower of the Greeks. The Wayside catalogue says it becomes established and remains for years, but it does not do that for me. A few flowers bloom the second season, but it has never come back in full force. Even so, the little wrinkled tubers are fairly cheap, and I am perfectly willing to take some trouble for the poppy-like flowers that come so early in the year, sometimes as early as February, and I have even known them to bloom in January.

In the mixed tubers the magentas and blue violets clash with the reds, so I like to get them in separate colors. These are hard to find, but

Wayside lists 'His Excellency' (red), 'Lieutenant', which I used to grow as 'Blue Poppy', and the exquisite early white one called 'The Bride'. I can never tell the top from the bottom of the tubers, so I always slip them in sideways and about two inches deep.

I depend upon the Dutch irises to fill in the gaps and keep the spring garden in bloom. If the early and late varieties are planted there is bloom for several weeks. 'Wedgwood' is the earliest—it comes around the first of April—and it is also one of the most persistent. A clump I have had for years still blooms every spring. The flowers are China blue, and there is a second flush after the main bloom is over. 'King Mauve' is the latest. The flowers are not bright, they are a much greyed lilac, but they are very plentiful, and the bulbs persist and increase. 'Golden Harvest', another late one, gives some bloom for a number of years, but never does as well after the first season. The white varieties are the most beautiful, but they seldom persist. 'White Perfection' is the finest; 'Joan of Arc' is handsome, but comes out with a yellow sheen.

Galanthus elwesii is the best snowdrop for this climate. It begins to bloom in January or February according to the season. With me *Scilla tubergeniana* is the most satisfactory of the early squills. It usually blooms soon after the middle of February, but may come earlier. *Scilla hispanica* (*S. campanulata*), the Spanish squill, is the most dependable of all spring bulbs. It multiplies rapidly in the garden, and even seeds itself. And it likes shade. I have the blue kinds—there are several varieties, all very much alike—and the white ones. The pinks are a muddy color, and they seldom persist. The Spanish squill blooms the latter part of April.

The satin hyacinth, *Ornithogalum nutans*, is a very old flower that used to be in southern gardens, but is seldom seen anymore, though P. De Jager still lists it. I have read that it is invasive, but it has never spread at all with me, though bulbs planted years ago in a shady place still produce a flower spike or two in March. The silvery flowers are pale green on the reverse of the petals, and some of the green shows through. It is a quiet flower that cannot hold its own in the perennial border, but is nice with wild flowers and ferns.

Several handsome alliums bloom the last of April, but none are really permanent with me. The last time I had *Allium rosenbachianum* the bulbs disappeared after the first season. I had more last year, and I am going to plant another dozen this fall in case those behave in the same way. The flower heads are of a rather dull purple, but their distinctive form makes them interesting. They are in dense balls on tall, straight stems. The flowers last a long time, and are attractive even after the color has faded. *Allium albopilosum* usually stays with me for several years, sending up enormous spherical flower heads, nine inches or more in diameter. The flowers are small, metallic, purple stars on pedicels over four inches long. In *Park's Flower Book* it is listed as *Allium christophii.*

September 12, 1965

Michaelmas

"The archangel, Michael, whose name in Hebrew means that he resembles God," Glenway Wescott says, in *A Calendar of Saints for Unbelievers,* "is the highest in rank of the seven archangels; the captain of the heavenly armies; the recorder; the master of intercession and revelation; the keeper of the souls of the dead; and the lord of mountains and high places." The feast of Saint Michael and All Angels comes on the 29th of September, and the flowers of the season are the Michaelmas daisy, meadow saffron, and yellow archangel:

The Michaelmas daisy, among dede weeds
    Blooms for St. Michael's valorous deeds,
And seems the last of flowers that stode,
    Till the reste of St. Simon and St. Jude.

The daisy first dedicated to Saint Michael was the Italian starwort, *Aster amellus,* long associated with religious ceremonies; Virgil says it often adorned the altars of the gods. He says the shepherds gathered it in the meadows along the winding stream of the Mella (for it is easy to find) and the country people called it "amellus" (aster). The roots were needed for sick bees.

In England country people gave the name to the little native starwort, *Aster tripolinum,* but the flowers we now know as Michaelmas daisies are the hybrids of our own native asters that went to England in the eighteenth century, and have returned to us from the hands of the hybridizers very much improved. The species and the hybrids bloom over a long period in summer and fall, and even up to Christmas, for "the Michaelmas Daisy blows lonely and late."

The Michaelmas crocus is the meadow saffron, *Colchicum autumnale.* The flowers are sometimes called naked nannies. In my garden some of its varieties have bloomed at Michaelmas, and the white form nearly always does. Although it grows and increases and blooms freely in dry shady parts of the garden, it is native to the English water meadows where it must be a fine sight if there are any such places left as those Bishop Mant described a hundred or more years ago:

go to Monmouth's level meads,
Where Wye the gentle Monmow weds;
Long brilliant tubes of purple hue
The ground in countless myriads strew.

The fall asters and the fall crocuses belong to Saint Michael because
they bloom at Michaelmas, but the yellow archangel blooms around the
eighth of May, which used to be in former times the feast day of the
archangel. It is *Lamium galeobdolon*, the pretty evergreen ground cover
that I wrote about last spring. The unwieldy name of the species comes
from two Greek words meaning weasel and ill-smelling, the pretty leaves
being foetid when crushed, and so it is called weasel snout. The leaves are
green and silver, and the lemon yellow flowers are in whorls. It is a bee
plant, and an astringent, said to be good for healing sores and ulcers.

In England, Michaelmas has its bird as well as its flowers, the Michaelmas blackbird, which is seen only in spring and fall, and there is a Michaelmas onion sown in August to harvest in the fall.

Michaelmas spring is a name for the fine spells of weather that sometimes come in September, and is sometimes used figuratively for a father's
having a son in his old age. The Michaelmas moon is the harvest moon,
and "they say so many days old the new moon is on Michaelmas day, so
many floods after." Another superstition of the season is that if crabapples
are gathered by young girls from the hedges and laid on the attic floor to
form the initials of their young men, those that keep in good condition for
more than a week will make the best husbands.

And everyone knows that the devil puts his foot on blackberries on
Michaelmas day. After that the berries are poisonous, or at least unwhole-
some, and whoever eats them is sure to die, or someone in his household
will, or at the very least he will be in great trouble before the year is out.

September 26, 1965

Oaks

When I asked an ensign in the Civil Engineer Corps of the United States
Navy why he wears oak leaves on his sleeve, he said the leaf and acorn are
used as the devices of several branches of the Navy. The device of the
Medical Corps, for example, is a gold oak leaf with a silver acorn in the
center. That of the Civil Engineer Corps is four gold oak leaves crossed,
with two silver acorns.

The Navy chose the oak because it is the "father of ships," its wood—
before the days of iron and steel—being the strongest material for construction. In England, as well as in this country, it has always been associ-

ated with mariners. The oaks of England, Canon Ellacombe says, are "the very emblems of unbroken strength and unflinching constancy. . . . The glories of the British Navy are linked with the growth of her oaks":

Our ships were British oak,
And hearts of oak our men.

The acorn, my ensign tells me, represents the source of strength of the mariners. The oak has always been the emblem of the brave. In Roman times the civil crown, a wreath of oak leaves, was the reward for saving the life of a citizen:

Most worthy of the oaken wreath
    The ancients him esteem'd,
Who in a battle had from death
    Some man of worth redeem'd.
—Drayton

Shakespeare made much of this custom in *Coriolanus*. Volumnia says, "To a cruel war I sent him; from whence he returned, his brows bound with oak." And later, "He comes the third time home with the Oaken Garland."

The oak appears frequently in heraldry. In the thirteenth century Sir Stephen Cheyndut bore an oak tree on his shield—a play on his name, as "chêne" is the French word for oak. The oak was also the badge of the ill-fated Stuarts, and their fate was said to be caused by their having chosen for their emblem a tree that dropped its leaves instead of an evergreen. In an old book that once belonged to Robert Cameron, I found his book plate with the Cameron arms: a shield in a wreath of oak leaves and acorns.

The Greeks looked upon the oak as the symbol of hospitality, but they always associated it with Zeus, the god of thunder and lightning, to whom the great oak of Dodona, the most ancient oracle of Greece, was sacred. The oak was also sacred to Jupiter, for he was born under one, and the Latin poets often speak of it as belonging to him; in the noonday heat, Virgil says, let the sheep and goats seek the shady valley, "wherever one of Jove's ancient and mighty oaks spreads out its giant branches."

When Caesar reached Gaul, he found the Druids also worshipping the oak. Fraser says, in *The Golden Bough*, that men must have noticed in very early times that lightning strikes the oak more often than any other tree, and that they must have taken this to be a sign from heaven that they were to hold it sacred. There is an old saying, "Beware the oak, it draws the stroke."

In England, oak leaves or apples are worn on the twenty-ninth of May, the day of the Restoration, and it is called oak-apple day in memory of the sturdy tree in which Charles II hid himself when pursued by his enemies.

Oak apples are galls that come in the spring on the leaf buds of *Quercus robur* (the English oak). When they are steeped in white wine vinegar and mixed with a little powder of brimstone and iris root, Gerard says, the decoction "maketh the haire blacke, consumeth proud and superfluous flesh, taketh away sun-burning, freckles, spots, the morphew, with all deformities of the face."

The oak and King Charles are connected with American as well as with English history. As every school boy knows, the charter that Charles II granted to the colony of Connecticut, in 1662, making it independent, was hidden in a hollow oak in Hartford when Sir Edmund Andros tried to seize it in 1687. The oak was blown down in 1856, but a marker was placed where it stood.

September 11, 1966

Mr. Hohman

One thing that has not changed in the last sixteen years is the Kingsville Nursery. The entrance is just as difficult to find as it was when I first looked for it in June 1950, and passed by several times, before I saw the inconspicuous sign on U.S. Route 1 just south of Kingsville, Maryland. The narrow lane is just the same as it winds across fields and through woods, and between rows of the rarest trees and shrubs in the country. After passing an ancient, weathered barn it arrives at the house. I think Henry Hohman told me that his house is over two hundred years old. It is called Quiet End.

Mrs. Hohman came to the door as before, and, as before, said Mr. Hohman was somewhere about the place. Mr. Hohman hasn't changed either, except that he is even thinner. When searched for, he is not to be found, but he can't resist a visitor who goes up and down the rows reading labels and taking notes, and once he speaks he meets enthusiasm with enthusiasm.

When we were discussing the stewartias (Mr. Hohman has the two American species in his collection as well as the Asiatic ones), I said I had discarded *Stewartia monadelpha* because the small white flowers are hidden by the foliage. He was horrified. He took me to a nearby tree, and pushing aside the branches showed me the tawny bark. In winter, he said, it is the most beautiful thing in the nursery.

All of the Asiatic species have beautiful bark. Usually it is dark grey, peeling in patches, revealing the tender pearl-grey coloring underneath. All are noted for autumn color. *Stewartia koreana* is said to be the most brilliant, but the leaves of mine are merely bronzed—at least that is the way they look to me; they match the burnt umber of the color chart. The mottled trunk is striking in winter (which seems to be the season for peeling, and therefore the contrast between the outer and inner layers is greater), and the prettily frilled flowers, much like those of a single white form of *Camellia sasanqua*, to which they are related, bloom in June and increase in number as the tree grows older.

Mr. Hohman has a choice collection of dogwoods. He has the weeping, willow-leaved, and variegated forms of *Cornus florida*, and also a dwarf variety found in Florida. He has the Chinese form of the Japanese dogwood, *Cornus kousa*. For flowers, fruit, and autumn color, the Chinese dogwood is considered one of the most beautiful of trees of suitable size for a small garden. It is little grown in Southern gardens and should be given a fair trial. The bracts are larger than those of the type, and the flowering season is longer. There were still flowers in August, though bloom begins in May. The curious little round red fruits are said to be edible and sweet. This is a woodland tree, but it needs a goodly amount of sun to make it bloom as profusely as it should.

Visiting the nursery in August gave me a chance to see some fruits I had never seen before. Though I have had obassia for thirteen years, and it began to bloom four years ago, it has not fruited in my garden. I had no idea that the small, velvety, pale green drupes would be so attractive. Everything about this tree is distinctive: the fragrant white flowers in long drooping racemes; the large, round, coarsely toothed leaves (to about eight inches in diameter); and the pearl grey markings on the dark grey trunk. It needs light shade (but more sun I think than it has in my garden) and a deep leafy soil; it must never lack for moisture. It grows to a height of twenty feet or more.

Another tree in fruit in the nursery was the Chinese fringe tree, *Chionanthus retusus*. The drupes were green, but they turn dark blue as they mature. There are only two species in this genus, ours and the Chinese.

In August the berries of *Viburnum rhytidophyllum* were beginning to color. I don't remember ever having seen the leather-leaf viburnum in fruit in Charlotte, and it is usually a bedraggled looking shrub hereabouts, but it is handsome in leaf and fruit in a cooler climate, and as it is very hardy, it should be used in the mountains. There is no use writing to Mr. Hohman or to order plants, or to ask for a catalogue. He is too busy to answer or ship. But many of these shrubs are listed by the Tingle Nursery.

September 18, 1966

A Dainty Dish

In 1617 John Goodyer grew the first Jerusalem artichokes in England, and wrote a history of the plant for Thomas Johnson's 1633 edition of Gerard's

Herbal. By the English name of this plant, Mr. Johnson said, "one may wel . . . perceive that those that vulgarly impose names upon plants have little either judgement or knowledge of them. For this plant hath no similitude in leafe, stalke, root or manner of growing with an Artichoke, but onely a little similitude of taste in the dressed root; neither came it from Jerusalem or out of Asia, but out of America. . . . All these that have written and mentioned it, bring it from America, but from far different places, as from Peru, Brasil, and Canada."

The Jerusalem artichoke is not, of course, native to Peru or Brazil, though it was once called Topinambour after a Brazilian tribe; it is a sunflower, *Helianthus tuberosus*, that ranges from Canada to Georgia, and blooms along the roadside in late summer and fall.

It was formerly supposed that Jerusalem is a corruption of *Girasóle*, as the plant was sent out from the Farnese gardens in Rome as *Girasóle Articiocco*, but the name is now considered the hawker's version of Ter Neusen, a town in Holland where the tubers were grown for the English market.

The French introduced the Jerusalem artichoke from Canada, probably before Goodyer grew his, for he got the tubers from Mr. Franquevill of London. Champlain, when he visited Cape Cod (in 1604), learned from the Indians that the tubers are good to eat both raw and cooked.

"These roots are dressed divers ways," Goodyer says. "Some boil them in water, and after stew them with sacke and butter, adding a little Ginger: Others bake them in pies, putting Marrow, Dates, Ginger, Raisons of the Sun, Sacke, etc." From the seventeenth century on, artichokes became a plant of the kitchen garden, as a winter vegetable. They were eaten raw in salad, boiled and served with French dressing, boiled in milk to go with roast beef, puree'd, or sliced thin and fried like potato chips. They were even made into a broth called Palestine soup.

Recently I read a recipe for sautéing the tubers in butter, with herbs and garlic, and then cooking them briefly in white wine. But, in the South at least, they are now used mostly for pickles. In South Carolina they are cooked in a vinegar sauce with chopped vegetables ad lib: green tomatoes, onions, cauliflower, cabbage, celery, green and red peppers, and so on. MacAlpine Cocktail Artichokes are pickled right here at Matthews, and sold in the grocery stores.

Artichokes are not appreciated by everyone. "Which way soever they be drest and eaten," John Goodyer says, "they . . . are a meat more fit for swine, than men." But Parkinson, who called them Canadian potatoes, considered them "a dainty dish for a Queen."

Goodyer says the artichoke is a "wonderful increasing plant." He set out one small tuber no bigger than a hen's egg, and harvested a peck. If even the smallest piece is left in the ground it will multiply alarmingly, and they say the only way to get rid of it is to turn hogs in to root it out. "Error," a seventeenth-century writer says, "being like the *Jerusalem-Artichoake*; plant it where you will, it overrunnes the ground and choakes the Heart." So perhaps it is better to buy artichokes from the curb market, than to plant it in the garden.

The tubers can be left in the ground all winter, and it is best to dig them as they are needed. After three years, they grow small and poor in quality and must be replaced. I have read that it is better to grow new plants from seed than to replant the old tubers.

There was some complaint that I left off the Latin name when writing about comfrey. It is *Symphytum officinale*. I used to wonder why so many plants are called *officinalis*. It means that they are medicinal. My comfrey has now made rather handsome rosettes of hairy, spinach green, deeply veined leaves that grow to a length of more than a foot.

September 3, 1967

Crinums

It seems odd that crinums, once the treasured lilies of southern gardens, should now be so completely ignored. I suppose it is because the colored catalogues advertise the real lilies, while the crinums are grown by collectors who send out mimeographed lists only to those who ask for them. A great deal of collection has been done since the days when milk-and-wine lilies were the common garden varieties, but most of it has been done in the Deep South and on the Gulf Coast, and it will take some time to learn which kinds are hardy and satisfactory in our area.

Last fall I ordered four crinums from Claude Davis in Baton Rouge; he sent another gratis. One of these, 'Southern Belle', failed to come up this spring. The others seem to be flourishing, but only one, 'George Harwood', has bloomed this summer. 'George Harwood', a hybrid raised in Australia, is supposed to be a cross between *Crinum moorei* and *C. scabrum*. As *Crinum scabrum* is one of the tender species—I have never succeeded in wintering it in North Carolina—Mr. Davis rates it as only moderately hardy; but *Crinum moorei* is one of the hardiest species, and looking over my records I see that hybrids with it as a parent have always survived our winters.

'George Harwood' began to bloom on the 26th of August. The chalice-shaped flowers are a brilliant rose color, with half-opened buds of a deeper color and tight buds rose-red. The contrast of these tones with the glistening white center of the open flowers makes this one of the most striking of all hybrids. The flowers have a delicate and delightful fragrance.

Crinum moorei was introduced into Glasnevin Gardens, in Dublin, in 1863 when David Moore, one of the most celebrated gardeners of his day, was curator. It is a South African species, native to Nepal. It is variable, and the form I have is the very pale one said to be common on the West Coast, and inferior to the more colorful makoyanum form, which so far as I know is not in the trade.

Another form, also a pale one, with very large flowers on scapes more than three feet tall, was sent to me from California by Edith Strout. I brought it to Charlotte from my Raleigh garden, and it increased so rapidly that I once had a fine clump, but as nearby shrubs have grown up it is now in such deep shade that it never blooms. All forms of *C. moorei* like part shade, but they won't bloom without some sunlight. *Crinum* 'Frank Leach' blooms at the end of July, and *C. moorei*, cultivar 'Schmidtii', blooms even earlier. This year the first flower opened on the last day of June. There were eight scapes, each with five to seven large white flowers, a fine sight when in full bloom.

When the flowers fade, large pale green seeds form. The stout scapes bend with their weight until they touch the ground. When the seed ripens, a little bulb grows out of it and takes root in the soil. Some seeds that I brought indoors and left on a table formed bulbs just the same. They are said to bloom, after planting, in five years. My original bulb came from the Oakhurst gardens as *Crinum* 'Herald'. It is no longer listed in the Oakhurst catalogue, but both seeds and bulbs of *Crinum moorei* are listed.

Mr. Davis says crinums can be moved at any time, but early fall is best. The bulbs will make good growth before cold weather if they are well watered, and will have a good chance of blooming the first year. I am sure he is right as to the Gulf Coast, but I think early spring is better in the Middle South. This gives the bulbs the longest possible season for becoming established before cold weather. Once planted, crinums should be left undisturbed. They grow larger and bloom more freely every year. They need a soil rich in humus with plenty of fertilizer. They like lots of water, although they will survive long periods of drought.

September 15, 1968

"The Southern Market Bulletin"

I was asked recently to give the address of the publisher and the price of subscription to "The Southern Market Bulletin," which I write about so often. I had better make myself clear. There is no "Southern Market Bulletin." There are about thirteen of them. The Department of Agriculture of each state, from Virginia to Florida and Louisiana, publishes its own. All are free. All you have to do is write and ask to have your name put on the mailing list. But North Carolina and South Carolina will not send theirs out of the state.

I have written about ours before. It is called the *Agricultural Review*, and is published twice a month. Fortunately, a friend who has a plantation near Camden gives me her *South Carolina Market Bulletin*, which is published weekly. In it I often find my heart's desire. The *Georgia Farmers and Consumers Market Bulletin* is published weekly and is one of the best. A new feature is a weekly article about the plants advertised in it. Each week an anonymous author writes a description of one plant, and tells about the folklore connected with it.

Caroline Dormon's favorite is the Alabama *Farmers' Bulletin*, published twice a month. My favorite is the *Mississippi Market Bulletin*. Perhaps because it is the one I knew first, thirty years or more ago, when Eudora Welty put my name on the mailing list. Eudora wrote about the market bulletin flowers in *The Golden Apples*, her chronicle of Morgana. The *Louisiana Weekly Market Bulletin* is colorful too, full of French herbs, vegetables and names—Yves Lancios, Camille Cazedessus, Gerard Saucier. I don't subscribe to the Virginia and West Virginia bulletins, as they advertise so few flowers, and the Florida bulletin lists mostly tropical and subtropical plants. It is a treasury of houseplants.

They are sometimes called "for sale, want, and exchange bulletins," because farmers and their wives advertise in them the things they have for sale, and tell about their wants, or are willing to swap. The farmers list livestock, farm machinery and farms. The women list seeds, plants, and bulbs. The bulbs are fairy lilies and milk-and-wine lilies and old daffodils that have been in country gardens since the early days.

The daffodils are gold dollars, buttercups, silver bells, the April white—and lately (in the South Carolina bulletin) I came upon the "Never-miss" yellow jonquil. There are old roses, too, 'Maréchal Niel', the Seven Sisters and Lady Bank's rose. I feel sure that many rare ones are there, listed by local names.

But a rose is not always a rose. The briar rose is *Rubus coronarius*. The thornless yellow rose, Rose Wharton found when she ordered it, is the double yellow kerria. She found that bush-jasmine is *Serissa foetida*, a dwarf, almost everblooming shrub that grows in old gardens. "Yard fern with pink flowers" proved to be bleeding heart.

There are rare plants too. In *Natives Preferred* Caroline Dormon tells about the pure white form of *Viola papilionacea* advertised by Miss Bonnie Black in the Alabama bulletin. She says it comes true from seed. Caroline also tells about cat-bells. They are a little native crotalaria with small seeds that tinkle delicately in the dried pods. She says when she was a child she tried to tie them around her cat's neck. I found plants advertised in the Mississippi bulletin.

There are give-away plants in the market bulletins: jewels-of-Opar, sultana (in seven colors) and false dragonheads, sometimes advertised as fake dragonheads; and some, such as kudzu (free for the digging), to be severely let alone; but delightful old-fashioned flowers are always turning up. One I have been hunting for for years, and just found it, is the little striped mallow that Mittie Wellford and I found last summer in the garden at Sabine Hall. It is a garden form of *Malva sylvestris*, and I think it is the variety *zebrina*. It is a European plant, but it was advertised as a Chinese hollyhock. I have just ordered some "shirt buttons." I'll have to tell later what they are. Or perhaps someone can tell me?

September 14, 1969

🖋 OCTOBER

. . . .

The Cuban Vine

One morning early in September, my neighbor, Mrs. P. W. Basinger, asked me to come to her garden to see a flowering vine that she had grown from seed. I asked what it was, and she said she didn't know, but it was given to her as the "Cuban vine."

I went through the little gate that leads to her wide, sunny terrace, and found a magnificent hyacinth bean climbing up a rain-spout. It is a great pleasure to find a handsome plant, perfectly grown, in the right place, and given plenty of room. The hyacinth bean needs room. A broad, 20-foot column of bold foliage and long slender spikes of violet flowers has grown from a single seed.

The flowers are like little sweet peas—but with no fragrance. They are in small clusters at intervals along stiff wine-colored stems more than a foot long. The spikes are well presented, standing out from the leaves so that all of the flowers show. The leaves are trifoliate, with broad, heart-shaped leaflets to six inches long. The leaflets are dark green with a net-work of wine-colored veins, and are on long, wine-colored stems. The brilliant, violet seed pods are as showy as the flowers. It is these varying tones of red violet in flower, stem, leaf and fruit that makes the vine so decorative.

The hyacinth bean is a tropical plant, perennial in hot countries, but planted as an annual in North Carolina. Mrs. Basinger's was planted very late, probably in May, and grew up overnight, like Jack's beanstalk—Jack bean is another name for it. The seed can be planted earlier, anytime after frost and the earlier the better for a long season. The plants begin to flower as soon as they begin to climb, and they bloom on until frost cuts them down. To bloom freely they must be in full sun, and the seeds must be sown where they are to grow, as they do not transplant well.

One of the virtues of this vine is that the foliage is very thick from the ground upwards, making a good screen. I asked Mrs. Basinger how she coaxed it up the rain spout. She said that she started it on a string, and once started it climbed on its own. Anyone who has ever struggled to make a vine rise up when it would rather lie on the ground will appreciate the advantage in that.

The Latin name of the hyacinth bean is *Dolichos lablab*. It can be found in most flower catalogues, and may turn up with either purple or white flowers. The white-flowered forms have green seed pods. I know of only one seedsman who lists the varieties separately. He offers one called 'White Pearl', with very large fruits; one called 'Princess Helene', with large clusters of pure white flowers; and the 'Purple Sudan' hyacinth bean, which he says is very decorative. I am still searching for a form called 'Darkness', with very dark purple flowers, and one called 'Daylight', with dazzling white flowers. I feel I must have 'Darkness' and 'Daylight' growing side by side.

Another fast-growing vine for covering up and screening out is the closely related scarlet runner bean, *Phaseolus multiflorus*. This is planted more for the large, edible beans than as a decoration, but the small, crinkled peas are poppy red—a color men like—and they look very gay among the bright green leaves. Like the hyacinth bean, it has clean, fresh foliage and no pests that I know of. One year I planted the scarlet runner early in May, and the vines were in bloom by the Fourth of July. Perhaps I did not give it enough sun, but as it grew for me, it did not live up to its name, for the flowers were few. The Aztec bean, said to have been found still viable in prehistoric cliff-dwellings, is a form of the scarlet runner.

Dolichos is also closely related to kudzu, for which I never like to miss a chance to say a bad word. When we went to live in Raleigh, a thin little vine, with small lilac flowers and large coarse leaves, was growing beside the barn.

No one thought to uproot it, as no one knew what it was, and as it grew it seemed a nice vine for a barn. It was not until it had taken over one end of the garden that we realized our fatal mistake. Every year the vines had to be torn off of trees and shrubs, and the tuberous roots dug out of the ground—as I remember them, the tubers were as big around as sweet potatoes and yards long. We never succeeded in getting them all up, and when we moved away the kudzu was still returning in full force every spring.

October 6, 1957

Sundials

The silence of sundials is suited to the stillness of gardens, where "time passes softly and no man knows." Charles Lamb says that the dial is "a measure appropriate for sweet plants and flowers to spring by." It tells the time without making a sound, "while on still wheels the hours softly turn." Without speaking it is understood; but it does not speak to the blind.

Hazlitt wanted sunflowers near his dial, and the buzzing of bees to make the silence more profound, but I like herbs near mine because both need the sun. The sundial in my garden stands in a bed of thyme. Children think this is very funny, for they love puns. So did the early dial makers: they liked to engrave a fly on the dial's face because the hours fly. A favorite inscription was: We must Die All, or simply We must——, leaving the dial to speak for itself.

No one knows when men learned to tell time by a shadow—perhaps the Babylonians thought of it four thousand years ago—but at least we know that God turned back the shadow ten degrees on the dial of Ahaz as a sign that he had lengthened the life of King Hezekiah. Old dials call this to mind: "It is a light thing for the shadow to go down ten degrees; Nay, but let the shadow return backwards ten degrees."

The association of sundials with churches is long and intimate. Before there were clocks, the dial on the church wall let the people know when it was time for the service to begin, and gave their spiritual pastors and masters an opportunity to moralize on the brevity of our mortal lives.

Gardens as well as churches can make use of more than one dial. It is not every garden that can afford a spot where the sun shines through all of the hours marked on the dial, from six o'clock in the morning until six in the evening, but there must be very few in which the sun does not shine on some spot at the beginning and at the end of the unclouded days. Vertical dials are made for east- and west-facing walls, and an old motto might be divided between the two. For the eastern one: At the rising of the sun—hope; and for the western one: At the setting of the sun—peace.

The way a dial is placed is more important than its design. There are charming reproductions of elaborate old dials, but a simple one on a plain pedestal will mark the time as well, and make a dignified garden ornament if it has a proper setting. It must be in a part of the garden where it is an integral feature of the design, preferably in the center. A good place is where two paths come together. It needs a suitable base of stone or brick, and should be raised a step or more above the ground level.

The hours are the daughters of the sun, and the dial says

I the sun my father call
But am a shadow after all.

Some legends stress the light: "I count the bright hours only"; and "The shadow passes, light remains." Others stress the dark finger: "Shadows we are and like shadows we depart"; or "Every day brings death nearer." For my own sundial I chose: "*Amicis Quaelibet Hora*" (To friends—any hour they please).

October 19, 1958

Silent Spring

As a gardener, I must have my say about *Silent Spring* (Houghton Mifflin, $5.00), Rachel Carson's argument for control of dangerous pesticides. I am in sympathy with Miss Carson. Before writing this, I made sure that the book is in the public library (and I hope in the branches, though I didn't check). It should be read.

The reason I am against poisonous sprays in the garden is they make me nervous. "Avoid contact with eyes, skin and clothing," the containers caution, but this is more easily said than done. Once when I was measuring, the stuff splashed up into my face. "Avoid spray drift" but the wind is swifter than I, and I have yet to find a windless day that is fit for spraying. I would rather share my garden with the bugs than worry about being poisoned. Like Miss Carson, I feel that the chance of being poisoned (even if it is a remote chance) is too high a price to pay for a mosquito-less patio.

With a not very open mind I have read all of the arguments that I could find against the book. Naturally chemical companies don't like it, but they are not the only ones who consider it one-sided. The writer of an unsigned editorial in the monthly *News of the Pennsylvania Horticultural Society* says, "We feel there are a few factors which must be pointed out. First of all," he says, "the author gives the impression that scientists, especially those who have been involved in pest control research, are a radical, nonthinking, irresponsible group. This is not so."

Miss Carson does not give me that impression. She is a scientist, herself, isn't she? I have always thought of biologists as scientists. And the whole book is based on the work of scientists, with fifty-five pages given to listing the principal sources of the scientific information that she spent four years in gathering. When she speaks of the "reckless and irresponsible poisoning of the world," she does not mean that it is done by scientists.

The next argument is that we can't go back to the balance of nature for control of pests. "Without pesticides," the writer of the editorial says, "it would be impossible to feed 180 million Americans and a large part of the world's population."

He must not have read the book very carefully, for Miss Carson says (page 12), "It is not my contention that chemical insecticides must never be used. I do contend that we have put poisonous and biologically potent chemicals indiscriminately into the hands of persons largely or wholly ignorant of their potentials for harm." I know this is true, for I am one of those ignorant persons.

Furthermore, she says, "we have allowed these chemicals to be used with little or no advance investigation of their effect on soil, water, wildlife, and man himself." She also says that the effect of poisons on an animal in a laboratory, the animal being exposed to a single chemical, may be very different from its effect on man, who is subjected to more than one chemical at a time.

What Miss Carson's detractors overlook is that, far from expecting nature to balance itself, she believes in using the "truly extraordinary variety of alternatives to the chemical control of insects. Some are already in use and have achieved brilliant success. Others are in the stage of laboratory testing." She considers these methods (all biological) not only safe, but very much more efficient than chemicals.

Miss Carson's word to gardeners is that "for most of us, mass spraying is of less importance than the innumerable small-scale exposures to which we are subjected day after day, year after year. . . . Each of these recurrent exposures, no matter how slight, contributes to the progressive buildup of chemicals in our bodies and so to cumulative poisoning."

Even my friend of the Pennsylvania Horticultural Society says that it is vastly important to use any chemical "only when necessary and only to the extent necessary. Spraying should never become a Saturday morning ritual." He doesn't seem to realize that it has become a Saturday morning ritual!

"Most serious of all," he adds, "is Miss Carson's charge that the actions of modern chemicals are irreversible. All forms of life are interdependent, and we cannot continually destroy more than we build. If Rachel Carson has made us more conscious of this fact, she will have accomplished much."

Which side is he on?

October 28, 1962

In Fruit and in Flower

One of the things I like best at the fall flower show is the display of fruits and berries: nandina and pyracantha and holly in profusion, of course, the lovely young green cones of the deodar, glowing pomegranates, the turquoise berry, and the French mulberry (*Callicarpa americana*). Then there is always something I have never seen before—this year it was the Amur honeysuckle, *Lonicera maackii*. It is a deciduous shrub, but like *Lonicera fragrantissima* it holds its leaves until midwinter.

As the leaves lie flat, and the red berries are borne above them, the fresh green of the foliage adds to the brilliance of the fruit. The berries are as shining as glass, and very freely borne, especially in the form *podocarpa*. Fragrant white flowers come at the end of May. The Amur honeysuckle is a large and fast-growing shrub, to fifteen feet tall with an equal spread. It needs sun, and must be pruned to keep it in shape.

Another thing that interested me was a branch of *Ilex crenata* 'Convexa' loaded with handsome black berries. I had never before thought that they added to the beauty of the shrub, but perhaps they are particularly good in this variety.

In *Trees of the Southeastern States*, the authors, Coker and Totten, say they have never seen a wild plant of *Rhamnus caroliniana*, the Indian cherry, though it grows well in the arboretum at Chapel Hill. This fall I saw one in a hedgerow where it had been sown by the birds. In October the leaves were still green. The berries were bright red, but they turn black as they ripen, and then they are sweet to taste. To dream of the Indian cherry means that misfortune is on the way, so I am trying to put it out of my mind.

Another native shrub with brilliant fruit is the American cranberry-bush, *Viburnum trilobum*. It is beautiful when the corymbs of white flowers are in bloom in the spring (April, as I remember), and again in fall when bunches of red berries hang from the branches. According to the books the fruits hang all winter, as the birds will not touch them, but Mrs. French says they are soon devoured in her garden in Gastonia. In my garden, the chokeberries are the only ones left until spring, but I cannot complain of this, as it is the birds that the fruiting shrubs are planted for.

Although birds love the beautiful frosted berries of *Elaeagnus umbellata*, the gardener is allowed to enjoy them first. Caroline Dormon sent me a small seedling of this, with directions to give it to someone with a larger garden than mine, but I am going to squeeze it in somehow and hope that it will get enough sun to make it fruit. In my Raleigh garden where the birds kept me well supplied with plants, they were under the oaks, and the silvery flowers came with the silvery leaves, but there was never any fruit.

The cotoneasters are outstanding for the brilliance of their berries, but in my garden *Cotoneaster lacteus* is the only one of the evergreen species that has not had fire blight. It is a handsome, very large shrub, but the berries are not as beautiful as those of *Cotoneaster henryanus* and *C. salicifolius floccosus*. I think the latter is the most beautiful berried evergreen that I have ever seen.

In the clerodendrums, the calyx is as showy as the fruit. When the bright blue berries and the rosy calyces of *Clerodendrum trichotomum* are fully colored they are quite spectacular. The large bunches of sweet-smelling flowers are nice to have in the garden the latter part of July, and the fruit colors in September or October. This species is sometimes a shrub, but usually a small tree. It has one bad feature. It suckers ferociously.

I like to have something in fruit as well as in flower at all seasons of the year, and so I try to keep on hand mahonias for the grape-like bunches of berries in spring, the rowan tree for summer, and as many shrubs as possible for berries in fall and winter.

October 27, 1963

St. Luke's Summer

Yet, for a moment, in these dying days,
   St. Luke will bring his little Summer, when
Faith may restore the tired hearts of men,
   Ready to doubt but readier to believe.
Oh sweet St. Luke, so happy to deceive!
—V. Sackville-West, *The Garden*

The feast of Saint Luke is on the eighteenth of October, when the weather is apt to be clear and warm after the equinoctial storms, a "golden revival, in a last reprieve," like a return of summer before cold weather begins. It is like Saint Martin's summer (around the eleventh of November) except it is earlier and warmer, and even more flowering.

This year, Saint Luke's summer came early; it began in late September when the mocking bird was starting to sing again, and the air was filled with the scent of the tea olives. There were three kinds in bloom at once; the sweet olive (*Osmanthus fragrans*), Fortune's tea olive, and the San José tea olive. I love the way fall begins with fragrance.

The cool nights and sunny days bring a last burst of bloom. No matter how much I pull it up in summer, the borders are blue with eupatorium, and I am glad to have it, for it is pretty with the pink of sultana and the hardy begonia. The porcelain white Korean daisies spill into the path, colchicums like large lilac tulips bloom in clumps in the shade, and under the stewartia the ground is sprinkled with tiny pink cyclamens.

Butterflies always appear during Saint Luke's summer. I don't know their names, but two large golden ones have been fluttering about for days. Bees have been as busy in the tea plant, which is unusually full of bloom this fall. I doubt whether I would have put a tea plant by the front door if the delightful evergreens that fill the nurseries now had been available sixteen years ago. And yet, I could not find a shrub that would suit the spot better, for it is low and spreading (between five and six feet high and wider than tall) and has an open, informal habit. Some plants get much taller; I remember one at Fruitland that was well on to twenty feet. The small white flowers and the lovely round white buds are not well presented on the branches, as they are under the leaves. I like to cut a branch and put it in a green glass bottle, and turn it so that the flowers and buds will show. The tea plant is at its best in moist shady places, but it will grow in dry soil and in full sun.

The seedling sasanquas in the hedge are always the first to bloom, and this year the next one was 'Velvety', one of Mr. Sawada's introductions, with a large single flower of a bright Tyrian rose. The seedlings fruit very freely, and just as the first buds begin to open, the fruits turn a warm soft red. They are almost as pretty as crab apples.

For many years a number of choice little bulbs have bloomed for me in September. *Sternbergia lutea* always seems unbelievably golden, as bright and as highly polished as a buttercup. It has not increased much, and it does not bloom freely—perhaps that is why I value the flowers as I do.

Oxalis bowieana is the handsomest of the wood sorrels. The flowers are large and of a clear bright rose color that is especially desirable so late in the year. The light green leaves are very large, to nearly four inches across, with almost round leaflets. I have mentioned the cyclamens already, and of course everyone has the charming white fairy lily in quantity, and the fall-flowering crocuses should be coming along soon if the chipmunks haven't eaten all of the corms.

Some of the summer flowers bloom on and on as if the season had not come to an end. *Salvia splendens* 'Evening Glow', has been in bloom since early June and seems to get even better as the cool weather comes. It is the best of the new introductions among the annuals, and I hope I can get plants again next year. I would certainly not be enterprising enough to raise it from the seed.

In spite of the warm bright days, the air seems chilly even before the sun sets, and I am reminded of the old motto for sundials: It is later than you think.

October 4, 1964

The Georgics

We used to have a cook who was fond of saying, "Life is sweet." I thought of her while I was sitting on the terrace one cool summer morning, reading the *Georgics*, and looking up now and then to enjoy the sunlight on the summer flowers. I was checking the references in *The Plants of Virgil's Georgics*, a commentary, with woodcuts by Elfriede Abbe, scientific illustrator in the Department of Botany at Cornell University (Cornell University Press, 1965, $7.50). It is a delightful book and the illustrations, done from living plants growing in Italy, have added greatly to my pleasure in it.

"The greater the work, the more is written about it," Miss Abbe says, "and every decade sees at least one new translation and commentary on the *Georgics*—all to the good, for every lover of the soil is rewarded by acquaintance with this classic of rural life." I wish that Saint Mary's, instead of sitting their pupils down to *Omnia Gallia divisa est*, had allowed us to translate *Quid faciat laetas segetes*, "What makes the crops joyous?" As it is, I came to the *Georgics* late in life, when I might have been enjoying it all along.

Although Virgil lived in the land of the olive tree, he writes of plants familiar to southern gardeners, the ivy, the box and the yew, and of flowers dear to all gardeners, the lily, the rose, and the violet. Miss Abbe takes Virgil's lily to be *Lilium candidum*. It grew in the garden of the old Corycian who in his worthless patch of ground had planted pot herbs along with poppies and vervain and white lilies. With honey from his own hives, and wine from his own vines, the old man sat in the shade of his plane tree, and thought himself a king. And his plane tree was already tall enough to sit under when he transplanted it.

The old Corycian picked fresh acanthus leaves soon after the plant had been frozen to the ground. In my garden, too, new foliage comes up whenever we have warm weather in winter. The species is *Acanthus mollis*, and mollis, which means soft, is the very word Virgil uses in describing the leaves. Acanthus is a bee plant, as most of Virgil's flowers are. It does not flower with me every year, but only after fairly mild winters. Just for the foliage, I consider it one of the handsomest plants I have.

The herbs of the *Georgics* are savory, saffron and smallage; rosemary and thyme; and balm and endive. All for the bees. Wild thyme, fragrant from afar, should be planted, Virgil says, and plenty of strong-smelling savory; and gardens should welcome bees with the breath of saffron flowers. Lemon balm is called melissa, from the Greek word for bee, because bees delight in it. And so, when bees begin to swarm, the crushed leaves should be scattered in the places where it is best for them to settle. When Virgil calls the yew injurious, he means that it is poisonous, and for that reason it should not be planted near bee hives. Dioscorides thought there was danger even in sitting in its shade.

John Martyn (in his commentary) takes the dark ivy to be the typical *Hedera helix*, which has black berries, and the pale ivy to be the variety 'Chrysocarpa', which has yellow berries. And the poet notes that box loves slopes. How pleasant it is, he says, to see the waving box on Mount Cyrtorus.

Buxus, taxus, hedera, lilium, viola, rosa—most of the plant names in the *Georgics* are the ones we still use, but sometimes Virgil uses a specific name for the genus. His *ilex*, for example, is not holly; it is the holly oak, *Quercus ilex*. *Ornus* is *Fraxinus ornus*, and *cerasus* is *Prunus cerasus*. A few names are given to entirely different plants from the ones that bear them now; *aesculus* is not the horse chestnut, it is the chestnut oak; *cytisus* is not broom, it is a shrubby trefoil; and *cassia* is not what we know as cassia, it is the garland flower, *Daphne cneorum*.

Some names will always be in doubt—Miss Abbe does not claim that her conclusions are definitive. And there is one plant, called siler, that no one has ever been able to identify. I am grateful to Miss Abbe for writing this book, and giving me such a pleasant task on a summer morning.

October 31, 1965

Potting up Tulips

My sister has decided to grow some tulips in pots to bloom on the terrace next spring. She thought all she needed to do was to plant the bulbs in pots and set the pots on the terrace for the winter. I told her I thought they would have to go in the ground, and that I would look for directions.

No one seems to consider leaving pots outdoors to bloom outdoors, but in her book *Hardy Garden Bulbs* (which is in the public library), Gertrude Wister gives detailed directions for leaving them out while the bulbs are growing roots, and then bringing them indoors to force. She says the pots should be set in a trench, on a layer of small stones, in a well-drained and shady place. Pack leaves or peat moss around the pots, and pile a deep layer of leaves or straw over the whole thing. Set the pots on a cool day, Mrs. Wister says, but do not cover them entirely until cold weather. An 18-inch mulch, extended beyond the borders of the trench, insulates against mild as well as cold weather. Hold the mulch in place with branches or wire.

As I do not think my sister is likely to dig a trench, I asked Ted Washington, at Hastings, if she couldn't simply sink the pots in the ground, with some small stones under them. He said he thought she could, and that the bulbs should be potted in November, at the time they are ordinarily planted in the garden. "Your sister can put them on the terrace in February," he said, "but once they are out of the ground she will have to keep them watered." If a heavy mulch were used, it would have to be removed gradually to allow the top growth to begin.

Mrs. Wister says the pots should be covered with hardware cloth to protect them from rodents. As I often find that it is difficult to get the materials recommended in books, I called a couple of hardware stores to see whether they have hardware cloth. Both have it. But you have to ask twice. The first time they say no, but the second time they look on the shelf, and there it is.

Mrs. Wister says hardware cloth can be used to cover bulbs planted in the garden to keep the squirrels and chipmunks from digging them up before the ground freezes. This is all right for her garden in Philadelphia, but the ground doesn't freeze much here, so it would have to be left on all winter. She says napthalene scattered around bulbs discourages the rodents, but it has to be renewed, and she doesn't think it does much good anyway.

Last year, the chipmunks, or squirrels, or both, dug up and ate most of the tulips that I planted. It wouldn't be practical for me to cover them with wire or cloth, as I have them tucked in among other plants. I thought I would try dusting the bulbs with red lead dust, as I had read somewhere that that is effective. I spent most of a morning in search of it. The seed stores and hardware stores had never heard of it, so I called the Charlotte Drug Co., which never fails me, and they said to call the chemical people.

After calling several I got hold of someone who looked it up in a book and said I must ask for lead oxide, and he thought Allied Chemicals might have it. At first they said they didn't, but then they looked on the shelf and said yes, they had one pound. I said I would take it, and then began to worry. I asked the chemist whether it is poison. "Of course," he said, "you know all lead is poisonous. You must wear gloves when you use it, and be careful not to breathe it or let it touch your skin. And it isn't a thing you would leave lying about."

So I decided to go back to napthalene flakes. Washington thinks better of them than Mrs. Wister does. He says he thinks I can get them at Eckerds. I looked in my files and found directions for applying them: "Sprinkle about half a teaspoonful over each bulb, after it has been set, and before it is covered. Do not put it under the bulb." Perhaps if this is done it will last long enough to do some good. But Mrs. Wister says too much will injure the bulbs. Another note in my files says to apply two ounces to a square yard and work in four inches deep.

October 15, 1967

The Blue Wonder

Mysteries are continually arising to divert gardeners. One just turned up in a letter from Sam Caldwell. "Please look at the enclosed slide," he wrote, "and see if you know what this flower is."

I looked and found a tall spike of pale blue-violet flowers, close together in the bud, but the wide open lower ones well separated and on pedicels more than an inch long. I hadn't the faintest idea what it could be, but when I turned to the letter and found that it had come from Mississippi, and had bloomed only once in seven years, I remembered some correspondence I had with Mrs. James Dormon (during the Second World

War) about the blue wonder lily that Eudora Welty got from an advertisement in the *Mississippi Market Bulletin*.

Eudora said it had never bloomed so she was still wondering. "I, too, am still wondering," Mrs. Dormon wrote when I told her about it. "Perhaps it is the seven-year hyacinth, *Scilla hyacinthoides*, found in old gardens. It is said to bloom every seven years."

Scilla hyacinthoides comes from the Mediterranean region, and has been in cultivation since 1585. At one time it was grown by California nurserymen. Cecil Houdyshel listed it for the first time in his little catalogue for fall 1941. "We were long doubtful of the identity of this rare species," he says. "It is one of the finest bulbs for the outside garden as it is perfectly winter hardy in the north. It is a strong grower, and will even recover if left out of the ground a year. Take my advice and plant it."

I took his advice, but it never bloomed for me. Later it did bloom for Eudora, and Elsie Hassan wrote that it bloomed for her in Alabama. Elsie said she had it from an old lady, and she wintered it in a tub. I have since read that it needs a thorough baking in summer, or else the bulbs must be taken up and dried for a few days in the sun. When left in the ground, I suppose, it blooms only those years when the summer before has been sufficiently dry.

Well, I think the mystery of the seven-year hyacinth has been solved, but I told Sam to send the slide to Caroline Dormon if there is any further doubt.

In the meantime Sam has solved a mystery for me. For a number of years most of the scapes of my red spider lilies (*Lycoris radiata*) have been blighted in the bud. I sent him one of these deformed flowerheads and he said it was swarming with thrips. I am sure the thrips are the trouble, but why should they suddenly attack the red spider lily, which I have grown since I was a little girl, and never known to have thrips or anything else. It is odd, too, Sam says, that they should attack the red ones and leave the pale ones alone, as they usually prefer the light to the dark colors, which I have found to be true with day lilies.

Sam says this has been a wonderful lycoris season in his garden in Nashville: "Several new crosses have bloomed for the first time. If I can get around to digging and mailing, I'll send you a few bulbs of my *L. radiata x sprengeri* which Dr. Hamilton Traub named *L. x jacksoniana*. This is my first and probably my best cross. There are pretty pink, rose, and ruby flowers, mostly with blue tints. They multiply fairly fast, and I have a lot of them now; I'd like to know how they perform in different localities." I hope he gets around to it, and I hope this and his other delightful lycorises will soon begin to seep into the trade. He showed fascinating slides of his collection when the Daffodil Society met in Nashville last spring.

In my garden this was the best year yet for *Lycoris caldwellii*, Sam's namesake, which Wyndham Hayward imported from Shanghai, as *L. aurea*, in 1948 just before the Communists took over in China. The bulb Mr. Hayward gave me fourteen years ago has become a very crowded clump, and I am sure I should divide it, but I am afraid to as long as it is doing so well: in mid-August it produced nine scapes with six peach-colored buds to an umbel. The flowers are a pale yellow that fades to cream. They come into bloom just as *Lycoris squamigera* is going, and just as *L. radiata* 'Alba' is beginning. *L. radiata* follows, and last of all (if it blooms) the golden *L. traubii*, giving continuous bloom from July into October.

October 12, 1969

International Growers' Exchange

The fall bulletin of the International Growers' Exchange came the first of October and I am writing about it at the earliest opportunity, as they ship plants only until November 15. Bulbs, I suppose, can be sent later. In a letter to customers, John Riordan says the old catalogue, *The Wide, Wide World of Bulbs and Plants*, is still in effect but a revision will be begun in 1970. It will be sent only to subscribers and will be good for three years. The price includes all addenda, supplements, price changes, and clearance sale bulletins.

The secretary says his pet peeve is, "Many of our good friends send us order after order for the rare and elusive items we offer, many of them not available elsewhere; but when it comes to the common items, they resort to their local chain store, garden center or what have you." I must be one of his most annoying customers, as I have ordered the rare things and nothing else for nearly 20 years. But he still puts up with me.

Few gardeners I should think, would order plants that they can get locally without the expense of shipping, which is not negligible. But the Growers' Exchange is the only retail source I know for many rare plants and bulbs from this country and the rest of the world.

In the fall bulletin there is a "choice selection of hardy perennials from Ohio's best grower." One is the beautiful, early-flowering phlox, 'Miss Lingard'. It begins to bloom about the middle of May, continues for a month or more, and will bloom at intervals throughout the summer if the dead flowerheads are clipped. 'Miss Lingard' is one of a series of crosses made in Europe of our native *Phlox carolina*, and known to horticulture as *Phlox suffruticosa*. The flowers are white and shining, with a pale pink center; the leaves thick and glossy; the stems to four feet. I have always wondered who Miss Lingard was. I think of her as painted by Sargent, tall and slender, playing croquet in a white muslin dress.

I was pleased to find *Thalictrum dipterocarpum* again. I haven't had it since the Raleigh days. In *Aristocrats of the Garden*, Ernest Wilson, who brought it to us from Western China in 1906, describes this species as "one of the loveliest herbs imaginable. It grows from eight to ten feet tall and the flower stems are very much branched and bear relatively large lavender-purple flowers in great quantity. The leaves are broad and much divided and the whole habit and appearance of the plant is elegant and graceful. It requires a good, well-drained soil, is fond of lime, and revels in sunshine." It grows only to three or four feet with us, and in Raleigh it bloomed in late May and early June. I also ordered 'Illuminator', a yellow-flowered meadow-rue, which will probably prove to be a form of *Thalictrum glaucum*.

Salvia nemorosa is another perennial that I haven't seen for many years. Its origin is uncertain and its names confusing. It is now known as *Salvia x superba* but was formerly considered a variety of *S. virgata*. It bloomed in Raleigh in May. I failed to note the length of the season, but it is said to bloom all summer. The Growers' Exchange lists a variety called 'East Friesland', a recent introduction from Europe. The flowers are an intense violet, and the red bracts persist when the flowers fall.

This is the first source I have found for the asphodel, *Asphodeline lutea*, since Henry Kohankie went out of business on a sad day for gardeners many years ago. Even so, I don't think I shall try it again, for Mr. Kohankie's perished at once and I have twice lost plants I brought back from Marion Becker's garden in Cincinnati. I have never yet seen it in bloom. The foliage is rushlike, and silver filigree, and beautiful all winter, but it disappears with hot weather and that is the end. The asphodel seems to do well in northern gardens and perhaps would do in the southern mountains.

October 19, 1969

Grapes

In her column in the August *Ozark Gardens*, Virginia Dahlke (Minnesota) says, "The pole by the pump which supported a wild grape vine was broken off in a summer storm. I'll miss that old vine, though all it was good for was the perfume of its blossoms."

I take this to be the riverbank grape, *Vitis riparia*, native from Canada to Florida and Texas. Its fruits are worthless, but Louise Beebe Wilder thought the scent of the tiny flowers "one of the most precious perfumes of the year. . . . As you walk or ride along the early summer roads, especially at night, you are suddenly enveloped, caught up so to speak, among tendrils of exquisite fragrance, indescribably gentle yet searching." She thought box, lilac and wild grape the most memory stirring of all fragrances.

She couldn't understand why Thoreau wrote on June 19, "The grape is in bloom, an agreeable perfume to many; not to me." But reactions to scents vary greatly; hawthorn, for example, is delicious to some, deathly to others. The flowers of the frost grape, *Vitis vulpina*, and of *Vitis californica* are also very fragrant. "There are doubtless others," Mrs. Wilder says, but I have not come across them.

One autumn Caroline Dormon wrote, "Wild sand hill grapes are ripe, and as beautiful as flowers, in addition to being delicious. And we've had rain and are enjoying a cool spell. I wish I had time to roam the hills and eat grapes. The fruit on no two vines has the same flavor."

Caroline says the Norsemen called America Vineland because we have so many native species of grapes. In the *Manual of the Vascular Flora* seven species are recognized in the Carolinas. From one of these, the fox grape, *Vitis labrusca*, a number of cultivated varieties such as 'Delaware', 'Concord', and 'Catawba' are derived. The Catawba grape came from Cain Creek in Buncombe County. The flowers of fox grapes are scentless, but the fruit has a musky fragrance. The muscadine, *Vitis rotundifolia*, is found in most counties in North Carolina, and ranges all the way from Dare to Cherokee.

In *The Shrubs and Vines of North Carolina* (1860), Rev. M. A. Curtis describes muscadines as "larger and thicker skinned than any of our other grapes, varying in color from whitish through different shades of red and purple to ebony black. The quality of the fruit varies as much as its color, being now of a sharp acid flavor, and again of a luscious sweetness." He says that the scuppernong, an amber-fruited variety of muscadine, was not found on Roanoke Island but comes from East Carolina. Two stories of its origin have been told to him, and it seems to me probable that both are true.

"Two men of the name of Alexander," Rev. E. M. Forges said, "while clearing land near Columbia, the county seat of Tyrrell, which stands on the east side of the Scuppernong River, discovered this grape, and were so much pleased with it that they preserved the vine and the tree upon which it grew. That was the vine I saw, from which other vines were propagated. They called it the White Grape, and from it made what they called country wine. This is the history given by a granddaughter of one of the discoverers, who was alive when I first went to scuppernong."

The other story came from C. L. Hunter of Lincoln, "who gave much attention to the history of our grapes." He told Curtis that according to tradition "about the year 1774, Rev. Charles Pettigrew found the scuppernong on the low grounds of Scuppernong River, and planted out several vines."

"Some of the dark muscadines," Curtis said, "have been brought under culture and are very nearly as luscious as the Scuppernong." Modern varieties of Scuppernong, U.S.D.A. introductions from Meridian, Mississippi, and other varieties of muscadines are found in the fall catalogues.

October 4, 1970

Solomon's Seal

Years ago I got a plant labelled *Polygonatum sibiricum* from the Gardenside Nurseries in Shelbourne, Vermont. I have never found a reference to any such species, so I think it must be a form of the European Solomon's seal, *Polygonatum multiflorum*, native to England also, but more frequently found in gardens than in the wild.

My plant blooms in April. It has made a nice clump now, with arching stalks to three feet tall, with one or several flowers hanging from each leaf axil, or as Turner said (in 1562), "about the springes of every leaf." I never thought to smell the little greenish bells—they look so cool and scentless, but I shall certainly do so next spring, for they are sometimes described as fragrant, and Eleanour Sinclair Rohde gives *Polygonatum officinale* a prominent place in the scented garden.

The common name is the same in England and the Latin countries, being a translation of *sigillum Solomonis*, Solomon having set his seal upon the root to let all men know its medicinal value. It is also associated with the Virgin, and called Our Lady's or Saint Mary's seal, *sigillum Mariae*. David's harp is another old name, and Parkinson says some call it ladder to heaven. Britton and Brown add sealwort and conquer-John.

Gerard agrees with Dioscorides "That the roots are excellent good for to seale or close up greene wounds, being stamped and laid thereon; whereupon it was called *Sigillum Salomonis*, of the singular vertue that it hath in sealing or healing up wounds, broken bones and such like." He adds that it "taketh away in one night, or two at the most, any bruise, blacke or blew spots gotten by falls or womens wilfulnesse, in stumbling upon their hasty husbands fists, or such like." At the end of the nineteenth century Anne Pratt wrote that the use of the root to remove bruises was still practiced in country places, and that she herself had often witnessed the success of the remedy.

Gerard found the taste of the berries sweet and pleasant, but elsewhere I have read that they are emetic. The starchy roots have been used to make bread, and the young shoots cooked as a vegetable. "The diluted water of the whole plant," another herbalist writes, "used to the face or other parts of the skin, cleanses it from freckles, spots or any marks whatever, leaving the place fresh, fair, and lovely."

Our native Solomon's seal, *Polygonatum biflorum*, is supposed to have all of the virtues of the European species, and I think it is still used as a medicinal herb in the southern mountains, for I find it advertised in the market bulletins along with mullein, catnip, penny royal, and wild cherry bark.

Dr. H. E. Ahies considers the giant Solomon's seal, *Polygonatum commutatum*, "hardly worthy of specific recognition," but it is listed under its own name by the Gardens of the Blue Ridge and other wild flower nurseries. Although it prefers moist ground, and grows along streams, we found a clump in our very dry scrap of woods when we first came to Charlotte. It was accidentally destroyed when the underbrush was cleared out, and I had difficulty in getting new plants established. They are flourishing at present. The five-foot stalks with their large ovate leaves, alternate and evenly spaced, make very sturdy ladders until they are weighted down in September by the large dark blue berries. The flowers bloom for me in May. Botanists allow for as many as eight to a bunch but by count I find only four or five springing from the lowest leaves, petering out to one near the top.

October 11, 1970

A Hummingbird and a Hammock

While we were having lunch on the terrace one day in early October, a hummingbird discovered the pineapple sage blooming by the terrace steps, and hovered over it, and kept coming back even though we were so near. It made small, shrill, almost inaudible sounds. "The Rubythroat needs no song," Chapman says. "Its beauty gives it distinction and its wings make music. Its only note, so far as I know, is a squeak, expressive of distrust or excitement." My hummingbird's body was a shimmering metallic-green, but it had no red at its throat, and so it was either a female or an immature male—a matron, I thought, as it was rather portly.

The pineapple sage, *Salvia rutilans*, is a tender perennial of uncertain origin. It is said to bloom the first year from seed, but it is easier for me to buy a plant from the greenhouse to put out in the spring. I plant it in the same place every year, where I can brush against the fragrant leaves all summer, and watch the low morning sun light up the slender carmine trumpets from late September to frost—usually in November.

"Potted plants of the pineapple sage have a more concentrated aroma than those in the open air," Eleanor Chalfin says; "the fruity scent dominates a small greenhouse, and winter plants—when in an ornate mood—

blossom with an unusual magnificence." I was surprised to find that she includes it with the useful herbs, "because the leaves may be added to jams, jellies and stewed fruits, as well as to potpourri."

Because they were unavailable in Charlotte I used to get plants from the Merry Gardens in the spring, and I would get *Salvia dorisiana* at the same time. *S. dorisiana* has leaves as large and as velvety as those of the peppermint geranium. Mrs. Chalfin used to say that they smell of ripe fruit and rose petals, and she called it the rose scented sage. A summer in the garden does not give it time to bloom before frost cuts it down, but it will bloom indoors, and the flowers are pink. I believe it is the best scent of any leaf I know—except, of course, lemon verbena.

Salvia rutilans is listed in *Hortus Second* as possibly a form of *Salvia splendens*, but they are unlike. *S. rutilans* is more of a shrub—to four feet tall, and wide spreading—and the long, slender, pineapple-scented flower stalks are not at all like those of the gaudy scarlet sage.

In the midst of the September drought, as I was turning one morning from Sharon Road into Sharon Lane, I found myself face to face with a stunning example of Victorian bedding-out. It was a round bed with a large central clump of tall spectrum-red cannas encircled by fireman's-red scarlet sage. Between the two fires were slender spires of ice-cold tuberoses. The circle was edged with dark green liriope, which made a pleasant contrast with the wide wine-tinted leaves of the cannas. After all those dry weeks, the flowers and their foliage were just as fresh as if they had been through a rainy season.

The traffic did not allow me to do it justice, and as I drove on I thought how Ida D. Bennett would have approved—only she would have edged the bed with alyssum 'Little Gem' instead of liriope. In *The Flower Garden*, published in 1903, she gives directions for planting beds of cannas, scarlet sage, castor beans, and caladiums. Such beds, she says, are "rich in tropical effects and give more distinction in a lawn than any other class of plants. On a small city lawn not more than one such bed should be allowed. On a large lawn three will give a better effect than a great number." When she has leisure, the amateur gardener will study these from the vantage point of the hammock, "noting all the peculiarities of plant growth that escape her when busy with trowel and watering-pot, so that the view from it should be the first consideration."

I believe the lawn on Sharon Road was perfect except for the lack of a hammock.

October 25, 1970

J∿ NOVEMBER

. . . .

Colchicum

When I was a child, my grandmother used to buy colchicum bulbs from the five-and-ten and lay them in the library to bloom. The way the pale, attenuated flowers came out of the dry bulbs was as wonderful to me as the unfurling of those little paper flowers that are released from a shell when it is dropped into a glass of water.

My grandmother would plant the bulbs after the flowers had faded, and another year they would bloom in the garden. It is in the garden, where they belong, that colchicum should bloom—yet they are seen there so seldom that I used to think that they would not grow in the South.

I was delighted to find that they are as satisfactory as daffodils if the bulbs are planted in partial shade with plenty of humus, and good drainage, and not more than three or four inches deep. They should be ordered in mid-summer and planted as soon as they come—preferably early in August, but imported bulbs are seldom available before September, and then sometimes the buds have already sprouted. When they are put in the ground, the flowers open promptly, but of course they are not so beautiful as when the bulbs are planted at the proper time. Once planted, they can be left undisturbed for years, unless you want to take them up and divide them. This should be done soon after the leaves die down.

Those who see the frail autumnal flowers for the first time are warned that these "naked nannies" are followed in the spring by large coarse foliage that may overshadow small early flowers, and may be objectionable when they turn yellow later on. In my garden I rather like the fresh, bold leaves, and in our hot climate they die down so quickly as not to be unsightly very long.

Colchicum has a long history as a medicine and a poison. The name comes from a part of Asia Minor once known as Colchis, the home of Medea, and the seat of the gentle art of poisoning. Theophrastus says that slaves, when too hard pressed, often staged a sit-down strike by taking the drug, a slow poison that caused a lingering death. When the pressure let up, they hastily took an antidote. Only sometimes they miscalculated, and outwitted themselves as well as their masters.

The flowers are described as crocus-like, but to me they are much more like tulips, and like tulips, they belong to the lily family. Some of them are as large as tulips. When the flowers open wide, they measure eight inches across. They are stemless, but their stem-like tubes are up to twelve inches long. The tubes are of a translucent whiteness that gives the flowers a look of unreality.

The showiest kinds are the large-flowered hybrids. One called 'The Giant' is the biggest. It is late-flowering, white at the base, with finely checkered, lilac petals. 'Autumn Queen' is large and early, and of the red violet color known as Matthew's purple. It bloomed once on the fourth of August. 'Violet Queen' is pansy violet, with white lines down the center of the petals forming a star. I wish there were not so many queens among the flowers. It is so confusing. 'Autumn Wonder' is the last to bloom. It comes at the end of September or early in October, is very free flowering, and one of the best. The finest of all is *Colchicum speciosum* 'Album', like a large, fall-flowering, pure white tulip. Unfortunately it is seldom offered in this country, but gardening would not be so much fun if there were not always something to search for.

Although not so spectacular as these hybrids, the small mauve flowers of *C. autumnale* are dependable, plentiful, and especially welcome, for the various forms bloom over a long season. The cultivar 'Majus' is the earliest, coming at the end of August, and the double form is the latest. It seldom blooms before October. There is also a silvery white one which comes at the end of September and blooms on for a long time.

November 10, 1957

Biennials

Biennials bloom when spring is already over, and summer is yet to come. Their charming names, foxglove, columbine, Canterbury bells, sweet rocket, and sweet William, have been part of the poetry of gardeners for hundreds of years. In *The Lady of the Lake*, Scott wrote of

Foxglove and night-shade, side by side,
Emblems of punishments and pride. . . .

Purple foxgloves must stand for pride, I think, holding themselves so high above the other flowers. The stalks are often five feet tall. In Great Britain, where they flower on hedge banks and may cover an acre or two at the foot of a sea cliff, they have local names such as ladies' thimbles, bloody fingers, and dead-men's-bells. In France they are called Our Lady's gloves.

The connection with foxes is obscure. Some think fox was originally folk, meaning fairy, and glove may be a corruption for glew, which means music. It is nice to think of a garden filled with fairy music, but I prefer to believe that foxes have gloves, and kittens have mittens.

In my garden, foxgloves bloom before the end of April and last more than a month. I buy plants every fall, and take any color I can get, though I like the all-white ones best. I wish I had patience to grow them from seed. Park offers separate colors, 'Yellow Queen', 'White Queen', and 'Rose Queen', as well as the Excelsior hybrids with flowers all around the stem, and the Shirley strain in a mixture of apricot, cream, yellow, pink and heliotrope.

Miss Jekyll liked to plant foxgloves in the wild garden among the ferns with white columbine and the tall stems of the white peach-leaved campanulas, in the woods in a tangle of brambles and wild honeysuckle, and in the borders with meadow sweet and Canterbury bells. The Canterbury bells are too difficult for me, though I sometimes see them in other gardens; and with us they do not bloom until the foxgloves have almost finished. The peach-leaved bellflower blooms earlier and is more satisfactory.

Columbine is the symbol of the seven gifts of the Holy Spirit. It was chosen because the inverted flower is like a circle of doves. There are only five doves to represent the seven gifts, so the Flemish painters added two more when they used it as a device. Columbine is also called *Herba Leonis*, because it is the lion's favorite flower. The ones I like best are the short-spurred kind called granny's sunbonnet. I brought seeds from the Busbees' garden in Raleigh, and I save some every spring and scatter them about. The flowers are pure white, dark blue, or a series of tones of rose and wine. Most gardeners prefer Mrs. Scott Elliott's long-spurred hybrids.

Miss Rohde, who nearly always answers my questions, thinks sweet William takes its name from William the Conqueror—perhaps because it is bearded. I can see no other connection. It is supposed to have been brought to England in the twelfth century by Carthusian monks, but at any rate it was there by the sixteenth century. "Sweet William with his homely cottage smell," usually blooms for us before the middle of April, making a good companion for tulips. Another season it may wait until the tulips are gone. Park advertises the variety 'Messenger', a mixture of bright hues, as blooming two weeks earlier than any other strain; if it does, it would be most desirable.

The violet-scented sweet rocket is called dame's violet because of its fragrance and hesperis because it is sweetest in the evening. I like to put out a few plants every fall, as they are so short-lived as to be practically biennial, and I never want to be without them. The white or violet flowers come into bloom between the end of March and the end of April, and last into July.

Mrs. Shipman used to say that the sequence of bloom moves from early bulbs to flowering trees and shrubs, to biennials, and then to perennials. She was right to stress the importance of the sweet, old-fashioned biennials, for they are essential to continuous bloom, and should not be forgotten when pansies are planted in the fall.

November 1, 1959

Out to Graze

When I was little, my family put me out to graze, without so much as mentioning the fact that some plants are poisonous. I tasted a great variety with no serious consequences, but I did munch a few that made me very uncomfortable for a while.

When I became responsible for two children in the garden, I taught them, as soon as they could walk, never to put any part of any plant in their mouths without asking me first. So far as I know, they never did.

They were obedient children, lacking in intellectual curiosity. I also showed them poison ivy and said, "Leaflets three—let it be." To this they paid no attention at all, and insisted upon playing in a bed of it. They were never seriously poisoned.

I have just gotten a copy of *Poisonous Plants of the United States*, by Walter Conrad Muenscher, which Dr. Totten tells me is the best book on the subject, and I was amazed at the list of common garden plants that are poisonous when eaten. They include aconite (all parts very dangerous), colchicum, lilies of the valley (leaves and flowers), leaves of delphinium, larkspur and foxglove, English ivy (whole plant, especially leaves and berries), poets' narcissus and trumpet daffodil, oleander (all parts very dangerous), opium poppy, and the deadly seeds of the castor-bean.

Checking the text I find that children have been poisoned from eating China berries, leaves and inner bark of black locust, bane-berries, fruits of the spindle tree, elderberry bark and buckeyes. All bulbs of members of the amaryllis family should be kept out of the way of children and animals; also those of two ornithogalums, the common Star-of-Bethlehem and the seldom-planted Chinkerinchee. Herb-doctors take note that people have died of an overdose of tansy tea.

Norman Taylor has a good article on poisonous plants in *The Garden Dictionary*. In addition to some of those mentioned, he lists as really serious poisons: seeds of laburnum, all parts of *Arum maculatum*, Jimsonweed (all parts deadly), the root of the Christmas rose, leaves of laurel and rhododendron, and the leaves and fruits of yew. I cannot find any mention of Carolina jessamine as poisonous when eaten, but I have always understood that it is. Holly berries are reported poisonous, also the rhizomes of bloodroot. All daturas are equally poisonous.

Muenscher lists a hundred plants that cause skin irritation when handled. One of these is trumpet vine. I suppose that is why yardmen call it cow-itch. The most common offenders (I mean those most likely to be met with in gardens) are the tree-of-heaven, *Aralia spinosa*, Jack-in-the-pulpit, borage, box, catalpa, *Clematis virginiana*, colchicum, lily of the valley, showy lady-slipper, larkspur, the juice of a number of euphorbias, including snow-on-the-mountain; Carolina jessamine, fruits of the ginkgo, English ivy, leaves of the Christmas rose if bruised, rhizomes of irises, *Juniperus virginiana*, juice of osage orange, *Sedum acre*, and bloodroot; oleander, roots of May-apple, primroses (some people are very allergic to them), buttercups, poison ivy and poison sumac, and rue.

Fortunately, few people are allergic to most of these. The gas plant is on the list, but when Mrs. White wrote to "Wayside Gardens" to ask if anyone who handled it had been poisoned, they answered that very few had, and those only from handling the seedpods.

As Dr. Muenscher is more interested in the welfare of livestock than that of human beings, I asked Miss Mary Lou Phillips at the Main Branch of the Public Library to check this material for me. She thinks "Fogg's Weeds of Lawn and Garden"; "Poisonous Plants," a pamphlet published by the Virginia Polytechnic Institute; and "American Medicinal Plants of Commercial Importance," a government bulletin, will supplement Dr. Muenscher's book.

Ellen Flood once said she would like to have a garden of fleurs de mal—with all plants in it poisonous. If I had set out to plant such a garden I could hardly have done better, for I have in mine, or have had, nearly every plant that I have listed.

November 29, 1959

Sally Battles

All gardens are friendship gardens and the flowers in them have the names of friends. "Go out and pick me some Sally Battles," my aunt said to me once. "They are down by the sundial—those yellow daisies." I picked a bunch of golden Marguerites, but when I brought them to my aunt, she said indignantly, "No, no! I wanted Sally Battles—those are Sally Bortches!" So I had to go back for coreopsis.

In the late nineteenth century the Countess of Warwick had just such a garden as my aunt's, only she might have said to a young relative, "Bring me the Prince of Wales." And there would be no excuse for picking the wrong flower: every one was marked with the donor's name on a little heart-shaped label.

In *An Old English Garden*, published in 1898, Lady Warwick describes her "Garden of Friendship":

> An apple tree stands, in the middle, up which a brilliant red honey-suckle twines, and all around are the mottoes, and references which tell of that true friendship which the poets sing, which the philosophers find so rare but which still does really exist to help us on the road that "winds uphill all the way—yes, to the very end!" In the book, there is a charming picture of the apple tree, encircled by a rustic bench that looks as if it were made of driftwood, and surrounded by a sea of hearts.

Since there are so many more hearts than plants, I think a number of the "kindly gifts" must have perished.

No matter how many specimens of the same plant were given to the countess, all went into the friendship border, and all were labeled; like Mittie Wellford, she would take anything, and never said, "Thank you, but I have plenty of that." There were three clumps of the common columbine, one from Lady Elcho, another from the Marchioness of Londonderry, and a third from Countess Cadogan. The seven Japanese anemones were from the Countess of Bradford, Madame de Falbé, Countess Howe, the Marchioness of Ormonde, the Lady Willoughby de Broke, Her Royal Highness the Duchess of York—later Queen Mary—and His Royal Highness the Prince of Wales, who became Edward VII. There was also phlox from the garden of Queen Mary's mother, Her Royal Highness the Duchess of Teck.

The flowers presented by dukes and duchesses were for the most part the same ones that grew in my aunt's garden or in the dooryard of any English cottager: snapdragons, bleeding-heart, phlox, meadow rue, delphinium, lemon lilies, lavender, Michaelmas daisies, scabiosa, snow-in-summer (from the Duchess of Leinster), spiderwort, coreopsis, Canterbury bells, sunflowers, black-eyed Susans, baby's-breath, Shasta daisies. But a few were more choice. The Earl of Chesterfield contributed *Delphinium sulphureum* (now called *D. zalil*), recently introduced from Persia. There was also a clump of *Eremurus robustus*, the foxtail lily, never a common perennial, and the recently rediscovered *Shortia galacifolia*, which must have been very rare at that time.

There was a shamrock in the garden, presented by the Countess of Listowell, and edelweiss from Mrs. Menzies—for not all of Lady Warwick's friends were titled. A Mr. Spiro gave her several kinds of spiraea, Mrs. Hartman a poker plant, Mr. Tyndale White a mock orange, and Mrs. Robert Woodhouse had her name on the hearts that stood before gaillardia, baby's breath, sunflower and rock-foil. I would dearly love to know who these Edwardian gardeners were.

From the *Encyclopedia Britannica* I find that the countess was the wife of the fifth earl of Warwick, and "well known in society." In her book she says she was always glad to get away from the distractions of the London season, and back to the fair green world of the country. In her book she invites the reader to wander across the park with her to the garden that she loves.

November 6, 1960

The Musk Rose

I wonder what it is that makes the musk rose so dear to the poet and so celebrated in literature. It cannot be the beauty of the small creamy flowers, perfect though they are in finish, and smooth as a shell. As to their mysterious fragrance, Bean says that the musky odor is faint, and it is said to elude those who come too near, though it fills the house and the yard, and maybe the whole street.

In the days when it was cherished, people liked to plant it against the house and near a window. "Do you remember the great bush by the drawing-room window?" someone asks in one of Mrs. Gaskell's novels, and adds, "That is the old musk-rose, Shakespeare's musk-rose, which is dying out through the kingdom now. The scent is unlike the scent of any other rose, or of any other flower."

I have never been sure what odor of musk is like. To me the rose breathes lemon and spice, but I cannot tell how Keats could single it out among the unseen flowers that perfumed the night as he stood in the darkness listening to the nightingale. Perhaps he didn't really know, but was echoing Shakespeare when he wrote of violet and musk and eglantine.

Bacon thought the scent of the musk rose surpassed that of all flowers except the violet, and he described it as blooming in July when the lime trees are in blossom, but Keats calls it "mid-May's eldest child, the coming musk-rose, full of dewy wine," and it does bloom in May in Hannah Withers's garden.

It was on the twenty-fifth of June that Miss Mitford and her young friend, Emily, found it at its best in the garden of the old house at Aberleigh. The lime trees were in bloom, and the ladies were walking in their fragrant shade when they were stopped by a rose thicket. They managed to get through, "at some expense of veils and flounces," but Emily stopped to admire the tall graceful shrub, whose long thorny stems now waved delicate clusters over their heads.

"Did I ever think," she exclaimed, "of standing under the shadow of a white rose tree! What an exquisite fragrance! And what a beautiful flower! so pale, and white, and tender, and the petals thin and smooth as silk! What rose is it?"

Miss Mitford replied that it was the musk rose, "that very musk rose of which Titania talks, and which is worthy of Shakespeare and of her.

"Did you never see it before? It is rare now, I believe, and seems rarer than it is, because it only blossoms in very hot summers. . . . No, do not smell to it; it is less sweet so than other roses; but one cluster in a vase, or even that bunch in your bosom, will perfume a large room, as it does the summer air." And Emily said, "Oh! . . . I wish grandmamma were here! She talks so often of a musk-rose tree that grew against one end of her father's house."

When the musk rose arrived in England by the way of Italy at the end of the sixteenth century, it became very popular with the Elizabethans. It must have come to this country in the early days, for Parsons wrote a century ago that the Old White Cluster was widely distributed. "The musk-rose grows naturally in Persia," he said, "and is doubtless the rose which has been celebrated by the Eastern poets. It is also found in India, where it is probably the species used for making attar. In this latitude [New York] it is quite hardy, and we have a plant of the old White Musk in our grounds, that has braved the severity of more than twenty winters."

Nowadays, the musk rose is little known in gardens—I have met with only one other than Hannah's, which was grown from a cutting taken from a bush against a house in Marietta, Ohio. Nevertheless it is still available to lovers of old roses, for it is one of the roses of yesterday that have been rescued and are now listed in the Tillotson catalogue.

November 20, 1960

Frost and Forks

This is the twenty-seventh day of November. As I sit in my studio window looking out over the garden, it is hard to believe that the spell of Indian summer is nearly over and cold weather will soon be upon us. It seems to me that we have never had a greener, more golden or more flowing fall, and there is still color on the trees, and there are still many things in bloom. All around me the last leaves of the dogwood are falling, and the white oaks are changing from rose to russet, but the sweet gums are still in a glow of topaz or wine. For weeks the tall, thin chokeberry at the end of the path has been a dazzling rose-red that outshines its scarlet berries.

The one black frost, early in the month, nipped the camellias that were in bloom, put an end to summer flowers, and ageratum and lantana, and ruined the last stalk of the tuberose; but the late chrysanthemums are untouched. I have two garden varieties, the old, brassy, pin-cushion kind and a many-petalled rose daisy. Now that the borders are more or less in order, these and bits of green make them gay and bright.

Last year I planted a lot of what seems to be a superior form of *Arum italicum* 'Marmoratum'. Yellow-veined, arrow-shaped leaves, some of them a foot long, are coming up all over the garden for winter color and for cutting. Mrs. Dwelle's yucca, an unusually beautiful form with foliage as blue as the leaves of *Eucalyptus rostrata*, always stands out when the summer flowers are gone. The eucalyptus was killed to the ground last winter, but came back up, and grew to a height of more than four feet. This species is called red gum, I suppose because of the bright red stems. The leaves are large, some to three inches in diameter, round and aromatic.

My autumn cherry has been in bloom for weeks. It is a form with very pale flowers, almost white in effect. It has two trunks, and I expect it is going to look more like a crepe myrtle than a cherry. The tea plant, well pruned by the March weather, has bloomed better and longer than ever, whether for that reason or not, and is still full of buds and flowers. The garden is gay with sasanquas, but in the hand the petals seem thin and slightly yellowed. There are sweet-smelling flowers on the sweet olive and the loquat, and odd flowers here and there on such things as the Carolina jessamine and a small plum that Miss Dormon sent me. Somewhere I saw a red quince in full bloom.

I have been trying to clear away dead annuals and the brown tops of perennials, and the fallen leaves, and to tidy the garden so that I can enjoy the little bulbs and small flowers that bloom in November. There are fall snowdrops, and fall crocuses and hardy cyclamens and *Oxalis bowieana*. This year the Chinese viola, which always blooms again at this season, has seemed to think that it is spring. But winter is coming, even though the garden year is just beginning.

I hope this winter will not be as devastating as the last, but in case it is (and the weather seems to come in cycles), Gilbert White's comments on the bitter winter of 1763 may be helpful. He said that after the snow on his evergreens had melted every day for four days and frozen again every night, they looked as if they had been burned by fire. But, he said, "A neighbor's plantation of the same kind, in a high cold situation where the snow never melted at all, remained uninjured. Therefore it highly behooves every planter who wishes to escape the cruel mortification of losing in a few days the labour and hopes of years, to bestir himself on such emergencies . . . and see that his people go about with prongs and forks, and carefully dislodge the snow from the boughs: since the naked foliage will shift much better for itself, than when the snow is partly melted and frozen again."

If we do have such another cold spell, I shall see that my people get out the prongs and forks.

November 27, 1960

Pomegranate

A pomegranate tree was one of the first plants to come into my garden when I started to make a new one, and it was one of the first to go, for I could never find a place where the burning scarlet of the flowers was not at war with its surroundings.

Now I often wish I had kept the pomegranate and let everything else go. I have nothing to match its beauty and brilliance in flower and fruit, and, as Lady Calcott says, "Whoever has seen the pomegranate in a favorable soil and climate has seen one of the most beautiful of green trees." Certainly I have no plant in my garden to remind me of so much.

It reminds me of the well-wrought garden of the *Romaunt of the Rose*, where it grew in such abundance, and of the nightingale that sang in the pomegranate tree outside Juliet's window, and of the single seed that doomed Persephone to the months underground and earth to the months of winter. It reminds me of the Emperor Baber's Garden of Fidelity, of the fruits of the Promised Land, of the hem of Aaron's robe, of the pillars of the Temple, and of Solomon's crown. Some say the pomegranate was the tree of knowledge of good and evil, and that it was the fruit that Eve gave to Adam. Some say that the apple of discord was really a pomegranate; when Paris awarded it to Venus it became the symbol of love and marriage.

Our names for the pomegranate, both Latin and English, come from the Romans, who called it *Malus punicum* because it was introduced from Carthage and *Pomum granatum* (apple full of grains) because of its many seeds.

The tree has been so long in cultivation that its provenance is no longer known. Although it has been considered native to North Africa, and Theophrastus said it was abundant on Mt. Tmolus and the Mysian Olympus, it is probably native only in the neighborhood of Persia.

The pomegranate is a thorny shrub that grows to a height of ten or fifteen feet, and may be wider than tall. It needs space and sunshine and likes heavy soil. It is drought resistant, and usually found to be free from pests, although Cynthia Westcott list bugs, scale, thrips and white flies as its enemies. A few years ago a number of varieties were listed: 'Ivory Queen', creamy white, 'Madame Legrelle', pink and white striped, variegated, and red—all with double flowers. At present I find only one of these, the scarlet, in southern nurseries.

At present I can find no source for fruiting pomegranates, but some nurseries must be growing them, for they are shown every fall at the annual flower show.

This year, Mrs. James Partington won a blue ribbon for a fruit so large I thought it must be the cultivar 'Wonderful', which Hamilton Mason recommends in *Your Garden in the South*. 'Wonderful' is one of the eight fruiting varieties described by L. A. Berckmans in *Bailey's Cyclopedia*.

Someone must eat them even now, for they appear in market this time of year. They are—or were—eaten as a dessert fruit. An old herbal says "wine is pressed forth of the berries," grenadine (also spelled granadine) is made from the pulp, and all parts of the plant have been used as medicine. "If one eats three small Pomegranate flowers (they say) for a whole year he shall be safe from all manner of eyesore."

The Chinese consider the dwarf pomegranate a subject for bonsai, and as a window plant (Mrs. Ballard says, in *Garden in Your House*) it is a longlived evergreen that will bloom off and on all year in a sunny window that is not too hot and dry.

I had one in my Raleigh garden where it was killed to the ground occasionally, but always came back to bloom from late summer until frost. Once it was still in bloom on the first of December. The plant was not over three feet, as I remember; the small scarlet flowers were double, and it never bore fruit, but I gather that there are dwarf forms that do fruit.

Everything about the pomegranate tree is delightful: the waxy buds, the silky petals, the globed fruit and the shining leaves. It is as much a part of the South as gardenias, crepe myrtles and camellias, and as Mr. Mason says: "If you could see the display in Savannah in May, you would want this for your own garden."

November 5, 1961

The Feast of Saint Martin

The mellow year is hastening to its close;
The little birds have almost sung their last. . . .

I think fall is my favorite time—especially this fall, when the clear days and frostless nights seem to go on forever, and the sweet-olive gives out a fragrance that is like a farewell to summer. The summer flowers have faded, and their spent stalks have been cleared away, but new buds unfurl as petals fall, and one door opens as another shuts.

Today is the eleventh of November, the Feast of Saint Martin, patron saint of fading leaves and budding branches. All week I have been putting out two wheelbarrow-loads of plants that I bought to replenish borders.

Every fall I plant lots of yellow alyssum and blue violas and white sweet Williams and freckled foxgloves. These bloom with the blue phlox that stays from year to year, and volunteers of the rosy *Silene pendula*. I love planting the violas when they are already in bloom.

This year, among the biennials and the perennials grown as biennials, I found a number of old friends that I had not seen for a long time. They looked so pretty in their little peat pots that I was unable to resist them, and I expect an unusually floriferous spring. One is doronicum, a very old garden plant that the sixteenth-century herbalists called leopard's bane though it seems to have been more terrifying to adders than to leopards. Adders are "utterly amased and Numm" when confronted by it. The great yellow daisies are charming with spring bulbs, but I never see them in gardens. Honesty is another garden flower of Gerard's day. When they bloom, in April, the brilliant violet flowers are as gay as tulips; they must be allowed to go to seed, for the transparent linings of the seed pods will be wanted for winter arrangements.

I also found the superior English strain of *Scabiosa caucasica* that has been developed by Isaac House. I don't think I have ever had this before, though I used to grow the annual pincushion flowers. All scabiosas are good for cutting. This is the first time in years that I have seen plants of the peach-leaved bellflower, and these are the beautiful cultivar 'Telham Beauty' which was an Award of Merit. The large, silvery blue-violet flowers bloom in May in the lull between spring and summer. I got another little bellflower, *Campanula carpatica*, to trail over the rock wall.

All the while I have been setting out these plants I have been enjoying the fall garden. There is little left in the borders except a few chrysanthemums and some greenery, but I am always glad to see some bare earth again. The chrysanthemums are unnamed kinds that came from Ridgewood gardens: a shaggy pale yellow star, a dark red button, and the golden pincushion—the last to bloom—that the Clarksons distribute. There is a little ageratum left, and there should be sweet alyssum, but I forgot to sow it this year. Under the pine trees the hardy cyclamen is blooming its head off, and the prettily marked leaves are coming up fast. My strawberry tree (arbutus) is blooming better than ever, little sprigs of pale green urns hanging from the tips of the branches. The camellia 'White Empress' is covered with flowers, and there is the tender pink of the sasanquas.

I think I like the double pink sasanquas best of all, and I don't believe there is much choice between 'Pink Snow', 'Agnes Solomon', and 'Jean May', but when I saw 'Cotton Candy' in the Trotter's garden I thought it superior. It is even more double and more frilly than 'Showa-no-Sakae'. Dave Blackwell introduced me to 'Gulf Breeze', a wide, deep pink flower that outshines all of the single varieties. Dave thinks it is a sport of 'Gulf Glory' which Mr. Sawada considers the finest single white sasanqua.

But the prettiest thing in my garden is a mullein that came up between the bricks around the pool, a great sea-green rosette with a soft silvery pile. It is a seedling of a common mullein that Mary Scruggs gave me last fall. And the little birds have not sung their last. They are singing as if, like the Chinese nightingale, they think spring comes on forever.

November 19, 1961

Miss Jekyll

It gave me great pleasure to write an introduction for *Miss Jekyll On Gardening* (Scribners, 1964; $6.00), an anthology drawn from ten of Gertrude Jekyll's fifteen books. As the books have long been out of print, and get more scarce and more expensive each year, the anthology is much needed, for Miss Jekyll's advice is as good today as it was at the turn of the century when American gardeners came under her influence. No one that I know of has gardened so well as Miss Jekyll or written of gardening so explicitly and so delightfully.

First of all Miss Jekyll was a dirt gardener. She gardened all her life. As a child she lived in the country, and had a little plot where she could plant what she liked; and not long before she died, at eighty-nine, she was still out in a wheel chair directing the gardeners, and grumbling because she could not do the chores herself.

"When I was a child," she says (in *Children and Gardens*), "I was very much alone, and nearly always in my playtime found my own amusements in the garden and shrubbery. There was a large rambling shrub garden with broad turf paths; and though it must even then have been planted for many years yet it contained many delightful shrubs and trees, such as are the very best to this day. There were several kinds of Magnolia, and Ailanthus and Hickory, the pretty cut-leaved Beech and the feathery deciduous cypress. And there were Ayrshire roses, and Cinnamon Roses and *Rosa lucida*, and the sweet Moss Rose, but hardly any herbaceous plants."

When she began to design gardens for herself and for other people, Miss Jekyll set to work to bring the herbaceous plants back to English gardens. She found them growing in the cottage dooryards, where they were still cherished after bedding out plants became the fashion, and brought them to Munstead Wood, and planted them in her celebrated borders, grouping them for the best effect in form and color.

Her other great contribution to modern gardens was her ways of using color. When poor eyesight made it impossible for her to go on painting, she composed pictures in gardens. "I am strongly for treating garden and wooded ground in a pictorial way," she says in *Wood and Garden*, "mainly with large effects, and in the second place with lesser beautiful incidents, and for so arranging plants and trees and grassy spaces that they look happy and at home, and make no parade of conscious effort. I try for beauty and harmony everywhere, and especially for harmony of color."

Miss Elinor Parker, who made the selections for the anthology, has chosen them to show the scope of Miss Jekyll's writing, taking the most useful and delightful garden passages and grouping them under six headings: A Gardening Credo; Design and Ornament; The Year in the Garden; Flowers, Shrubs, Trees; Colour and Scent; and Special Gardens. The special gardens are rose and rock gardens, the dry wall, water gardens, the wood, the vegetable, fruit and herb gardens. There is also a section on cut flowers, and one on subjects related to gardening.

Through it all the reader is able to picture Miss Jekyll's own garden at Munstead Wood, and that is the only way it can now be seen, for after her death the property was sold and divided into smaller lots. But I know that garden as I know my own, and I can see it as Marion Cran saw it not long before Miss Jekyll died: "There were blue poppies out in a shady glade; drifts of gentian; a carpet of lilies of the valley; trillums, azaleas in glory. . . . There were beauty and great peace there—abundant growth in wood and garden; her choice peculiar trees were strong and tall, birds sang everywhere; the paths wound beautifully among ferny mosses and rare pretty undergrowth." When Mrs. Cran said good-bye, Miss Jekyll said, "I have tried to make a little peace and some surprises."

November 15, 1964

Hostas

In my great-grandmother's garden plantain lilies were called funkias. As funkias, they were popular with the Victorians, who liked the bold foliage of the large-leaved kinds. Now, after long neglect, they have reappeared as hostas, and are in such demand that some growers specialize in them. The plantain lily is one of the permanent perennials that makes few demands on the gardener's time, and not only holds its own but even improves with age.

Gertrude Jekyll knew how to use plantain lilies to best advantage. Her favorite were *Hosta sieboldiana* and *H. plantaginea*, our old August lily, sometimes called Corfu lily—no one seems to know why. I have never been able to discover any connection between the hosta and the island, but I find that corfu is an old spelling of curfew. Perhaps it was called the curfew lily because, unlike the other species, it blooms in the evening.

Miss Jekyll liked the effect of its pale green leaves with pale yellow calceolarias and pale blue delphiniums, and she liked to see tall white lilies spring from clumps of hosta and lady fern. She planted quantities in pots to decorate the paved courtyard at the garden entrance to her house in Munstead Wood.

Hosta sieboldiana, the other Victorian favorite, is called the short-cluster plantain lily because the flower scapes scarcely rise above the enormous blue-green leaves. The leaves are sometimes a foot long, and they are so deeply ribbed they look like seersucker. I had this originally from Kohankie, and I am not sure where the true species can be found at the present time, though I think H. A. Zager has it. I find that it takes about five years for a plant from a nursery to become established and produce characteristic foliage. Once established, it continues to improve if conditions are favorable, and if not it soon begins to dwindle.

H. fortunei gigantea, a robust form of the tall-cluster plantain lily, is also described as having very large, blue-green, wrinkled leaves, but I have had it only two years, and I suppose this, too, develops slowly. *H. nakaiana*, on the other hand, makes a fine clump in two years, and Mr. Zager says when well established it often blooms a second time.

The first plantain lily of the season is *H. sieboldiana*. It begins to bloom the last of May. The next, *H. caerulea*, blooms in June. The others come along in July and August, and the last are two forms of *H. lancifolia fortis* and *tardiflora*, which bloom from September into October. *Hosta minor* 'Alba', also late blooming, is the smallest of all, and is the only hosta I have never been able to grow. I have planted it a number of times, but it always dies before the year is out. I think it dislikes hot climates. 'Honey Bells', a hybrid between *Hosta plantaginea* and *H. lancifolia*, was developed by Alex Cumming at the Bristol Nurseries. The flowers are lavender; they open in the morning, and are described as smelling like trailing arbutus. Wayside Gardens offers two other hybrids, 'June Beauty' and the fragrant 'Royal Standard'.

There are variegated forms of all or almost all of the species. The prettiest and best known is 'Thomas Hogg', a form of the blunt-leaved plantain lily, *Hosta decorata*. The leaves are dark green with narrow white rims. This is a slow-growing plant that keeps itself in a neat clump indefinitely, but a variegated hosta with creamy margins, found in local gardens, increases so fast it is a give-away plant, and makes a splendid ground cover. Another one that increases rapidly is *Hosta undulata*, which has a wavy leaf with a wide creamy stripe in the center and dark green edges. The green-rim plantain lily, a form of *H. fortunei*, has pale green leaves edged with dark green.

I have read that some hostas tolerate sun, and that a few even prefer it, but I think that must be for northern gardens. The ones I have grown need shade. And even though they are recommended for "places where nothing else will grow," I find they prosper only in good soil with plenty of humus and continuous moisture. Fertilize with manure and superphosphate, and leave them undisturbed indefinitely.

November 6, 1966

November Blossoms

This year the frosts that always come in late October were so light that scarcely any damage was done to the late fall flowers. The only mark that I noticed was a brown spot on *Camellia sasanqua* 'Snow-on-the-Mountain'. Now, in November, the other sasanquas and the tea plant are in full bloom and the garden is filled with the vanilla scent of the loquat. It begins blooming at the top and I can't see the flowers, but I knew the minute the first one opened.

When warmer days came, the cup and saucer vine was still hung with buds and untouched flowers. I planted it in June from a pot. It slowly covered a bamboo trellis that I had made at the end of the terrace, and then when it reached the top it caught the lower branches of a pink locust that grows there and rapidly climbed the trunk.

Even before the first bud opens (late in September) the calyx is a fancy affair, frilled and plaited and apple green. When the cup-like flower blooms, the calyx serves as a saucer, and the whole is like a Canterbury bell. The flower is white at first, and then becomes tinged with violet and then a deep violet. When the cup falls, the pale green saucer persists. It has a pale star in the center and then in a little while it is filled with a fruit like a tiny striped watermelon. I had never seen the fruits before. It is described as large, but here it will probably be frost bitten before it matures. The cup and saucer (*Cobaea scandens*) is a perennial vine, but we must grow it as an annual and the seeds must be started indoors.

On All Saints a few fall crocuses were still in bloom and the first (and last) flowers of saffron (*Crocus sativus*) were opening in the sunshine. Saffron is a distinct flower because of the deep but glowing violet of its petals. The color seems all the more intense because the flowers come up through a ferny grey mat of Roman wormwood. Cyclamens (both rose and white) were still in bloom, and one little bird's foot violet (*Viola pedata*). The violet was in bloom when Rosalie Holziner brought it to me the first of October, and it had been blooming all summer. Repeating is a characteristic of the species.

In her book of southern wild flowers Alice Lounsberry writes of finding several flowers on Satula Mountain early in September and I have a note of bloom in Reidsville, North Carolina, a few days before Christmas. Mrs. Lounsberry says they are what the Japanese call "returning flowers," and given to departing travelers as a token of a safe homecoming. *Viola pedata* is one of the most variable species as to form and color. Ezra Brainerd, who devoted his life to the study of violets, considered the bicolor flowers, with two dark upper petals, typical. He called the violet-flowered variety *concolor*. It varies from Bradley's violet to wisteria violet or paler, and there is a rare white form.

Another returning flower is *Berberis candidula*, a dwarf evergreen barberry that blooms in April but always produces a few small, pale yellow flowers in October and November. The flowers are like tiny roses on stems as fine as hairs. They spring from bunches of small leaves along slender arching branches. The leaves are bright green and shining on top, but silver underneath. I have read that the dark purple berries, being freely borne, show up well against the foliage, but my shrub has never fruited. After 10 years or more it is still less than three feet tall, and not much wider.

On Election Day I found the first pearly buds of the fall snowdrop. They have bloomed now for many years, but they have never increased although they seem to hold their own.

At the same time a curious bulb of the bunch-flower family begins to bloom. It is *Schoenocaulen texanum*. The generic name means rush stem, and it seems to have no common name. I got it from Dr. Thad Howard, who sends me many rare and interesting bulbs from Texas. The flowers of this one are not spectacular in the garden, but in the hand they appear as finely wrought as the most delicate filigree. As the moss-green buds open along the slender, tapered spike, the stamens spring like hoarfrost from tiny green corollas.

As I looked for, but did not find, the buds of the white hoop-petticoats, I thought how pleasant it is to know that all through the winter little frosty flowers will continue to bud and blossom.

November 17, 1968

The Saffron Crocus

This summer Linda Lamm brought Rose Wharton a little package of *azafran puro*, which she bought in Spain at the shop of Jesu Navarro. Azafran is the Arabic name for saffron, the dried stigmata of *Crocus sativus*. It was introduced into Spain by the Moors, and the best quality still comes from there. When I opened the package, the fiery stigmata produced such a strong aroma I wondered whether it was really *azafran puro*. But when I took out a stigma and dropped a little water on it, the water was at once suffused with the beautiful golden color that the Greeks and Romans valued so highly for dyeing their robes.

In October I watched eagerly for my one little clump of *Crocus sativus* (which has survived for ten years, but increased very little) to come into bloom, for I had never remembered their having any scent other than a faint, fresh crocus fragrance. When they did bloom, on the twentieth, it was just as I remembered, though I sniffed and sniffed. I picked a flower and brought it indoors to see if that would bring out another scent, but it didn't. I laid it on my desk and forgot about it until it was dry, and then I sniffed again, and there was the aroma of Jesu Navarro's *azafran puro*.

I looked through all the books I have, and *Gerard's Herball* is the only one that mentions the fact that the stigmata have no odor until they are dried. "His floure doth first rise out of the ground nakedly in September," Gerard says, "and his long smal grassy leaves shortly after the floure, never bearing floure and leafe at once. . . . The floure consisteth of six small blew leaves tending to purple, having in the middle many small yellow strings or threds; among which are two, three, or more thicke fat chives of a fierie colour somewhat reddish, of a strong smell when they be dried, which doth stuffe and trouble the head."

Headaches and insomnia are caused from too much saffron, Gerard says, but "moderate use of it is good for the head, and maketh the sences more quicke and lively." It also strengthens the heart, and is a special remedy for consumptives who are, "as wee terme it, at deaths doore, and almost past breathing, that it bringeth breath again, and prolongeth life for certaine days, if ten, or twenty graines at the most be given with new or sweet Wine."

Another herbalist says saffron "is an herb of the Sun, and under the Lion; and therefore you need not demand the reason why it strengthens the heart so exceedingly. Let not above ten grains be given at a time; for the sun, which is the fountain of light, may dazzle the eyes and make them blind; a cordial being taken in an inordinate quantity hurts the heart instead of healing it." Francis Bacon said it was the liberal use of saffron in their drinks and cordials that made the English people sprightly.

In *A Garden of Herbs*, Eleanour Sinclair Rohde gives a recipe from *The Compleat Housewife*, 1736, for Syrup of Saffron: "Take a pint of the best canary, as much balm-water, and two ounces of English saffron; open and pull the saffron very well, and put it into the liquor to infuse; let it stand covered (so as to be hot but not boil) twelve hours; then strain it out as hot as you can, and add two pounds of double refined sugar; boil it until it is well incorporated, and when it is cold, bottle it, and take one spoonful in a little sack or small cordial, as occasion serves."

My saffron came from the Plantation Gardens. In her booklet "Herbs

Described," Eleanor Chalfin says the corms should be planted in part shade or under creeping thyme and given a dressing of bone meal in summer. Mine are planted with Roman wormwood, *Artemisia pontica*. I wonder whether its bitter pungence is what has saved the saffron corms from the rodents. Under the same protection *Crocus speciosus* has increased wonderfully in the past two years. This fall it bloomed freely for nearly a month. The large flowers are the most beautiful blue violet in the color chart.

After writing this I thought I'd see what Louise Beebe Wilder and Miles Hadfield have to say. Mrs. Wilder says saffron is one of the most famous of flowers, but a disappointment in the garden and not worth growing except for its antique interest; Mr. Hadfield says *Crocus speciosus* is a "dull purple flower." I sometimes think all men are color blind.

November 23, 1969

❧ DECEMBER

. . . .

Queen Anne's Pocket Melon

Dr. Walter Brem Mayer, who takes delight in asking people questions that they can't answer, came by one morning, early in October, with a most deliciously scented little fruit the size of a small orange, of a warm cinnamon brown, evenly striped with pale yellow. He said a patient of his had brought it from Newton. The patient called it a pomegranate, and Dr. Mayer's father said he had known it all his life by that name. Neither of them knew any other name, or to what genus it belonged. I spent the morning trying to find its scientific name, and when I had to give up, I sent it by air mail to Mr. Morrison. He couldn't identify it without more information, but said he would send the seed on to a friend who was expert at identifying plants by their seeds.

Later on I happened to look through an issue of that invaluable little leaflet, *Saier's Garden Magazine* (published in "conjunction with the *Saier Catalogue of Seeds*"), and came upon a paragraph headed "Queen Anne's pocket melon." It seems that someone had written, in an Illinois newspaper, about a small melon "about the size of a baseball and very spicy and fragrant" that was called a pomegranate, seeds of which could be had from Mr. Saier for twenty-five cents a package. A number of people wrote to Mr. Saier for pomegranate seeds, and he, of course, sent the seeds of *Punica granatum*. When he discovered that what they wanted was a vine, not a shrub, he put the notice in his magazine, asking if anyone could tell him what the melon is.

I next looked up melon in the *Oxford English Dictionary*, and found a quotation from Delamer's *Kitchen Garden* (1861): "A pretty little old-fashioned variety,—Queen Anne's pocket melon . . . produces green-fleshed well-flavoured fruit, the size of a large orange." (They must have grown them bigger in those days.) But still no Latin name.

As I was going to Monroe, Louisiana, to lecture on vines, Helen Mayer brought me a melon to take with me. When I held it up before the Monroe gardeners, two of them smiled. They were the two oldest gardeners there. One of them said: "We used to grow it long ago, and when I was a girl I used to wrap one in a handkerchief and put it in my pocket when I went to school." Still no one knew the Latin name.

While I was in Louisiana, the Mayers went to Pawley's Island and there, of all places, they found in the Hammock Shop a pile of second-hand books—among them one by Liberty Hyde Bailey on gourds. Dr. Mayer thumbed through it and found: *Cucumis melo* variety 'Dudaim', Queen Anne's pocket melon. It is also called the pomegranate melon, and is of the genus that cucumbers and musk melons belong to. I looked in Mr. Saier's catalogue, and sure enough, *Cucumis melo* is listed there—but the seeds have gone up; they are now thirty-five cents. I wrote him a postcard and asked him to send me a package of seeds in the spring. That is the time to plant them, about April, as the vine is a tender annual.

December 7, 1958

Scotch Hall

In East Carolina time stands still. Scotch Hall revisited seemed to me unchanged since I saw it last, over twenty years ago. As I entered the house, the door to the piazza was open to let in the warm October sunlight, and looking down the long boxwood walk I could see the blue waters of Albemarle Sound. The walk between double rows of box, tree box without, dwarf box within, was just as I remembered it, but looking up I saw that the old trees that form an avenue from the house to the water had suffered from the hurricanes. By the time a tree has sheltered several generations I begin to think of it as permanent, and it is always a shock to find that it is not. Unlike the brick that the wind blew off of the tall graceful chimneys of the house, the branches of the trees cannot be put back.

The trees are pecans planted by George Washington Capehart soon after he built the house in 1838. His daughter planted the box, and his wife planted the Seven Sisters rose at the end of the piazza. The rose, a form of multiflora that was brought to England from China in 1817, was exceedingly popular in Victorian days, especially in the South. "It was planted by the mistress of every Southern home," Mrs. Earle says, in *Old Time Gardens*, "from the power of association, because it was loved by her grandmother." In *Parsons on the Rose* it is described as "of but temporary duration," but at Scotch Hall the same shrub has bloomed every spring for more than a hundred years.

In describing the famous plant that he saw in the Goldworth Nursery in 1826, Loudon says (*Arboretum et Fruticetum*) that it covered a hundred square feet and had three thousand flower buds, but the "variety of colour produced by the buds at first opening was not less astonishing than their number. White, light blush, deeper blush, light red, darker red, scarlet and purple flowers, all appeared in the same corymb, and the production of these seven colors at once is said to be the reason why this plant is called the Seven Sisters rose."

The Seven Sisters is deliciously fragrant, and the other end of the piazza is made fragrant all summer by the little white flowers of the Confederate jessamine. The jessamine is barely hardy in Charlotte, so I had no idea that it would grow that far north, but it seems to flourish in old gardens along the coast. This one came from Mrs. Slade's garden in Hamilton.

The flower garden is a modern one, planted thirty years ago by Mrs. Capehart, the present mistress of Scotch Hall. She drew the intricate design of triangles around circles, laid out the beds and walks, and in order to save transplanting, rooted the box cuttings in place. The box-bordered triangles are filled with the sort of plants that pass from one old garden to another.

On my first visit, in May, the old roses were in bloom. There was a moss rose, a little China rose, called 'Archduke Charles', as sweet smelling and as deeply pink as a carnation; and two old remontants, 'Giant of Battles' from the yard of the parish church and 'General Jacqueminot', described by Dean Hole as "a glory and a grace, its petals, soft and smooth as velvet, glowing with vivid crimson, and its growth being free and healthful."

When I was there in October there were only a few late flowers, but the garden was no less beautiful, for of all plants boxwood is the least touched by time and season.

Scotch Hall is on Bachelor's Bay, across from the mouth of the Roanoke River and not far from Windsor. The name was given to the place early in the eighteenth century and appears in a deed to James Lockhart in 1727. The Capeharts' house was built on the site of an older house, and every spring bulbs planted in the old garden come up and bloom. They are out of line with the later plantings, but the Capeharts have always liked these small ghosts from the past, and have left them where they were planted so many years ago.

December 18, 1960

Thirty Years' Bloom

I suppose there are gardeners whose pleasure in their flowers would be lost if they were asked to keep records, but to me old garden notebooks are as fascinating as old diaries. They give me almost as much pleasure as the garden itself. My mother and I, between us, have recorded the bloom of thirty years. Looking back to the first garden book I find that on the last day of 1931 my mother picked three roses, a paper white narcissus, and some sweet alyssum. That must have been the year we went to see the Virginia gardens, for the empty pages are filled with plans and details and lists of plants that we saw on our trip.

One of the sketches is the plan of the little gardens on either side of the River Walk at Brandon. I could never forget that long green vista with the river at the end and the wide borders of yellow cowslips, but I had forgotten the charming plan of the little hidden tea garden with a table in the center. I had forgotten the yews on the lawn, and the poets' laurel and the andromeda that I saw in bloom for the first time. I had forgotten the climbing rose, 'Gold of Ophir', that grew on the gate, and that honesty and Chinese forget-me-nots were in bloom. There were also notes of plum yews at Montpelier; and of crocuses, snowdrops and winter aconites blooming in the grass at the Governor's Palace in Williamsburg.

Along with our garden notes some extraneous things have crept in. One is a recipe for Mrs. Burgwyn's spice cakes; it is sandwiched between a list of plants set out on Ash Wednesday and a list of things in bloom the day after. This reminds me of a gardener who kept her kitchen and garden notes in the same book. Her cook was startled, when following a recipe which called for two eggs and a cup of sugar, to turn the page and find that the next ingredient was a tablespoon of nicotine sulfate.

My mother recorded the weather and the date of the first flower of every plant as it came into bloom. At intervals, such as high spring, mid-summer and Thanksgiving, she would take a census of everything in bloom at that time. She was very systematic about her daily records. Each morning she would go out with her little black book and write down the names of the flowers that had bloomed since the day before. This is the way records should be kept. Mine are not as well done, for one day I may go my rounds in the morning, and the next I may go in the afternoon. Then I may skip a few days, and when I do, it is hard to remember whether the lily bloomed on Monday or on Tuesday.

My own blooming dates are kept in a series of small loose-leaf note books that I get from the five-and-ten. I find loose-leaf books more practical than the diaries my mother used, for on some days there is not enough room on a page, and on others there is nothing to report. I also keep a card index, with a card for each plant. I try to tell where it came from, and when, and to check the color of flowers and fruit against the chart, and to give measurement of the whole and the parts. Far from being a chore, I find that making these notes brings out beauty that I would have missed if I had looked at the flowers only in the garden.

The best record book I have seen is a garden log that Hannah Craighill gave me. It allows a page for each week (but of course it need not be a week, it could be a day or a month, or irregular intervals) with space for notes under the following headings: weather (high and low temperatures), planting, transplanting, fertilizing, spraying, pruning, blooming dates, general notes, and suggestions for next year. At the back of the book there are yellow pages for garden plans, expenses, hints, sources of supply, and a very useful large envelope for clippings. It is published by Fred H. Beach & Co., 200 Fifth Avenue, New York.

December 31, 1961

Earthworms

In *The Illustrated London News* (August 17, 1963), Maurice Burton says Americans think of earthworms mainly in connection with fishing, but the British, prejudiced perhaps by Darwin's preaching, "think of them first and foremost as one of the essential elements in maintaining the fertility of the soil. . . . Worms not only draw humus materials into the soil and turn the soil over, thus justifying one of their nicknames 'nature's ploughmen,' but their burrows running down into the earth to a depth of five feet help to aerate and drain the ground. They have, indeed, been described as 'among the world's most important animals.'"

This sent me to my files and book shelves to see what I could find about earthworms. The first thing I found is that some gardeners want to get rid of them. In a clipping from *The New York Times* garden page, Victor Ries says that soil high in organic matter attracts moles that feed on earthworms, but if the gardener kills the earthworms with chlordane the moles will go elsewhere. In another article ("Better Compost") Mr. Ries says earthworms can be eliminated from the compost pile by adding a half pound of 50 percent chlordane to each cubic yard of material.

In *A Book about Soils for the Home Gardener*, those two mild and amiable gentlemen, Mr. Ortloff and Mr. Raymore, say, "Fussy gardeners sometimes deplore the unsightly worm castings, even going to the extreme of applying various chemicals to rid the area of these 'pests.' Nothing could be more foolish. The wise gardener knows that an abundant working population of worms indicates a good, friable, fertile soil and avoids the use of the strong chemical fertilizers in large doses." It is debatable, they say, whether the worms increase the fertility of the soil, but some think they make plant nutrients more available.

In the Brooklyn Botanic Garden's *Handbook on Soils*, Emil Trogg (Emeritus Professor of Soils, University of Wisconsin) says there is no scientific evidence to support the belief that commercial fertilizers are toxic to earthworms and soil bacteria. On the contrary, "experiments have shown that an application of commercial fertilizers tends to increase the numbers of bacteria and earthworms in soils." In the same handbook, Henry Hopp (U.S. Dept. of Agriculture) advocates taking care of earthworms by covering the garden in the fall with a mulch of organic material and raking it off in spring. Otherwise the worms will die, or else they will depart to a more protected place. Earthworms, he goes on to say, are not necessary to good crop growth in sandy soils, but they are needed in loam and clay.

As to whether earthworms should be planted, Mr. Hopp says this is rarely necessary. If there are no earthworms in the garden, it is because something is wrong with the soil, and any worms that are introduced will die. If the soil is habitable, the worms will be there, and the only thing needed to increase their numbers is the winter mulch. Chemical fertilizers, he says, do not kill earthworms out, but do increase their soil-improving activities.

In *The War in the Soil* Sir Albert Howard presents the views of the organic gardeners. When worm casts are examined, he says, it is found that important chemical changes have taken place: "It was recently found at the Connecticut Experiment Station that the content of humus had been increased by fifty per cent. The available nitrogen was multiplied by five, the soluble phosphate by seven, and the available potash by eleven. . . . When the soil is managed so that it is well supplied with earthworms, everything else follows. The crops thrive and there is no need to apply artificial manure."

Well, I take care of my earthworms, and would not dream of pouring chlordane over them, but my real reason for mulching as much of the garden as possible with pine straw and oak leaves in winter, is that I think the mulch looks better than bare ground. I don't rake it off in spring. Encouraging the worms has not brought moles to the garden. My greatest problem is the chipmunks. If anyone knows how to get rid of them without hurting their feelings, I'd like to hear about it.

December 8, 1963

Mistletoe

The mistletoe that Americans kiss under at Christmas time is not the mistletoe of tradition. Ours is *Phoradendron flavescens*, a parasite which grows on deciduous trees from Florida to New Jersey. The mystic plant of the Old World is the viscum of Virgil and Pliny, which grows on many trees, even evergreens, but is most prized, because most rare, when it grows on the oak.

It had a long history in medicine and mythology before it came to be associated with Christmas. It was an ancient cure-all in Europe, and in parts of Japan and Africa, and I expect there are still some who put their trust in it, though it is not recognized in modern medicine. In addition to curing the falling sickness (epilepsy) and other bodily ills, it was believed to be an antidote to poison, a safeguard against fire, a protection from witches, trolls, and all evil beings, and a talisman against all evil. A sprig laid on the threshold would keep bad dreams away. It was said to open all locks, and with it Aeneas unlocked even the gates of death.

When Aeneas wanted to visit the land of the dead, he sought advice from the Cumaean Sibyl, who said: "Hidden in a dark tree deep in the forest, is a bough with golden leaves, sacred to Persephone. No one can enter the secret places of the earth without plucking the bough, and when it is plucked another will grow, also of gold. It is easily plucked if Fate is calling; if not, no force can remove it."

As Aeneas set out on his search, two white doves flew before him through the forest, and on the shore of Lake Avernus they settled on an evergreen oak. In the oak was a golden light, that was (Virgil said) like the mistletoe, which grows fresh and green on its alien tree, in the midst of the cold winter woods. The bough was easily picked, and with it Aeneas and the Sibyl began their descent to the lower regions. When the boatman refused to take them across the Styx they had only to show him the gleam of gold and when they came to the gate of the Groves of the Blest, entered only by those bearing appointed gifts, Aeneas gained entrance by leaving the golden bough on the threshold.

Mistletoe kept Aeneas safe, but it caused the death of the Norse god Balder, the best loved of all immortals—loved by everyone but the jealous Loki. When Balder dreamed that he was about to die, he told his mother, who immediately went to sticks and stones and all hurtful things and made them swear that they would never harm him, but she thought the mistletoe too young to swear and too weak to hurt anyone. Loki found this out, and breaking a branch he put it in the hand of the blind god Hodur, who stood aside while others threw things at Balder for the fun of seeing them drop to the ground before they reached him. "Here is something for you to throw," he said, "and I will direct your aim."

Perhaps there is some connection between the instrument of Balder's death and the Aryan reverence for the oak that bears the mistletoe. Fraser thinks there is. He thinks the god may be a personification of the tree that was worshipped by the Druids. Pliny said the Druids held the mistletoe sacred only when it grew on the oak. Since it was held aloft and did not grow in the earth, he believed it was sent from heaven; they said it must be cut with a golden sickle (for iron is taboo), and must never touch the ground.

The Druids called mistletoe all-heal; they considered it a protection from evil as well as from disease. It was their custom to send a boy with a branch from house to house to announce the new year. Up to modern times little boys in Brittany ran about the villages on New Year's Day crying, "À gui l'an neuf," expecting presents. "Gui" comes from the Celtic name for mistletoe.

No one seems to know where the kissing comes from, though some say that after the death of Balder it was decreed that mistletoe must never again bring destruction, and that those who pass under it must exchange the kiss of love and peace. The kissing ball, made with hoops covered with evergreens and a bunch of mistletoe hung beneath, is peculiar to England, and was hung up in English houses at Christmas time long before the Christmas tree was known.

December 22, 1963

Evergreen Vines

One of the nicest things about gardening in the South is the variety of evergreen vines that can be grown. Two of the best are natives, *Smilax lanceolata* and the Carolina jessamine, *Gelsemium sempervirens*.

One year, Carolina jessamine bloomed in my garden from the middle of February to the middle of April, but it usually comes about the end of March and has not so long a season. When it is in bloom, the garden is filled with the fragrance of the yellow flowers.

The jessamine is difficult to transplant from the woods, and anyway, it is not likely to be found nearby, for Dr. Hechenbleikner says the vine at the entrance of the Charlotte College Arboretum is the only wild one he knows about in this area, but now that it is sold in cans it is easily established in sun or shade, and it climbs into a pine tree or covers a fence very rapidly.

It takes training to get the long stems to climb. They would much rather run along the ground, rooting as they go, and once up, they get themselves into such a tangle I have to cut them back once in a while and start over. Fortunately I have three vines, and they can be cut back one at a time, for it takes more than a season for them to get back to blooming, and I would not like a spring to go by without the fragrant flowers.

Along the coast smilax is in every garden, but it is not so often seen in the Piedmont, though it grows here just as well. I think this is because it is not in the nurseries (but if anyone has it, please let me know). I got mine from Alabama, and the only source I have at present is one of the advertisers in the *Mississippi Market Bulletin*.

The most beautiful evergreen vine for the South is *Clematis armandii*, but it makes tremendous growth and needs a strong support and plenty of room. Mine is on an arch over the garden gate where it has to be hacked at continually to keep it from closing the entrance, and even then most people have to duck in order to get through. Like the rest of the genus, it has a way of suddenly wilting when it is in its prime. They say this can be prevented by deep planting; if the plant dies, the soil must be treated with a fungicide before another is set out. Plants from containers may grow to ten or twelve feet in one year and bloom the second season. The foliage is handsome at all seasons, and in March or April there is a profusion of large fragrant white flowers.

After searching for *Stauntonia hexaphylla* for many years, I finally got it from a rhododendron specialist in Oregon. Like most evergreen vines, it gets off to a slow start, and mine has just begun to climb with reluctance after three years of standing still. I hope it will now go ahead in leaps and bounds, and produce the airy sprays of fragrant spring flowers and the edible fall fruit that I have read about. It is called *hexaphylla* because the compound leaves may have as many as six leaflets, but mine have only three so far. It has shown no sign of winter injury, and I expect it to be perfectly hardy, as it comes from Japan and Korea.

Kadsura japonica is a vine that gets off to a very, very slow start. It grew for years in our Raleigh garden without making any progress at all, and then suddenly it had covered the summerhouse. And then one day in June, when we were having tea in the garden, someone looked up and saw that little waxen flowers were hanging from the vine on long threadlike stems. In the fall these thin stems were tipped with balls of tiny red berries.

Soon after we came to Charlotte I planted kadsura on the fence, but it grew so slowly I forgot about it and a volunteer cherry laurel covered it up. This summer I crawled under the cherry laurel to see what had become of the vine, and found that it had grown up, branched out and begun to fruit. The kadsura on the summerhouse used to shed its leaves in late winter, but in another Raleigh garden, on the house wall, it was evergreen. I must observe what happens here. This is a rare vine in the trade, but I find it in the Monrovia catalogue. Mine came from Fruitland, and I doubt whether they have it now.

December 12, 1965

Tennyson's Garden

Tennyson's garden in the Isle of Wight bloomed "not wholly in the busy world nor quite beyond it." It was near enough to the village for the poet to hear:

The windy clanging of the minster clock;
Altho' between it and the garden lies
A league of grass, wash'd by a slow broad stream.

It was a "careless-ordered" garden, the garden of Farringford, a little island farm. In his poems Tennyson describes it in detail, and in all seasons, but I like it best on a May morning when two young men, "brothers in art," paid a visit to the gardener's daughter:

> All the land in flowery squares,
> Beneath a broad and equal-blowing wind,
> Smelt of the coming summer
> . . . .
> From the woods
> Came voices of the well-contented doves.
> The lark could scarce get out his notes for joy
> . . . .
>
> To left and right,
> The cuckoo told his name to all the hills;
> The mellow ouzel fluted in the elm;
> The redcap whistled; and the nightingale
> Sang loud, as tho' he were the bird of day.

The dew was still on the grass when the young men crossed the meadow and followed a worn path across a field that slanted north, and came to a green wicket in a privet hedge; they entered a grassy walk that ran through crowded lilacs in full bloom and led to the garden on the southern slope:

> In the midst
> A cedar spread his dark-green layers of shade.
> The garden-glasses shone, and momently
> The twinkling laurel scatter'd silver lights.

The cedar, "sighing for Lebanon," often appears in Tennyson's poems, and so does the yew tree opposite the window of the morning room; and so do the hawthorns along the drive whose flowers are "pearls of May."

> The daughters of the year,
> One after one, thro' that still garden pass'd;
> Each garlanded with her peculiar flower. . . .

The crocus, the primrose and the snowdrop were followed by bluebells and forget-me-nots; and "Thick by ashen roots" the violets bloomed.

Within the ancient walls of the kitchen garden, flowers sunned themselves in the fragrance of long beds of lavender and rosemary. And in summer, as in Maud's garden, there were lilies and larkspur, and the spice of the woodbine and the musk of the rose:

The slender acacia would not shake
One long milk-bloom on the tree;
The white lake-blossom fell into the lake
As the pimpernel dozed on the lea.

During "the year's last hours,"

Heavily hangs the broad sunflower
Over its grave i' the earth so chilly;
Heavily hangs the hollyhock,
Heavily hangs the tiger-lily.

But the yucca "which no winter quells" blooms on, and so does "the year's last rose."

The garden had many visitors. They would find Tennyson raking the lawn or planting trees, and Mrs. Tennyson being pushed in her long chair carriage by one of her tall, attentive sons. The boys, dressed in black velvet, reminded the poet's friends of the picture Millais painted of the princes in the tower. One of the visitors to Farringford was Garibaldi, who came to plant a Wellingtonia. And one day a visitor, who found the poet away from home, said to the maid, "Tell him the Prince of Wales called."

One of the last visitors to the garden was Mrs. Boyle (E. V. B.). She went on an April evening in 1892 when the aubretia was in bloom. Ever afterward, when aubretia bloomed in her garden at Huntercombe, she thought of how she had found the poet talking with his friends in the summerhouse, while they watched "the twilight turning brown."

When he was persuaded at last to go indoors, Tennyson pointed out to his guests some bushes of "small-leaved laurel" along the path. I think it must have been *Danae racemosa*, for he called it the victor's laurel of ancient Greece. It was well, Mrs. Boyle said (in a style more Tennysonian than mine), that, when she said farewell, no voice whispered that it was for the last time. Tennyson died on October the sixth. His garden was afterward opened to the public, and I wonder if it still is. I would love to go there.

December 19, 1965

Roses at Christmas

Jove can at will the winter send
Or call the spring at will.

In all climates where spring-like days come at the end of the year, roses sometimes bloom for Christmas. In *A Garden of Pleasure*, E. V. B. (Mrs.

Boyle) wrote on the twenty-fourth of December, "There are roses, real pink roses, full blown in the garden still. Tea roses are there also, showing large firm buds which look resolved to open. There are little white strawberry blossoms shining among the wild strawberry leaves in the south border under the windows of the houses."

Roses have bloomed for me at Christmas when they were not expected, but the expected Christmas rose, *Helleborus niger*, has never shown itself in my garden before January. The reason for this is that I have never had the proper forms, the cultivars 'Praecox' and 'Maximus'. That is, I have had them, but they never lived long enough to bloom. Last year a slice of each came to me from Heatherfell's the last of November. Both had buds, but the flowers did not come out perfectly. Though the plants are so slow to become established, I think maximus is going to bloom this year.

Another December, Mrs. Boyle wrote, in *Days and Hours in a Garden*, about her Christmas rose. She had only one plant, a very large one, which grew under the east wall of the house, with a covering of spruce fir branches to protect the flowers. When left unprotected, she said, frost stained the flower with red, and if covered too heavily the flowers became green.

My hellebores bloom under pine trees without any protection at all, and seem to get on very well. But they have never increased much, nor bloomed very freely, though I have had them for eight years.

"I never saw such Christmas roses as I have just now," Henry Bright wrote on the fifth of January. "Clustering beneath their dark serrated leaves rise masses of bloom—bud and blossom—the bud often tinged with a faint pink colour, the blossom a snowy white guarding a center of yellow stamens. I have counted thirty to forty blooms upon a single root, and I sometimes think the Eucharis is not a finer flower."

In Henry Bright's day, at the turn of the century, thirty-year-old clumps of hellebores were not uncommon in English cottage gardens, and fifty-year-old clumps were not unheard of. Once settled they do not like to be disturbed, and as Mrs. Boyle says, "will sooner die than take to a new place."

No one can say why hellebores flourish in one garden and perish in the garden next door, but their needs are few and simple: part shade, a soil rich in humus (some say leaf mould, some say lots of manure), and water in dry weather. The flowers are excellent for cutting and last for many days, but the leaves should never be cut, and the flowers should never be allowed to go to seed. Hellebores, if they live at all, are healthy plants, and seem to have no enemies. But sometimes the buds are found lying on the ground, and this is said to be the work of mice. The mice don't eat the buds, they just chew the stems. Though the Christmas rose comes from the Carpathian mountains, it can be grown at low elevations, and even in climates with hot summers.

We know that it can be well grown in Charlotte, for Mrs. Huffman has often written of Mrs. E. A. Anderson's successful plantings. But I have been told by more than one good gardener that after ten or fifteen years the plants begin to deteriorate. The answer to this is to have young plants coming on. They are available, though expensive, and I shall be glad to provide addresses.

It seems to be well established that the Christmas rose is not the hellebore of the Greek and Latin writers, and of Spencer and Cowley, but Parkinson and Gerard described it as a garden flower in the sixteenth century, and it is the plant that Darwin wrote of in *The Loves of the Plants*:

> Bright as the silvery plume, or pearly shell,
>   The snow-white rose or lily's virgin bell,
> The fair helleborus attractive shone,
>   Warmed every sage and every shepherd won."

December 26, 1965

December's Flowers

In *Down the Garden Path*, Beverley Nichols gives a list of flowers in a bouquet he picked from his bleak garden on the sixth of December: a rose (a little frost weary); a spray of pink larkspur; one snowdrop; three blooms of purple stock; a dandelion; one of those little white flowers with thousands of blossoms that grow in fields in summer; several yellow wall-flowers; two marigolds in exceptionally fine condition; a late chrysanthe-mum; a few pansies; a Michaelmas daisy; two violets; a yellow daisy. "I love as much as anybody to go out in spring and to come in again . . . with armfuls of white lilac," he said. "But this search for winter flowers— this foraging in a barren land—with all the elements against you, and darkness so swiftly descending, is to me a keener pleasure."

And to me. On the fourth of December, after a night when the tem-perature dropped to 20, and on a day when it did not rise above 35, I went out to pick a bouquet for Mrs. Stuart Gaul who was in the hospital. This is what I found: an Algerian iris that was beginning to unfurl when I went to church at 7:30 (when I brought it in the house, the warmth brought out the perfume of violets); a sprig of the arbutus tree with its cold greenish bells; a twig of the fragrant viburnum; a spray of the winter clematis; rosemary; one flower out on the first stalk of the paper white narcissus; violas ('Blue Perfection'); camellia 'Dawn' (slightly discolored);

one frozen rose bud (the old pink climbing daily); yellow chrysanthemums; the aster I got from Mrs. Tate in Belmont, and the one Elizabeth Clarkson brought from Texas; and a snip of *Erica carnea*—but that was really cheating, for it was not quite out.

The hardy cyclamens were gone (but I picked a beautiful silver patterned leaf), and so were the fall snowdrops, and it was an interval without white hoopskirt daffodils. The hoopskirts are blooming unusually well this year. One clump came into bloom on the seventh of November, and lasted until the end of the month. 'Nylon' has a bud ready to burst as soon as it warms up a little. 'Jessamy' has its first bud in four years, and my old clump which has bloomed faithfully for 16 years is crowded with the points of tiny buds just poking through the ground. I expect I will have blooms well into the new year.

I could not find a dandelion, though I had seen one a few days before, and I couldn't find a crocus, though there had been bloom from the few corms the chipmunks left me, and would be more. The first was *Crocus zonatus* at the end of September, a small, pale, lilac flower lighted by a golden throat. This multiplies rapidly, and I would have a garden full by now (from a few corms put out along with the hoopskirts 16 years ago) but for my greedy friends. The next flowers were the white and the violet forms of *Crocus speciosus*. They bloomed during the first half of October. Speciosus means splendid, and they really are the finest of the fall-flowering species. They have pointed petals in tints of glowing spectrum violet. Before October was over, I found the little sweet-scented flowers of *Crocus longiflorus*; they continued to appear until the last of November, when the pallid wraith *Crocus ochroleucus* comes along.

I wish Mrs. Price, or Mrs. Muse, or someone, would keep a supply of wall-flowers. I always want them, and never have any because they are biennial, and I can't raise things from seed. One year there were a lot growing in a dooryard at the foot of Ridgewood Avenue, and they were a glow of brown and orange all winter long, and deliciously fragrant.

After picking my December bouquet, I realized that I had completely forgotten the first fragrant flowers of the winter-sweet. They had opened under their papery, fading leaves, and their scent was not noticeable in the chilly air. Later, when the leaves have fallen and the air is warm it will be impossible to pass them by.

Winter is the time I like to pick flowers. In the summer when the garden is so full I seldom feel the need of flowers in the house, but when they must be searched for, it is nice to bring them in. And I am like Mary Horsley, who says she cannot bear to leave them out in the cold.

December 18, 1966

Greens and Berries

When I was little we lived in Hamlet. Every Christmas, country people brought greens and berries to our door: holly and mistletoe and longleaf pine, and the lovely coral berries of *Smilax walteri*, which they called red bamboo. Though it grows in swamps all along the coastal plain from New Jersey to Florida, I think Walter's smilax is rather rare, and I have never found it in the trade at all. Perhaps this is as well, for it is said to be as troublesome in the garden as the less decorative cat briers are; it may be one of those things that are better to read about than to grow. But I often think of those bright and shining clusters of red berries hanging in leafless thread-like stems, and wish I could have them in the house for Christmas.

In Raleigh, the Christmas greens used to be brought into the Capitol Square and laid on the grassy bank by the sidewalk along Morgan Street. Along with the holly and mistletoe and pine they brought running cedar and twin flower. The twin flowers were rooted, and there were always shiny red berries among the tiny oval leaves. We would put them in a finger bowl with damp moss, and later on plant them in the garden. Although they always berried so well, those I have now in the garden cover the ground but bloom little and never have fruit. I don't know whether this is because I have plants of only one sex, or whether they find the soil not acid enough, or too dry.

Some of the mountain people advertise Christmas greens in the *North Carolina Agricultural Review*: galax, ferns, teaberry, running pine, hemlock branches with cones, and balsam. I think running pine is the plant we call running-cedar, but I have never been sure about the differences in lycopodiums. Teaberry is the mountain name for *Gaultheria procumbens*. Alice Morse Earle calls it checkerberry. In *Old Time Gardens* she tells how Appoline, the milkman's little daughter, brought the aromatic new green leaves to church in spring Sundays, and the spicy berries in the fall. The children liked to chew them during the long sermons. The leaves were called pippins. They taste like wintergreen. Teaberry demands a very acid soil mixed with leafmold and sharp sand. As it grows under evergreens it likes complete shade.

Galax will grow in shady gardens if the soil is acid enough, and it is said to cover the ground quickly, but it doesn't do that for me. I doubt very much whether it will ever be thick enough to allow of picking for Christmas, but the clump of round, deep green wine-tinted leaves is pleasant to come upon in the winter garden. If there are enough leaves to pick, they should be snipped with scissors—pulling them is likely to disturb the roots.

Alice Lounsberry says (in *Southern Wild Flowers and Trees*) Mrs. Kibbee, the widow of a doctor who died in a yellow fever epidemic, was the first person to think of selling the leaves at Christmas, and that she largely supported her children by the sales. In May, when the slender spikes of creamy flowers stand on thin stems above the glossy new leaves, Mrs. Lounsberry says they look like a milky way. I suppose she thought of this because the generic name comes from the Greek word for milk, or because the mountain people call it galaxy.

Boxes of Christmas greens are usually advertised in the *Mississippi Market Bulletin*, but this year the only offering I found was Mrs. W. L. Radau's "Partridge berry vines, moss and sphagnum moss for making berry-bowl or terrarium." Mrs. Radau also advertises interesting dried material.

I like to bring in the Old World greens—holly and mistletoe, ivy and yew, rosemary, laurel, box and bay—as well as those of the New World:

> With Holly and ivy
> So green and so gay,
> We deck up our houses
> As fresh as the day.
> With bays and rosemary,
> And laurel complete:
> And Every one now
> Is a king in conceit.
> —*Poor Robin's Almanac*, 1695

December 25, 1966

Pomanders

We have always made pomanders at Christmastime, but I have just learned that they are traditional presents for New Year's Day. They are made by sticking whole cloves in an orange. This sounds easy enough, but the stems of the cloves are apt to be blunt, and it may be necessary to make holes first with a darning needle. That takes more time, and also makes it more difficult to space the cloves evenly and to keep them close together. Success depends upon finding a small and perfect orange with a thin smooth skin. As soon as the fruit is covered with cloves, it is rolled in a mixture of powdered spices. We always used cinnamon and orris root, but orris root is hard to find. Rosetta Clarkson suggests cinnamon and nutmeg. Cardamon is also used.

Oranges stuck with cloves are the poor man's pomanders. The earliest reference to them that I have found is in Ben Jonson's *Christmas, his Masque*: "New-yeares-gift ha's an Orenge, and Rosmarie, but not a clove to sticke in't." Originally, pomanders were little perforated cases, often in the shape of an apple or orange, made of ivory, silver, or gold, or even of crystal, and filled with a paste of perfumes and spices.

One of the often quoted receipts comes from William Ram's *Little Dodoens*: "Take Labdanum one ounce, Benjamin and Storax of each two drams, Damaske powder finely sieved, one dram, Cloves and Mace of each a little, a Nutmeg and a little Camphire, Muske and Civit a little." The labdanum was heated until it was soft, two or three drops of "oyl of spike" were added, and then the rest of the ingredients, finely powdered. The paste was made into beads which were pierced with a bodkin and worn as girdles, or necklaces, or as bracelets such as the one Julia gave to Herrick:

"How can I choose but love, and follow her," the poet said, "whose shadow smels like milder Pomander! How can I chuse but kisse her, whence dos come The *Storax, Spiknard, Myrrhe,* and *Ladanum.*"

Along with his receipt for "A comfortable Pomander for the brain," William Ram tells how to renew its scent: "Take one grain of Civet, and two of Musk, or if you double the proportion, it will be so much the sweeter; grinde them upon a stone with a little Rosewater; and after wetting your hands with Rose-water you may worke the same in your Pomander. This is a sleight to pass away an old Pomander; but my intention is honest."

Pomanders are associated with the Elizabethans, but they are much older than that, and must have originated in France, for their name comes from old French: pome ambre, the amber being ambergris. There is a reference to it in the *Roman de la Rose* (thirteenth century), "Plus olant que pomme d'embre." Pomanders were worn as a protection against plagues and pestilence, and to counteract evil odors; and they were held in the hand to cure insomnia. Mrs. Clarkson gives a receipt that calls for "opium, mandrake, juice of hemlock, henbane seed, and winelees, to which must be added musk, that by the scent it may provoke him that smells unto it. Make a ball as big as a man may grasp in his hand; by often smelling to this, it will cause him to shut his eyes and fall asleep."

In *Old Time Gardens*, Alice Morse Earle says that in country places apples stuck with cloves were presented as a token of sympathy to friends in sorrow or distress. They were called "comfort apples." She says pomanders were made of "the maste of a Sweet Apple tree gathered betwixt two Lady Days." Lady Day is March 25, the Feast of the Annunciation, which doesn't seem a likely time to gather apples, but it used to be a name for any day kept in celebration of an event in the life of the Virgin Mary—such as the Assumption on August 15 or the Nativity on September 8.

The old poets liked to write about pomanders—perhaps because it is such a pretty word, but they pronounced it two ways. Some, like Herrick, put the accent on the first syllable; others, like Skelton, put it on the second. I like Skelton's way: "Colyaunder, Swete Pomaunder, Good cassaunder."

December 28, 1969

Looking Ahead

When the monks made up a calendar of saints and their flowers for the year, they left out December 31. There is no flower for New Year's Eve. In the floral dictionary from Hone's *Every Day Book* (London, 1826) a verse fills the empty space:

> It betokens warmth and growth;
> If West, much milk, and fish in the sea;
> If North, much cold and storms there will be;
> If East, the trees will bear much fruit;
> If North-east, flee it man and brute.

I looked in the 1968 almanac, which I picked up while Christmas shopping, and I see that New Year's Day will be fair and pleasant southward to the Gulf Coast.

The present-day almanacs are very like the early garden books. Just before Christmas I got from a dealer in garden books, *Every Man his own Gardener, being a new, and much more complete Gardener's Kalendar than any One hitherto published,* by Thomas Mawe (Gardener to His Grace the Duke of Leed's), London 1776. Among the many things to do in the kitchen garden in January, Mawe says: "On a small spot of ground you may sow a little spinach, to come in early spring; at which time it will be very acceptable in most families. The smooth-seeded, or round leaved spinnach, is the best to sow at this season." In the January calendar for the flower garden Mawe says "plant ranunculuses and annemonies, if you have any now out of the ground; these now planted will succeed those which were put in the ground in October or November. Choose a dry mild day for planting these roots, and see that the ground is not very wet, for that would rob them. Lay the bed rounding, that the wet may run off. . . . Tulips, if you have any out of the ground, should now be planted to bloom late, and to succeed those planted in last autumn." Tulips planted as late as mid-January have bloomed well in Charlotte.

Most of the January saints have mosses or evergreens for their emblems, but there are several winter flowers in the floral dictionary. On New Year's Day where the weather is mild *Viburnum tinus* blooms for Saint Faine, an Irish abbess of the sixth century; and *Iris persica* for Saint Genevieve, patroness of Paris, who by her prayers saved the city from Attila in the fifth century. The feast of Saint Genevieve is the third of January, and I have never known this beautiful little iris to bloom before February, but Darnell says it does "in warm forward seasons."

Helleborus niger, the Christmas rose, is the flower of Saint Agnes, the pure, who was beheaded at the age of thirteen, and whose feast is January 21. A white lamb is a better-known emblem of Saint Agnes. The flower for the 25th, the conversion of Saint Paul, is the winter aconite, *Eranthis hyemalis*, which Linnaeus classed as a hellebore. It does bloom in my garden on Saint Paul's day in some seasons. The flowers are like stemless buttercups. Eranthis is difficult to establish, as the tubers deteriorate very quickly when they are taken from the ground. Mine came from Mr. Krippendorf, who dug the plants from his woods and sent the clump with the soil still around it. Those who have been disappointed by the results from imported tubers might try growing eranthis from seed scattered in woods soil in part shade and covered lightly with fine compost. They are said to bloom by January 3, and I can give an address for seeds from Mr. Krippendorf's woods.

December 31, 1967

 INDEX

Editor's note: The authority for botanical nomenclature when
Elizabeth Lawrence wrote these columns was *Hortus II*. *Hortus
III* equivalents are shown here in bold type.